PRAISE FOR

THE POWER OF BROKE

"Daymond knows how to make things happen. He knows the difference between a want-preneur and an entrepreneur, and he lays it out for us in these pages. What a kick it is to read over his shoulder as he shares his hard-won wisdom. This guy built an empire from the streets of Hollis, Queens, and here he compares notes with other visionaries who've also found ways to beat the odds and make it to the top. His new book is so inspiring, so insightful, so invigorating. I'm glad that he took the time to share this mind-set with the world."

—Mark Cuban, entrepreneur and owner of the Dallas Mavericks

"Daymond John's journey proves that desperation breeds innovation, and *The Power of Broke* breaks it down for us with straight talk from a guy who knows what it takes to make something out of nothing."

—Steve Case, chairman and CEO of
Revolution LLC and cofounder of America Online

"Money can't buy you strength or spirit. It can't get you peace or power. In his empowering new book, Daymond John sets out a blueprint for folks looking to put their God-given assets to work to build a business or a brand. Nobody knows better than Daymond that it doesn't matter how you start out in life—the will to win resides in us all."

—Russell Simmons, business mogul and philanthropist

"I firmly believe that you should only read business books from people who have actually built businesses. Daymond has done just that, and here he breaks down the thesis and the religion behind exactly how he did it. You have to understand that 'broke' isn't what happens in your wallet; 'broke' is a mind-set. It's about tapping into that state of desperation that leads you to tremendous creativity. I was in the game of broke before I even knew what the game was, and, here, Daymond John deconstructs this crucial concept in detail."

—Gary Vaynerchuk, VaynerMedia CEO and
three-time *New York Times* bestselling author

THE POWER OF BROKE

HOW EMPTY POCKETS,

A TIGHT BUDGET,

AND A HUNGER FOR SUCCESS

CAN BECOME

YOUR GREATEST

COMPETITIVE ADVANTAGE

Daymond John

WITH DANIEL PAISNER

CROWN
BUSINESS
New York

Published in the United States by Crown Business, an imprint of the Crown
Publishing Group, a division of Penguin Random House LLC, New York.
crownpublishing.com

CROWN BUSINESS is a trademark and CROWN and the Rising Sun colophon
are registered trademarks of Penguin Random House LLC.

Crown Business books are available at special discounts for bulk purchases for
sales promotions or corporate use. Special editions, including personalized covers,
excerpts of existing books, or books with corporate logos, can be created in large
quantities for special needs. For more information, contact Premium Sales at
(212) 572-2232 or e-mail specialmarkets@penguinrandomhouse.com.

Library of Congress Cataloging-in-Publication Data
John, Daymond, author.
The power of broke : how empty pockets, a tight budget, and a hunger for success
can become your greatest competitive advantage / Daymond John with Daniel
Paisner.—First edition.
    pages cm
1. New business enterprises.   2. Success in business.   3. Creative ability in
business.   4. Strategic planning.   5. Entrepreneurship.   I. Paisner, Daniel,
author.   II. Title.
HD62.5.J6336 2015
658.1'1—dc23   2015021158

ISBN 978-1-101-90361-2
Ebook ISBN 978-1-101-90360-5

Printed in the United States of America

Book design by Elina D. Nudelman
Cover design by Michael Nagin
Cover photograph by Geordie Wood

10 9 8 7 6 5 4 3 2 1

First Paperback Edition

This book is dedicated to David Freschman, a man who embodied the very best qualities of entrepreneurship and friendship. David always fought for what he believed in. A great father, a great husband, and a great contributor to his community, he never saw the color of a man's skin but focused only on the integrity of a man's heart. David was one of the great "early adaptors" in the small business space, before the days of incubators and angel investors and venture capitalists, who saw the value of focusing in this area. I can't thank David enough for always being there for me, and for investing in me—with his faith, love, and knowledge. The world was richer for his being here, and it's a poorer place without him. May he rest in peace.

"Yes, there were times, I'm sure you knew,
When I bit off more than I could chew.
But through it all, when there was doubt,
I ate it up and spit it out.
I faced it all and I stood tall;
And did it my way."

−Frank Sinatra, "My Way"
(I know Paul Anka wrote the song,
but it's the Sinatra version that gets me going)

CONTENTS

THE POWER OF BROKE

ONE

THE POWER OF BROKE

THE POWER OF BROKE is a mind-set. It exists in all of us, whether we have money, opportunities, or advantages. Trouble is, most people don't recognize this power for what it is. They leave it alone, or maybe they don't even know it's there. Instead, they buy into the line from people in suits, fancy offices, or business schools who tell us that there's a certain way to start businesses—we need money to jump-start our business.

But that only works for a few of us—and only for a while. Why? Because, take it from me, the *power of broke* is all about substance over flash. It's about creativity over certainty. It's about taking a shot over playing it safe. And here's another thing: The money runs out after a while. Those deep pockets you may or may not have, they'll never be deep enough to buy all the passion, ingenuity, and determination it takes to have success over the long haul. Even if you've got money behind you, there's no guarantee that it will see you through. It's the money in front of you that counts, after all. It's the money you need, not the money you have, that makes all the difference. And this book is all about that difference, and how to put it to work for you.

Let's face it, when you're up against all odds, when you've exhausted every opportunity, when you're down to your last dime . . . that's when you've got no choice but to succeed. You're out of options, man. So you double down, dig deep, and switch into that relentless turbo mode we've all got kicking around in our machinery. And that's when the real magic happens. Are we clear on this? **The *power of broke* is the half-court shot you fire up with time running out and the game on the line.** It's the shot your teammates won't take because the likelihood of that ball kissing the net is pretty damn thin and they don't want to mess with their stat lines. They're playing the percentages while you're playing to win—and this can mean everything. I don't mean to mix my sports metaphors here, but I'm reminded of that great Wayne Gretzky line, "We miss one hundred percent of the shots we don't take." So, take the shot! Absolutely, take the shot. **The *power of broke* is all about taking that shot.** The *power of broke* is looking up at the sky, wondering what you've got to do to catch a break, and saying, "God, why am I doing this?" It's living with the constant fear that you've gone crazy for putting it all on the line—but putting it out there anyway. There might be a million reasons for you to throw up your hands, throw in the towel, throw away your dreams, and put an end to whatever craziness you're pursuing, but the *power of broke* is that one reason you keep going. Maybe you've been rejected by thirty loan officers, but that green light could be waiting for you on the thirty-first try. Perhaps your product or service has been totally slammed by the first thirty people who try it, but the thirty-first review is a rave. And that comes from the one guy whose opinion really matters.

Whatever it is, keep at it—absolutely, keep at it! Because, hey, you never know. **When you've got nothing to lose, you've got everything to gain.** Sometimes it takes having your back against the wall, leveraging your last dollar, and having no place to go but up, up, up if you expect something to happen. Because if you've got to succeed to survive, you will. Trust me on this.

BE A TRUE INNOVATOR

Here's my take: Innovation happens from the bottom up, not the top down.

Break dancing, rap music, slam poetry, iPods, smart watches, electric cars . . . all the most creative, the most successful, the most dynamic innovations pop in an organic way, and then grow. Or not. You put your idea out there, no big thing, and it just kind of happens. Or not. People either respond to it or they don't, and it doesn't matter how much money you throw at it, how much you try to dress it up, it is what it is and that's that.

It has its own beating heart.

You don't need me to tell you this—just take a look at the world around you. Our favorite movies, the ones that win all the awards, the ones we talk about with our friends, tend to be the indie films that come from a small, sweet voice, a singular vision, and not the slick, big-budget, mainstream movies from the major studios. Yeah, those big blockbusters make the big bucks, and they can be a lot of fun, but they don't *always* light our imaginations or stir our souls—at least, not in the same way.

Just look what goes on at Art Basel in Miami Beach, the biggest gathering of international artists on the calendar. Hundreds and hundreds of the best artists in the world come to Florida every December to share their work, strut their stuff, do their thing. It's an amazing thing to see, what some of these folks are up to, but it's not *just* the fine art displayed on the walls by the top galleries that makes all the noise. A lot of folks, they'll tell you the real excitement of the show, the raw energy, is off to the side. That's where you'll find the street artists, the pop-up displays, the next big thing. And that's where you'll find the crowds—because, when it comes down to it, people want to experience something pure, something real. They want to be lifted from their everyday experiences, from what's expected, and set down in the middle of something completely and breathtakingly *new.*

I come from the world of fashion—that's where I made my name. But at FUBU we were never about *high* fashion. Our designs came from the streets, from our own hard-won style, our pride of place. The spirit of our clothes was in our name—For Us By Us—and one of the reasons we captured a good chunk of the market was because we were authentic. We were true to ourselves. Were we completely and breathtakingly *new?* Not really, but what was exciting about our clothes, what a lot of folks connected to, was that we wore them proudly. They were a reflection of our world.

FUBU isn't the only successful brand that launched in this way. A lot of the most iconic fashion brands started out in a small, hand-sewn way. *Haute couture,* at the high end of high fashion, is based on the same principle—high-quality clothing, made by hand, with a personal touch. In French, the word *couture* simply means "dressmaking," and when it started out it just referred to plain folks figuring out a way to dress nicely, to turn their rags and loose fabrics into clothing that made them feel a little more like nobles. But today the term has come to symbolize the best of the best. Why? Because it came about in this genuine way.

The same goes for architecture, literature, music, technology, design, fashion . . . every important innovation, every lasting impression, every meaningful trend, and every successful business comes from a singular vision, put out into the world with a small, sweet voice. It starts from the bottom and it grows from there—or not.

Or not . . .

Those two little words, suggesting the possibility that things might not go my way . . . they're at the heart of everything I do. They're why I give myself the same marching orders every morning when I get out of bed: rise and grind. Because in *those* three words I find tremendous power—the power to do anything, to get past anything, to become anything. They remind me that the choice of whether to succeed—*or not*—is all mine.

POWER FACT: **Eight out of 10 new businesses fail within the first 18 months.** . . . It's not enough to have a good idea for a start-up or a hot new product; execution is key, and part of that execution comes in finding your "voice" as an entrepreneur. Why do so many new businesses fail? Many times, it's because they've been cashed to death. It's because businesses built on steroids and on injections of capital are living on borrowed time. When the money runs out, the business runs its course.

This idea that the best concepts and innovations tend to happen organically, authentically, is not limited to art and discovery. It cuts to our personal lives, too. Think about it: Our most lasting relationships are built on the same solid foundation. It's got to be pure, got to be real . . . or else it just won't work. If you're a guy, and you pull up to meet a girl in a hot car, you'll make a certain kind of first impression, right? The two of you get together, you take her out for an expensive dinner, buy her a nice pair of shoes and maybe some bling, you sip the finest champagne . . . by the end of the night she's into you. And if you keep it up, at end of the week, she's *totally* into you. Doesn't matter what you look like. Doesn't matter if you're a brilliant conversationalist or even if you share the same views. In some cases, you could be fat, bald, stupid . . . whatever. It only matters that you showered her with power, bought her a bunch of gifts and flowers, took her away on romantic weekends, and whatever the case may be. It all adds up. You've presented yourself to her in a certain way. And if she responds to that certain way, that's great, I'm happy for you . . . *really*. But what happens to that kind of relationship in the long run? What happens when all that money goes away and there's nothing left but to be yourself? What happens when you buy her a present every time you see her, and then all of a sudden you lose your job? Then what?

Don't be surprised if you find your relationship was only as strong as the money you put into it. When the jewelry runs out, no more fancy dinners, and the getaway vacations end . . . what's left? You've been riding a superficial high, a false emotion—and it's bound to catch up to you. It will.

Or maybe you're a woman looking to snag your dream man. So you slip yourself into a fine, beautiful dress, get yourself *done* with hair and makeup, work out like crazy so you can't help but turn all kinds of heads. You finally meet this amazing guy, and you really, really want him to pay attention to you, ask you out a second time, and a third. And he does, and the two of you have a good thing going . . . for a while. Again, I'm happy for you. That's great. But then you get a little older, you gain a couple of pounds, the dress no longer fits. Or maybe you're living together, and you're stuck in bed with the flu, looking all a mess in your footie pajamas. What happens then?

BE GENUINE

Now, before you start beating up on me for presenting such superficial examples, let me just say that they're *meant* to be superficial examples. I'm trying to make my point in the extreme. No, women aren't just out for money and fine things—and men aren't just out for sass and sex appeal. The point is that if it's not authentic, if there's no *there* there, your relationship is not about to work in any kind of long-term way, no matter how you dress it up, or how much money you throw at it. You might hang in for a while and have a nice little run, but it won't last. It *can't* last. It's the same in business. Let's say you open a new restaurant. You design a gorgeous new space, in the best part of town. You have no experience in the kitchen, but you have the money to hire a top chef, the best decorators. You have no vision, no specific market you're trying to serve, no style of cooking that speaks to you, but your research tells you that a certain kind of cuisine is crazy popular right now, the *edge* of the cutting edge, so that's what you decide to pursue. Basically, you focus-group the crap out of the place, spend all kinds of money throwing in all the bells and whistles and every conceivable amenity, open your doors, and wait for the tables to fill. But it doesn't always work out that way, does it?

Why is that, do you think?

Or let's say you're in the soda business, and you decide for some reason to shake things up, tweak your formula, try something new. You've already got the biggest, most successful brand in the world, and your market projections show steady growth for years and years. But you get it in your head that the soda-drinking public is fickle, ready for a change, so you shave off a chunk of that money and hire a bunch of chemists to engineer a new flavor, a bunch of marketing experts to redesign your logo, a bunch of advertisers to help get the word out. You can afford to bring in the best of the best to work with you on this. Trouble is, you haven't taken the time to stir up any real interest in the marketplace. You haven't even *identified* any interest for what you're selling. There's been no demand for a new formula, folks haven't really tried it or asked for it—and nobody's even saying they're tired of the old formula. You've gone down this road for no good reason and you end up with New Coke—one of the biggest thuds in the history of product launches.

Remember what happened there?

Well, truth is, nobody outside the Coca-Cola Company really

knows what happened back in 1985 when New Coke hit the market, because nobody's talking. Nobody will cop to it. But I have some ideas. They teach case study classes on this New Coke fiasco at some of our top business schools, and I certainly don't have that kind of insight or expertise. And obviously I can't put myself in the boardroom at Coca-Cola when these big-time executives made the series of decisions that set them down this path. But if I had to guess, I'd say that all their money got in the way, confused the issue. Probably, they were just making change for the sake of change—because they could *afford* to, and not because they *needed* to. Probably, there was a collective and colossal failure to acknowledge the simple fact that business is like any other innovation, any other relationship. It grows from the bottom up—only here it's not about a guy and a girl, an artist and her audience, a designer and his muse. No, here it's about your brand and your relationship with your customer, with the marketplace. It's a marriage: *I'm giving to you, and you're giving to me.* It's a partnership: *I'm here for you, and you're here for me.* If the authenticity is there, if the business is built on a solid foundation, you'll have a shot to succeed. If it's just a superficial enterprise, built on flashy gimmicks, inflated hopes, and a big budget, the odds run a little longer.

In today's digital age, even *governments* have got to keep it real. Just look at the so-called "Facebook Revolution" that basically kickstarted the overthrow of an oppressive regime in Egypt in 2011; the revolution in Tunisia that same year; Hong Kong's Umbrella Revolution of 2014, where protesters changed their profile pictures to images of yellow umbrellas to rail against election reforms; and on and on. These movements didn't succeed because they had big marketing budgets. They succeeded because they were *real*. It's gotten to where an entire nation can be energized by the force of a single idea put out into the world in a passionate way through social media—at little or no cost.

POWER FACT: **According to WebDAM, a leading digital marketing platform, 25 percent of the world's total advertising budget is devoted to online promotions.** . . . *Clearly, if you're out to make some noise, if you want your message to pop, it's never been easier to reach your target audience with a direct hit, but you've got to keep it real if you want to make an impact.*

Doesn't matter what you're selling—the power has shifted to the people. Doesn't matter if you're in government, in business, in a relationship, today's buzz words are *transparency* and *authenticity.* You've got to keep it real, people—and you can't keep it real in business today if your strategy is to simply throw money at whatever roadblocks come your way, because chances are, money alone won't get you past them. It's the force of that *single idea,* offered in a genuine way, that gets results—no matter how much money you put behind it.

STAY HUNGRY

My point here is that there's great value in being true to yourself, and that it helps to have your back against the wall when you're starting out. It helps to be up against it. It helps to have to scrape, hustle, dream your way to the top. It helps to have a passion for your pursuit, especially when passion is the only resource you can afford. It helps you to realize your dream because it forces you to keep that dream real.

Bottom line: *It helps to be so hungry you have no choice but to succeed.* Better believe it . . . it helps. It does. Trust me, I know—because that's where I was coming from when I started FUBU with three of my boys from my neighborhood in Hollis,

Queens. I know—because now that I've turned my focus to helping others launch their own businesses and grow their own brands,
I see it all the time.

Take it from me, "the People's Shark." That's how folks have
come to know me on the ABC-TV reality show *Shark Tank,* where
I sit on the panel with four other investors, listening to the pitches
and proposals of our entrepreneur-contestants. Anyway, that's how
I come across, because that's who I am. Some of my colleagues on
the show have developed reputations as ruthless dealmakers, and
some as easy marks, easily won over by flash and publicity. Me, I've
worked hard to champion the underdogs on the show, to shine a
light on the hardworking success stories, and to help people recognize a good idea—a real idea, a winning idea.

So here's the big idea at the heart of this book: When you start
from a place of nothing much at all, when you're *hungry* and laser-
focused on succeeding at whatever it is you're out to do, when you're
flat-out determined to get where you're going *no matter what . . .*
well, then you've got a running start. You're moving in the right
direction, for the right reasons. On the flip side of that, when you
start with all kinds of resources, when funding isn't an issue, when
failure isn't about to break you . . . well, then you're standing still.

Absolutely, there's tremendous power in being broke. The more
you *need* to succeed, the more likely it is that you *will* succeed. The
more you've *invested*—and here I'm talking about emotional and
personal investment, not a financial investment—the more you'll
get back in return.

And so I'll say it again: there's great power in having to scrape
and scramble. The people I've met in business, the ones who've
had their first breaks handed to them, they're missing a kind of fire
inside, a hunger, a willingness to do whatever it takes to succeed.
I'm generalizing, I know, and there are exceptions everywhere you
look, but for the most part it takes this certain fire, this certain
hunger, to build any kind of real and lasting success. At least, that's

how it was with me—and chances are, if you've grabbed this book, that's how it is with you too.

But here's the thing: the *power of broke* only works in your favor if you recognize it, tap into it, put it to work. Broke, on its own, is just broke. If you let broke beat you down, if you let it *break* you, you'll never find a way to thrive or even survive. You'll never lift yourself up and out and on to great things. But if you look broke in the face, if you define it, own it, make it a part of who you are and how you go about your business . . . well, then you've got something, people.

GO BACK TO THE BEGINNING

Remember those great *Rocky* movies? They came from a personal place, from the mind and heart of one artist—the first movie anyway. After that the small, sweet voice started to get drowned out by the Hollywood blockbuster machine . . . but that's a whole other point, so let's double-back: When does Sylvester Stallone's Rocky character start to stumble? When he starts throwing all this money around, letting success go to his head, right? When he starts to surround himself with all these luxuries, starts to work out in a plush, cushy gym, sleeps in a nice big bed . . . that's when he loses his edge. It's all right there in the song they use on the soundtrack, "The Eye of the Tiger." When Rocky is coming up, running up and down those steps in Philadelphia, working out in those meat lockers, he has the eye of the tiger, man. He is determined, driven. He has this mentality that says, "Nobody's gonna stop me from getting over this wall." Over, under, around, through . . . that wall means nothing to Rocky Balboa, because he is focused. Because he has *no choice* but to fight his way past. Because he's been down so long he can't breathe unless he finds a way to lift himself up and out.

But then he isn't the underdog anymore. Then he's the champ, riding high, getting all kinds of endorsement deals, all kinds of distractions. And what happens? He starts to relax a little bit, takes his eyes off the prize, and he gets himself an ass-whupping from Clubber Lang—Mr. T! It isn't until Rocky goes back to his old rival, Apollo Creed, and starts training again in the same rough-and-tumble, broke, desperate way he did before that he's able to get back on his game. And it's not just about training in a dirty old gym. Apollo Creed tells Rocky he's got to buy into that whole *power of broke* mind-set he had when he was facing his first title fight. He's got to move into a crappy room in the nastiest part of town. He's got to live in the 'hood. He's got to hustle. He's got to get down so low there's no place for him to go but up.

Basically, he's got to get his roots back into his DNA, shake the glitz and glamour from his thinking, and get back to work.

Apollo puts it to him plain in one of the movie's key scenes. He tells Rocky why he lost that fight, what he has to do to win back the title:

"You lost your edge. . . . You didn't look hungry. No, when we fought, you had the eye of the tiger, man. The edge. And now you got to get it back. And the way to get it back is to go back to the beginning."

Rocky Balboa (at least, *Rocky III* Balboa) gets away from wanting it, gets away from needing it . . . and it costs him. The same goes in business. When you *want* it, when you *need* it, you find a way to make good things happen. When you *expect* it, when you feel *entitled* to it, you might just be headed for an ass-whupping.

Now, I'm not suggesting that you *can't* start a business with a ton of money and great contacts behind you—because, hey, too much of a good thing can still be a good thing. And I'm not suggesting that the *only* way to start a business is from a place of desperation—because, hey, why struggle if you don't have to? But I *am* suggesting that there are all kinds of ways to turn every strike against you into an opportunity. I am suggesting that if you're dealt a lousy hand, you can find a way to play it in a winning way. And I am suggesting that being broke can actually be an *advantage* for you in business—being broke forces you to be aggressive, creative, resourceful . . . all those good things. It forces you to be realistic about your pace of growth and keeps you from letting your hopes and dreams run away from you. It pushes you to think about what's in reach. And it reminds you to keep true to yourself.

Sure, broke can have its downsides. You're behind on your rent? You don't have the cash flow to fill all those orders? Not exactly what you had in mind when you started out, is it? But keep your head up. Hang in there. Move ever-forward. Trust me, if you do, all these drags on your bottom line can become empowering, liberating. They can become assets—the counterpunch to that great Notorious B.I.G. song, "Mo' Money, Mo' Problems." If you buy into that type of thinking, then it follows that the *less* you have, the more you stand to gain, right?

DON'T OUTRUN YOUR RESOURCES

Let's take a look at a *Shark Tank* pitch from the show's sixth season to help us frame the conversation we're about to have in the pages ahead. Sometimes it helps to see a living, breathing example of a theory so you can get your head around it, and I've got just the story to do the job for us.

First, a quick word on the show: that's how a lot of folks know me these days, from my role as a panelist/investor/entrepreneur on the hit ABC reality series. *Shark Tank* invites inventors and entrepreneurs into the studio to pitch business ideas and opportunities to a panel of hungry Sharks who listen carefully to the pitches and then decide whether or not to invest their own money in the product or business. When we started back in 2009, our producer, Mark Burnett, tapped a bunch of Sharks from all different backgrounds, all different industries. He didn't put a bunch of stars together and assemble this glitzy panel of famous entrepreneurs to help draw viewers. No, he put his own spin on the *power of broke* and cast a bunch of hungry, dynamic, aggressive personalities who'd basically lived the spirit of entrepreneurship that would drive the program. All of us were successful in our own ways and in our own worlds, but none of us were what you would consider a household name. The network actually fought Mark on this, but he dug in. He wanted to fill his panel with people who would keep it real, who wouldn't be afraid to sweat to make these businesses work. The concept was that each Shark would have a certain area of expertise, and that together we'd be in a good position to respond to any pitch on a business or product. I was the fashion guru, with a good gut for trends in pop culture and lifestyle, but over the years, all of the Sharks on the show have developed a knack for spotting opportunities across a broad spectrum. We might have started out as experts—in real estate, fashion, direct marketing, technology, whatever—but by now we've become generalists.

We've got our teeth into everything.

Now, you have to realize that the *Shark Tank* pitches that get edited down to ten- or twelve-minute segments on the show can run an hour or two hours or even longer in the studio. A lot of times we'll tape a segment that never makes it onto the show, and we never really know what pitches will be featured on an upcoming episode until the week it's on. I try to catch the show every time we air a first-run episode, but because my travel schedule is so crazy, I'm not always able to watch it. So there I was, watching a pitch we'd heard a couple of months earlier—a story I'd pretty much forgotten about after the taping.

Here's how it went down: We were visited in the tank by two young guys—Joel Vinocur and Arsene Ecj—who'd developed a line of running, walking, and workout shoes called Forus. (Pay close attention to the name—*Forus*—because it factors in.) They were seeking a $200,000 investment, in exchange for a 15 percent stake in their company. Like a lot of our contestants, they had all these gimmicks attached to their pitch. They sprinted onto the set to really sell the point that they were marketing athletic shoes. (Cute, right?) They brought a pair of shoes for each of us on the panel, which they'd sized ahead of time and encouraged us to put on. (A personal touch, don't you think?) And they'd set up an impressive display of their various shoe lines, in a bunch of different colors and styles. (How's *that* for an eye-catching reminder of the potential reach of the brand?)

What struck me about these guys, though, wasn't their stunts—it was their enthusiasm for their product. It was in the way they carried themselves, in the way they presented their shoes, in the way they spoke of their mission. But then, as I listened to their pitch, I was struck by the name of their company—Forus Athletics. It reminded me, of course, of FUBU—an acronym that stood for For Us By Us and was meant back in the day to reinforce for our customers that we were just like them, making clothes we wore ourselves. At the time my partners and I thought it was the kind of name that could start a movement—away from the big department-store brands that seemed to cater to rich white kids and toward a self-styled clothing line that was inclusive, affordable, and shot through with street cred. And it did. Folks came to know us on the back of our name, to *connect* with us, and it got to where people could tell you the story behind our name even if they'd never tried on any of our clothes.

POWER FACT: Small business optimism is higher than it's been at any time since the Great Recession, according to Capital One's Small Business Confidence Score. We see evidence of this stat all around, but optimism will only take you so far. *Small business owners know better than anyone how important it is to stick to a core business plan, to make great strides with small steps. And, they know that imagination and patience will see them through.*

Right away I felt a certain kinship with these Forus guys, because I had to think they were looking to make the same kind of personal connection with their target market. They were athletes themselves, and they'd designed a shoe that was lighter and more flexible than other shoes on the market—with greater shock absorption and a memory foam core that helped to form a custom fit over time. Plus, their shoes were affordably priced, retailing for between $75 and $85.

There was every good reason to think these guys would be a runaway success—but for some reason they were here on the show, looking for money. So what we wanted from them wasn't their profit projections or branding strategies. We wanted to hear their story.

KNOW YOUR MARKET, KNOW YOUR MISSION

One of the guys, Arsene, talked a little bit about his background, growing up in Côte d'Ivoire, on the coast of West Africa. He told us he had to flee the country after the civil war there. He spoke about how his father had died in his arms. He said he literally had to run to this country—earning a track and field scholarship to a school in the United States, eventually making it to law school. What this young man had to endure in order to get an education, stand on his own two feet, and get to a place in his life and his business where he could go on national television and make a passionate appeal for what he and his partner believed was much-needed funding . . . well, it was the *power of broke* on full display.

And yet my fellow panelists weren't buying it.

Each Shark had a good reason for passing on the pitch:

- Mark Cuban, owner of the Dallas Mavericks, already had a shoe endorsement deal for his basketball team, so he was out.
- Lori Greiner, "the queen of QVC," worried that Forus wouldn't be able to knock the big boys like Nike, Saucony, and Adidas off the shelves, so she was out too.
- Kevin O'Leary, our serial entrepreneur, praised the team for growing their business to this point, but said he thought there were too many challenges ahead of them to justify the valuation they were seeking. Also out.

That left me and Robert Herjavec, our tech guy–turned–*Dancing with the Stars* hoofer—and frankly, I was concerned that these entrepreneurs were looking to do too much. They were caught between wanting to be a performance brand and a fashion brand, and they had a licensing deal with NASCAR that didn't make a whole lot of sense to me. They had so many lines and styles that they were looking at an inventory nightmare, because they had to stock and ship shoes in all these different sizes and half-sizes, so I was out. Robert, meanwhile, seemed to like the business. He loved that these two guys were go-getters, hard-chargers. He loved that they'd scraped and clawed their way to this point. And he thought they were on to something with these lightweight performance shoes. But Robert had no experience in this end of retail—specifically, in managing such a complicated inventory setup. So what did he do? He tried to bring me—the fashion guy—back into the deal. He said he would invest if I'd join him as a partner.

I hated that Robert put this back on me, set it up so I could make or break a deal when I'd already passed on it. But, hey, I took his point. Retail was an area of strength for me—especially when it involved so many styles and sizes. Robert's strengths were in finance, technology—and he saw that there was an opportunity here that had yet to be realized; he wasn't out to throw me under the bus so much as to invite me to hop back on and join him for the ride.

So I thought about it some more. It was tempting, because I really liked Joel and Arsene, liked what they'd accomplished, and I wanted to see them succeed, but I didn't see how a deal could work. So I went back to Arsene, who seemed to run the pitch, but I couldn't get him to rethink his approach, and as I worked it over in my head I realized that this was a textbook example of the *power of broke* idea at the heart of this book. From what I could tell, outside looking in, Forus had once been a bare-bones operation. These guys had started with an idea, a passion for running, and a firm belief that they could build a better running shoe. As far as we could tell on the panel, they had done just that. And they were successful, in a limited way. As a result, they'd reached a point where they were having trouble filling their orders, but instead of digging in and focusing on this one piece that was probably within their control, they'd set their sights too high and started in on all these different line extensions, setting it up so that they could count on having even more trouble filling those orders and managing their inventory going forward.

In the end, I passed on a Forus investment a second time, and we sent these guys away empty-handed. All of us were rooting for them to succeed, but none of us were willing to back that success with our own money.

I caught a lot of social media heat for turning these guys away—and the way it worked out, for keeping Robert from doing a deal he was only interested in making if I was involved. The feedback that came in on this pitch seemed to single me out, almost like folks were expecting me to do the deal. It's like I'd cast the deciding vote, and now I was the bad guy, even though that's not exactly how it went down. Still, I couldn't see how money was the answer to the growing pains this company was facing. Already, Forus had taken in over $500,000 in sales over the previous six months, and at that level the business would pull Joel and Arsene in the direction they needed to go. It would happen organically . . . or not at all . . . but it wasn't something money could buy.

Sometimes you need an infusion of cash to grow your business to the next level, but this didn't feel like one of those times. No, this felt to me like these entrepreneurs had reached a tipping point. They could lean one way, branch out in all these different directions, and continue to struggle. Or they could lean back the way they'd started out, get a handle on their inventory, scale back on the number of product lines and extensions, and grow in a more organic way.

I hated to turn these guys down—but I believe I did them a favor. Was I out to do them a solid by refusing to invest with them? No—I was looking out for myself. Let's face it, I'm in the business of making money, not subsidizing people just because I like them or I like their story. The *solid* came as a kind of by-product, because I honestly believed that they were better off without the $200,000 they were seeking. It didn't matter if that money came from me, or Robert, or Mark, or Lori, or Kevin, or if they went out and found a way to raise some money away from the show. It only mattered that it would have tempted Joel and Arsene to continue veering off in the wrong direction.

More money would have just confused the issue, left these Forus guys thinking they could do anything, pushed them more and more from their core concept, encouraged them to spend more time on their software or their ill-conceived NASCAR line—instead of taking the time to engage authentically with their customers and learn what they really wanted. Point is, sometimes money isn't the answer.

That's the *power of broke,* baby . . . it can make you or it can break you. And it's on you which way it will go.

SHARPEN YOUR SHARK POINTS

On *Shark Tank,* if someone comes in with a product and tells the panel he has $50 worth of sales, he gets laughed off the set. We fall out of our seats. But if that same someone then tells us his product only cost a dollar, and that $50 in sales came in under three minutes, selling from the trunk of his car in the parking lot of the local mall . . . well, then it's a whole other equation. Then everyone on the panel goes quiet, wondering which of their fellow Sharks will start bidding, and next thing you know there's a feeding frenzy. Why? Because without even realizing it, this wannabe entrepreneur has stumbled onto a proof of concept that opens doors and generates business. He's sold his first widgets or gadgets or whatever and taken the pulse of his market in a meaningful way.

Put another way, he's maximized the *power of broke* and put it to work *for* him. That's just what happened for me and my partners when we launched FUBU in the early 1990s, but the world has changed. The strategies that worked back then won't necessarily work today, but there are whole new strategies that have now come into play. At the same time, just as the world has changed, the key elements to any start-up remain the same—in an eat-or-be-eaten, kill-or-be-killed kind of way.

Understand, the *principles* behind those strategies are still very much in play, and I return to them constantly when I speak to business and student groups. Lately, I've bundled these principles into an easy-to-remember acronym, which I call SHARK Points. The idea is to get audiences to start thinking like a shark, the same way we do on the show as panelist-investors. It's the perfect metaphor for the *power of broke,* when you think about it. What do we know about sharks? They're ruthless, right? They're hungry. They feed on the weakness of lesser creatures. They're smart and swift and used to getting their way—all in all, the same characteristics that could help you out in a business setting, which of course was why the producers of the show hit on that whole *Shark Tank* theme in the first place.

But what else do we know about sharks? They're majestic creatures, right? They're powerful, resourceful, aggressive, hungry—all the qualities you'll need to take a bite out of your business. Plus, a shark has all these pilot fish swimming around him that he helps to feed. But at the same time they help to feed the shark. Meaning, there's a symbiotic relationship in place—as big and majestic and powerful as he is, a shark can't go it alone. A shark also smells opportunity from a great distance, like a drop of blood in the water five miles away. A shark does not spend its energy on small things because it has to reserve its energy. And a shark travels the entire world—it's very hard to hold a shark back as he sets off and does his thing.

So, what are my SHARK Point basics?

SET A GOAL. This first point is about as basic as it gets. What it comes down to is knowing where you're headed. Be realistic on this. Aim too high and you're bound to be frustrated, disappointed. Aim too low and you might leave some opportunities on the table, so take the time to get it right. Think what's possible in a best-case scenario. Think what's possible in a worst-case scenario. Think what's in reach. Then reach a little more—but set it all down on paper. Commit to it.

HOMEWORK, DO YOURS. In almost every business, analytics are key. Know your field, know your competitors, know your *stuff*. After all, if you don't know your stuff, how can you hope to know what's possible? How can you prepare yourself for what's coming? Think of it this way: out in the ocean, a shark doesn't attack unless it knows its prey; here on land, a "shark" needs the same mix of insight, instincts, and information to keep out in front. And a shark needs to know that there's nothing new under the sun. Face up to this fact, people. I hate to be the one to have to tell you this, but let me give it to you straight: You will never create anything new. Twitter is just an updated version of a note tied to a pigeon's leg. Facebook is nothing more than an endless chain letter, or another way to look at it, scribbles on the bathroom wall. Instagram is the scrapbook you used to keep and share with your friends. All there is, all there will ever be is a new form of delivery, a new way to market, and a new way to figure it out. On *Shark Tank* we see it all the time. Someone comes on the show and says, "I have the newest thing." No, you don't. What you have is maybe a new way or a new approach. So part of doing your homework means appreciating the history of your idea, your market, and your competition. "A fool can learn from his own mistakes, but a wise man learns from the mistakes of others." That's a line I picked up from Mr. Magic, an old-school radio deejay from New York. The thought behind it reinforces this concept that there are no new ideas—only new ways to execute those ideas.

ADORE WHAT YOU DO. It comes down to passion. You've got to love, love, love what you're doing—otherwise, why not do something else? That was my deal starting out: I loved clothes, loved seeing people in my designs, loved dreaming up new concepts. And that's the deal for every one of the successful entrepreneurs, influencers, and innovators you're about to meet in this book—they *love* what they do. "The only way to do great work is to do what you love." That one's from Steve Jobs, and it's been repeated into the ground, but I'm repeating it here because it's an all-important point. Own it, love it, live it . . . and you can find a way to make it work.

REMEMBER, *YOU* ARE THE BRAND. I wrote a whole book about this called *The Brand Within,* and here's how I opened it: "You are what you eat. You are what you wear. You are what you drive, where you live, what you drink, how you vote, what you stand for, how you love, hate, dedicate . . . you with me on this?" I still feel the same way, especially when it comes to building a business or career. It all starts with how you carry yourself, what you put out into the world, the way you interact with your audience, your customers, the marketplace. It's on you. Just *you*.

KEEP SWIMMING. Even when they're asleep, sharks are slipping through the ocean, swimming, scheming, getting ready to attack—which is pretty much the approach you have to take when you're starting out in business. You have to be relentless, nimble, moving ever forward. No matter what. And real sharks out in the ocean, if they don't keep swimming, they die—so keep this in mind, too.

To understand these SHARK Points more fully, check out the guide I've created specifically for you at: DaymondJohn.com/ PowerofBroke. It's a dynamic resource designed to help you wrap your head around this SHARK mind-set, and to guide you as you begin to tap into assets you might not even know you have.

DON'T JUST TAKE MY WORD FOR IT

So here's what's about to happen in the pages ahead. I'm going to introduce you to a dozen or so successful individuals from all different backgrounds, with different skill sets, different visions, different approaches, different lines of business. And let's be clear: these people aren't just successful, they're *wildly* successful—at the top of the top of whatever it is they do, wherever they find their passion, their purpose. You'll meet Gigi Butler, a cleaning lady from Nashville who found a way to build a cupcake empire on the back of some simple family recipes and a sound, simple strategy; Rob Dyrdek, the fearless (and peerless) professional skateboarder who turned his passion for extreme sports into a global franchise;

Kevin Plank, the founder and CEO of the ridiculously successful Under Armour sports apparel line; Acacia Brinley, a pioneering "influencer" on social media who learned as a teenager to leverage her personal brand into a personal fortune; Christopher Gray, the high school student from Birmingham, Alabama, who found a better way for students and families to access millions of dollars in unused scholarship funds; and on and on.

POWER FACT: **The initial $10,000 raised by Nick Woodman to fund his GoPro launch came from selling bead-and-shell belts out of his VW van....** *What a great example of doing whatever you have to do to get it done.*

The common thread knitting all of these uncommonly successful individuals together is that they've come at their achievements from essentially the same place. The paths they've had to take and the businesses and opportunities they're pursuing are all wildly different. But there are common themes running through their stories. They share a lot of the same traits. They're all hungry and determined. They all practice the *power of broke,* except in different ways. They've all had to scramble, with little or no money, to get to where they are today, at the very top of their fields. In some cases, they might have grown up with a certain level of privilege. You know, maybe there was family money, or professional contacts, that could have certainly offered a leg up—but that *edge* never really came into play. And all of them would probably tell you they wouldn't have had it any other way—meaning, if they had to do it all over again and could relaunch their business or product with unlimited resources, they'd still reach for the up-against-it, seat-of-the-pants approach.

That's the power of broke.

My idea here is to *show* rather than *tell*. I can pound my chest all I want and tell you there are all kinds of smart, creative, desperate ways for you to make the best of a bad situation and get your business going without a whole lot of cash, but end of the day, that's just me, pounding my chest. That's just me, telling my FUBU story—a story I take out on the road with me when I talk to business and student groups, more and more these days, ever since *Shark Tank* premiered in August 2009. When the show started out, the world knew me as just a hip-hop fashion mogul. I'd had my hand in a bunch of different businesses—fragrances, music, movies, spirits, jewelry, and accessories. But folks mostly knew me as the FUBU guy until *Shark Tank*. By the end of that first season, I was getting tons of invitations to appear before this or that group of entrepreneurs and tons of interview requests to share my thoughts on what it takes to start and sustain a business from a place of nothing much at all. Out of those conversations I've learned that we lift each other up by sharing our stories.

But like I said, you don't need to hear only from me. Better to shine a light on the innovators you're about to meet—creative, hard-charging, resourceful visionaries who found a way to make *something* out of *nothing*. Check out *their* stories and you just might be inspired to find a way to put the *power of broke* to work for you.

TWO

RISE AND GRIND

THERE ARE THOSE three words again, right at the top of this chapter . . . my reminder to myself, and to the hundreds of thousands of
people who follow me on social media, to get up and get to it.

So let's get to it here—and to start, let's take a look back at some
of the formative influences of my childhood and how they formed
this mantra that still guides me today.

I didn't have much growing up. I lived with my mother in Hollis, Queens. Just the two of us. She worked constantly—two or
three jobs, most of the time. Home late, up early, constantly moving, *doing*. She was disciplined, diligent, determined to set me up
so I could have some kind of shot. The thing is, in my neighborhood, "some kind of shot" had lots of double meanings . . . sad to
say, most of them with the emphasis on the word *shot*. Can't lie,
won't lie: the crowd I grew up with was getting into all kinds of
trouble. Trouble with guns, drugs, school, stolen cars, you name
it. Some serious stuff. And me, I got into my share, right alongside. Wasn't so deep into it as some of my boys, mostly because my

mother was on me to keep my head down and steer clear, but it was there. Close enough to taste, touch.

There were bad decisions all around—mine to make if I leaned the wrong way, mine to avoid if I could make the right call.

My mother was a smart lady—*real* smart. She knew the deal. She knew I was a mostly good kid with a mostly good head on my shoulders, but she also knew what it meant to run in this kind of traffic, especially growing up with a mom who wasn't around, so when I started high school she took out a mortgage on our house for $80,000. Funny how I remember the details; it was a lifetime ago, but it's like it was yesterday too. That might seem like a lot of money, but when you break it down, it didn't go very far, because my mother's plan was to use the loan to replace the money she'd been earning on all those jobs. We had to *live* off of that for the next three years, until I finished high school. We had to pay all our bills off of that, service the debt on the house off of that . . . so, no, it didn't go very far at all.

And look at it another way: Her other option would have been to keep working all those jobs and to send me off to boarding school, military school, some place where I would have been watched over constantly, but we couldn't afford that—no way, no how. Even if she dug deep, took out loans, tapped into some scholarship or grant monies, it wouldn't have worked. It might have been what I needed, but it would have been out of reach.

Anyway, $80,000—just enough, my mother thought, to let her dial things down at work and spend some more time at home with me, peeping and sweating my every move, helping me to skate past all those negative influences in our neighborhood. Guess she figured if she didn't make sure I had at least a toe on the straight-and-narrow, I might set off on the completely wrong path.

One way to look at it: that $80,000 was like my mother's investment in *me*. Another way to look at it: mothers are the ultimate start-ups, our true angel investors.

POWER FACT: **Steve Jobs sold his car and Steve Wozniak sold his calculator so they could scrape together enough money to build the prototype of the computer circuit board that would become known as the Apple I.** *Sometimes you can find the equity you need in the stuff you already have.*

Couldn't have been an easy decision for my mother to shut off that income stream the way she did, especially knowing it'd be tough to get back the good jobs she was leaving, but she didn't think she had a choice. This was what she felt she had to do to keep me on track; this was what it cost to keep me safe and focused. I don't think I appreciated her sacrifice at the time—didn't even recognize it for what it was. It's like she did a complete 180, changed her entire MO, just to give me a shot. In her bones, she knew I needed a kind of compass to make sure I was headed in the right direction. And she knew, as compasses go, she was the closest I'd ever get to true north.

Looking back, I see what my mother saw, feel what she felt. You have to realize, when I was little, I'd mostly made little kid–type trouble, but when I got bigger, the trouble got bigger too—and the consequences even bigger. Like I said, my friends were into all kinds of crazy stuff. Wasn't long before this one was getting shot, this one was getting arrested, this one was getting murdered on the back of a drug deal gone bad. Every month or so there'd be some new tragedy, some epic human fail that could have been avoided. So she just figured, *Hey, let me stop working a little bit and get in Daymond's face a little bit, and I'll be there to pick him up if he stumbles, you know. Whatever happens, whatever he's into, he'll have somewhere to turn.*

And that's how it went down. My mother ran the numbers in her head and figured the $80,000 she took out in cash would last us three to four years. And it did—it kept us going while she kept me in line. It was a good trade, far as she was concerned. She didn't count the money she might have lost, the opportunity cost of stepping away from all that work. She didn't care about the change to her routines. None of that mattered. What mattered, she always said, was that she kept me out of trouble. What counted was that she was there for me—always there. And from that point forward my mother was always around. She didn't hover, like some of the helicopter-type moms you see in some of our more affluent communities. No, sir—wasn't her style. She didn't walk me to school or demand that I check in with her after my last class. But she was there. She was present—and I got to say, it made all the difference.

My mother kept it real, watched over me like a hawk. Her big thing was I had to be home by a certain time each night. I didn't wear a watch, didn't pay attention to the time; no, the Concorde was my clock. Check it out: We lived at 103rd Street and Farmers Boulevard, a couple miles from JFK Airport, and you could hear that plane rumble each night as it came in for a landing. My mother used to say, "Daymond, as long as you're faster than the Concorde, you're okay."

So I'd be out playing stickball, chasing girls, hanging on the corner with my friends, whatever. I'd be a couple blocks from home. But as soon as those neighborhood streets started to rumble and rattle with the noise of the Concorde, I took off. Oh, man . . . I *ran*. Faster than the Concorde! Because I knew what was waiting for me on the other side of that door if I was late.

One other thing: during the summer, when the sun was out longer, I got an extra couple hours to be outside—and at *those* times the Empire State Building was my clock. Every night the lights at the top of the building would come on when it got dark, and you could see them from all over the city—from my neighborhood, definitely. The cool piece to this story is that my office is now on the 66th floor of the Empire State Building, and every time I ride that elevator I think back on how things were on the streets of Hollis.

Those two "clocks"—the Concorde and the Empire State Building—were such powerful symbols when I was growing up. I always told myself I would fly on the Concorde someday, but it stopped flying by the time I started making decent money, so that's not happening. But I do sit pretty close to the top of the Empire State Building, and every night when it gets dark I imagine little kids all over the city racing home to keep from troubling their mothers.

So there was that.

Money was tight, though. Let's be honest, it had been tight before, and now it was tighter still—and going over that time in my life, I think it shaped my outlook on money, not having all that much of it. We were up against it, constantly. There was a nice-enough roof over our heads, nice-enough clothes on our backs, but in almost every other way we were scrambling, scraping. Some months we'd have to let the electric bill slide to pay for groceries. Winters, we'd sometimes go without heat for a week or two. But we got by. We were okay, and soon as I could make some kind of meaningful contribution I started working my butt off—I guess to try and fill up some of those bank accounts where my mom's paychecks used to go.

TAP THE POWER

So here's my takeaway on how I grew up: adversity, on its own, isn't necessarily a bad thing. In fact, my whole premise here is that being broke can be like a godsend, if you find a way to harness the *power of broke* and use it to your advantage. What do I mean by that? Well, in my case, it meant finding some piece of motivation in my mother's example to help lift us up and out of our situation. It meant finding inspiration in her perspiration. It meant recognizing that my back was against the wall and the only direction was up and forward. It meant making the most out of whatever resources we had. It meant digging deep, and keeping focused, and going at it hard.

It meant waking up every morning and saying those three little words: *rise and grind*.

Over and over.

Again and again.

Think about how you might apply this same mind-set to your own life, your own circumstances. Do you have money? That's great—you're off to a running start. Do you *need* money? That's great too—you've got something to prove. You've got to work harder, smarter, faster, longer, just to level the playing field, and if you go at it the right way, somewhere in that *harder, smarter, faster, longer* you'll find a kind of competitive edge. You'll separate yourself from the rest of the pack.

I'm not suggesting we'd all be better off if we started from nothing, because hey, money can buy you a whole lot of advantages. Better schools. A financial cushion if things don't go your way. Investors you might be able to call on to help you start a business or fund your research. And on and on. But there's a whole lot of *silver lining* out there for those of us who haven't been lucky enough to be born with *silver spoons* in our mouths. And for a lot of us, the silver lining covers the whole damn cloud. What it comes down to, I think, is mind-set—the poverty of the mind. Are you a *have* or a *have-not* type of person? Are you a *want* or a *want-not*? It's how you approach your situation, and what you do to make the best of your situation, that makes all the difference.

POWER FACT: In 1982, over 60 percent of the richest Americans on the Forbes 400 list came from wealthy families; 30 years later only 32 percent could make the same claim. *Inherited wealth is no longer the common denominator among our wealthiest individuals and families.* Do the math, people: that means 68 percent of the wealthiest people started with nothing. That means today's entrepreneurs have greater opportunities and richer backstories than at any other time in our recent history, no matter how they started out in life. That means there is always opportunity—as long as you know where and how to look for it.

There's a great line I heard from Liz Claman, an anchor on the Fox Business Network. She told me once that her father used to say, "I've given you every advantage in life except for being disadvantaged."

That cuts right to it, doesn't it? It reminds us that when you grow up on the side of *have-not*, you're used to hearing the word *no*. In fact, you probably hear it more than any other word in the English language. *No, you can't afford this. No, you can't have that. No, that's impossible.* When you finally do hear the word *yes*, you tear off after it—whatever it is you're chasing. You've heard *no* so often, you're numb to it. But *yes*—it lights you up, fills you with possibilities. On the other side of that, when you grow up privileged, you never hear *no*, so as soon as those resources are gone, you're in a tough spot. You hear *no* for the first time, it's tough to recover, tough to look for another way to get to *yes*.

GO FOR IT

Okay, so if a willingness to do whatever it takes is fine and good, what happens when *whatever it takes* is a necessity? What happens when you've got no choice but to bust your butt and bring good things to light? And on the flip side, what happens to the guts, the swagger, the drive, the hard-charging attitude you'll need to make it to the top when you know, deep down, there's a safety net to catch you if you fall?

My mother's thing was to think big. Always. No matter what. We lived small, but there was no cap on our dreaming, no ceiling on what was possible, so I made it my business to stay out of real trouble and push myself to achieve. *Think big*—that was like her mantra. She even kept a supersized can opener on the wall of our kitchen, like the kind you used to find in home decorator stores back then. It was up there for inspiration, because in my mother's book it wasn't enough to hustle, to make a couple extra bucks. You had to hustle, but then you had to do a little something more besides. I had no choice but to be smart about it, to be creative, to think from a place of desperation. And let me tell you, when you're always reaching for that *little something more besides,* the commitment to finding it, the dead-solid-certain belief that it's there for the taking . . . it comes to define you. It becomes an important part of your personality. When you come at the world from that place of desperation (or aspiration), it's like you're wired in a whole different way. And it was that sense of desperation that would become my fuel—that feeling that I had no option but to succeed, no place to go but up, up, up . . . *that's* what powered my first successes.

Like a lot of kids in my neighborhood, I was in the snow removal business—mostly because it didn't take much more than a shovel and some elbow grease to get started. But I went these kids one better, because I out-hustled them. See, even at ten, eleven years old, I was out there looking for ways to drum up repeat business. I didn't understand terms like "leveraging" or "up-selling," but I guess I understood the concepts, because I was putting them to work. I'd go around the neighborhood and offer a free spring cleanup to anyone who'd give me an exclusive contract to shovel their driveway and their front walk for the season. I made deals like that with six or seven people on my block, and then I went out and hired other kids to help me with a lawn mowing business I'd started up. But not before I told them that if they wanted the job they'd have to help me on those free spring cleanups I'd promised those folks during the winter—you know, cleaning out the gutters, tidying up fallen branches and other debris before the start of the season.

I didn't understand a term like the *power of broke* either—but there it was.

Here's another way I tapped that power early on: In my neighborhood, it was all about the car. Kids used to hustle, steal, connive, save their way to have enough cash to buy a Jetta or a Sterling or a Cadillac 98. Those were the rides everybody wanted—used, typically, but the car had to look good to mean something. So up and down the street my boys were stashing their money, hoping against hope they could buy a hot car, only when my turn came and I'd saved up enough I went another way. By this time I'd graduated from the lawn business and I worked crazy hours at two jobs—at Church's Fried Chicken and at Red Lobster. I walked around smelling like grease from the deep fryer, like melted butter from all those half-eaten lobsters, but the money was decent. The hours? They were crazy, wall-to-wall, but that was part of the transaction. Managed to make some serious paper—enough to help out around the house, hit the town every now and then, put a little something away for later.

Back of my mind, that *little something for later* had four wheels and a motor. Clothes were a big deal to me—my kicks, especially. They helped to make a statement, announce my arrival . . . all of that. But as I got older it was more and more about the car, which I guess came from the same place, wanting to move around the neighborhood in style, only the buy-in was a whole lot steeper. I scrimped and saved, same as everyone else, but I came at it in an entrepreneurial way. I decided to buy a beat-up old van instead of a Caddy—one of those 15-passenger vans that wasn't about to turn any heads. Why? Because I saw an opportunity. Don't know that I could have put a name to it just then, but it was the *power of broke* on full display. It was me, putting my money to work, because I had no other choice but to double-down and look for an edge—and at that age, at that stage, *any* kind of edge would have done me just fine.

For about $12,000 cash, I bought a red-and-white 15-passenger Ford van, 1979. The van had over 100,000 miles on it, and it had been on the road for over ten years, but it was in pretty good shape—a little beat-up, but reliable. I took a lot of heat from my boys for driving around in such a boring ride, but this was my *little something more besides.* This was me making an investment in my future. It wasn't enough for my ride to just get me around town. No, for $12,000, my ride had to grow my game, take me to some new opportunities, and here I'd set it up so I could go into the share-a-ride business. Told myself it'd be like buying a ride *and* a business, so I set my street cred aside and went for it.

Told myself it didn't matter if my ride didn't turn heads—it only mattered that it turned things around for me.

MAKE A PLAN, TEAR IT UP, MAKE A NEW PLAN

The way it worked in my neighborhood, there was money to be made shadowing the MTA city buses, providing more of a door-to-door service, like a rogue limo driver. These days ride-sharing services like Uber and Lyft are plugging into the same concept in a big-time way, changing the landscape of the taxi industry—but my take was capped by the technology, the times, and my empty pockets. Still, break it down and you'll see the germ of the same idea. I was out to offer a service you could get elsewhere, but I was out to do it cheaper and more efficiently. Here's how I set things up. I'd drive along Parsons Boulevard, all the way down Guy R. Brewer Boulevard, and then to the Rockaways and Beach 116. People would come off and on, off and on, and if you hit it right, you could make $40 to $50 in a two-hour round-trip. I'd charge a dollar, which was 15 cents cheaper than the city bus, but I'd stop wherever you wanted along the route, so that was like the big value-added piece of my service. You know, if you were on one of the main streets, like Merrick Boulevard, it could be ten or twelve long blocks between stops, which meant people could be six or seven blocks from their apartment, so I'd just pull up right in front of their building. For a lot of women it was a whole lot safer than riding the bus at night, and when it rained or when it was cold, it was a great way to beat the weather.

Riding with me was cheaper, and it was more convenient, and as an added bonus I also extended credit. I was like one of those mom-and-pop bodega operators in the neighborhood. I came to know my customers, and they came to know me. *What's that, you don't have the money today? No problem, you can take care of me tomorrow.* So that brought me a whole other mess of customers, because you needed exact change to ride the city bus, and ain't no way Ralph Kramden was gonna let you ride for free.

POWER FACT: **There are over 600,000 new business start-ups every year in the United States—fewer than half of them (44 percent) survive eight years.** The message here is that *the barriers to entry are coming down in a lot of industries, but success is never guaranteed.* No, the odds aren't exactly in your favor, but they're not against you either, so find a way to get out in front—then find a way to stay there.

All these extra perks added up, to the point where folks started looking for *me.* No, the technology didn't exist yet for me to offer the kind of integrated service customers have come to expect from Uber, but my customers and I did what we could with the technology that was available at the time, which was basically common sense. My regulars, they knew my schedule, and I knew the best times of day to get the biggest return on my investment. Obviously, I couldn't just drive up and down the street looking for fares. It cost too much in gas, and there was wear and tear on the van—expenses I could only justify if I was riding full.

Better believe it, I took a lot of grief from my buddies for showing up everywhere in my run-down van, but the girls didn't seem to mind. There was a lot of room in those backseats for us to mess around in—not like those cramped little Jettas. And nobody seemed to mind if I asked them to ride along with me for a while on a busy night. It was never dull . . . I'll say that.

That van became a symbol for me—a reminder that the way forward in business isn't always to spend. Today I'm always telling young entrepreneurs to take *affordable next steps*—in other words, to think within reach. And this was me practicing what I would go on to preach. Here's how I looked at it: Even if I had the money for a new van, it wouldn't have made a ton of sense to buy one. At $40,000, which was about what a high-end van would have run me back then—leather seats, tinted windows, the works—I would have been behind on the deal. Why? Because the moment I drove it off the lot, the new van would be worth $20,000. Because the used van I bought for $12,000 was *still* worth about $12,000 after I'd been driving it for a year. After I put on 80,000 miles or so, I would probably need a new transmission, maybe a brake job, so let's say that would have run me another $5,000. That still means, all in, I'd be into that used van for $17,000, while the brand-new car, after putting 80,000 miles on it, would be inching closer in value to what I paid for the used van in the first place.

So you see, the *power of broke* keeps us from making the easy decisions that come back to bite us.

What put me out of business eventually were the tickets. There were gypsy cabs and share-a-ride vehicles all over the city, and few of us had legitimate livery licenses, and pretty soon the Department of Transportation started cracking down on us. We were taking money from the MTA and from medallion cab drivers, so I could understand that. First time I got a ticket, I just chalked it up to the cost of doing business, but after a while the tickets started coming in waves. And the fines! They could run me $1,500 a pop, which was a real hit to my pockets. Every here and there, fine, no problem, you find a way to deal. But every month, every other week, that kind of hit punches all kinds of holes in your budget. *Affordable next steps?* For a time, this van business fit the bill, but it started to hurt—especially after I'd been at it a couple years and my beat-up ride started needing maintenance.

Before I got out of the share-a-ride game, though, the van proved pretty useful in the launch of my next business—and here again, it was knowing I had to keep scrambling that kept me focused. I could have probably gotten $10,000 for the van at this point, and a lot of guys I know would have jumped at that kind of money, but by this point I was getting into the clothing business, and the van was turning out to be a real windfall once I started using it to truck all my T-shirts and other gear to Black Expos up and down the East Coast. A couple times, when I had nothing else on the calendar, I'd even driven to the Apollo Theater, slid open the doors, and started selling T-shirts and tie-top hats right out of the van. It was like having a *hoopty* boutique.

Truth was, I couldn't really afford to keep the van once I gave up on the share-a-ride business, but it was a real boost to my new clothing line, so I kept it—and I look back on that decision now as another example of the *power of broke* on full display. It's not that I wasn't strapped for cash, but I'd been strapped for cash my whole life, so I told myself I could ride out this little rough patch and make the most out of my investment in the van while it was still running. I could just roll on up and start slinging clothes.

If I'd had some money behind me—if I'd come at it from a place of success, from where I am today—I don't think I would have bumped into this outlet for sales, not quite in the same way.

Don't think I would have been *driven* in quite the same way. (Sorry about the bad pun—couldn't resist.) My head would have been someplace else, and I'd have probably been looking to make more of a big hit–type splash with my clothes. But I didn't have those kinds of resources, that kind of mind-set, and looking back I can't shake the belief this was a good thing. It forced me to grow this idea I had for a clothing line in a ground-up kind of way.

STEP OUTSIDE YOURSELF

This right here is the essence of this book. It's all about tapping into the mind-set that finds us when we're in that place of hunger, that place of desperation . . . and putting it to work. It's about embracing the up-against-it mentality that might have stamped your childhood, the paycheck-to-paycheck, make-every-penny-count culture that defines so many American households . . . and putting it to work *for* you instead of *against* you. It's also about the kinds of pitfalls that can find you if you get your hands on too much money too soon in the development of your business. I see it all the time on the *Shark Tank* set, where my fellow panelists and I are regularly pitched by entrepreneurs looking for funding or guidance on a start-up or new product launch.

Let's be clear: this book is for people of all ages, at all stages of life. Maybe you're just starting out, unsure of where you're going and how you want to make your mark. You'll find stories to inspire you to follow your own path with just a compass and a flashlight to help you find your way. Or what if you've been working for the man your whole life and are looking to make a change—looking to embrace those entrepreneurial passions before it's too late? You'll also hear from folks just like you—maybe they've hit some kind of dead end or brick wall and needed a harsh wake-up call before doubling back and hitting the restart button.

No matter who you are, in almost every situation, at almost every turn, the *power of broke* can work for you—but it doesn't always work on its own. No, you've got to be willing to try new approaches, adapt to changing technologies, adjust your thinking.

Don't believe me that the world is changing? Check out these two stories, one from each end of the age spectrum. The first is about a young guy—looked to be in his early twenties—I met as I was coming out of a hotel in Vegas. We were each waiting for the valets to drive up with our cars, and this kid asked me if I had any advice for him. He recognized me from television, said he was a rapper, trying to catch a break, wanted to know if I could help him out.

I said, "That's not really my area of expertise."

Just as I was saying that, the valet drove up with this guy's car—a sweet Aston Martin. So I turned to the guy and said, "Homey, it looks like you're doing okay for yourself."

It was interesting—the kid was out for advice, but from the looks of things he was doing better than me.

He said, "No, I'm making plenty of money. But it's not what I want to be doing."

So I asked him how he was making money, and it turned out he was a fairly well-known artist, a painter. He told me he'd hit upon a great way to monetize his work. Somehow, he'd built a platform of over 100,000 Instagram followers, and each week he'd put up an original painting and announce to his followers that the design would be available on a T-shirt for the next twenty-four hours. It was a "one day and one day only" type deal, and off of that he would collect all these preorders for the limited-edition shirt, which he'd price at $40, $50, $75, whatever the case might be. Next day, he'd take his design to the screen printer, run off the precise number of shirts in all the right sizes to fill his order, and ship everything out. Every week, he'd repeat the process with a new design.

Right away I thought, *What a great business model*. The guy was getting full margin on his orders, because he was selling directly to his customer. He didn't have to deal with returns, or sizing issues, or warehouse issues. There was no overstock, no inventory. No special software, no significant start-up costs. And the best part—he'd set it up so his customers had to prepay, meaning he never had to raise any capital to fill his orders.

I said, "How much money you making on this deal?"

He said, "Last year, we did $1.3 million."

One point three million dollars! On a business run entirely from this guy's cell phone—I couldn't have found a better *power of broke* story if I'd hired a Hollywood screenwriter to think something up. And underneath this great success was a reminder that the more things change, the more they stay the same. Why do I say that? Because this guy's business model was basically exactly the same as the one direct-mail marketers have been counting on since the 1960s. And so was his conversion rate—one-half of one percent. He was averaging about 500 T-shirt sales each week off that 100,000-follower base. That's the same return they used to get at Publishers Clearing House, at Columbia Record Club, at pretty much every other direct-mail company on the planet—the same return you can *still* expect. The only difference was that his method of reaching that customer had changed. So even though this kid had found a way to tap into today's technology, he was basically borrowing a page from an old playbook. Same formula, different platform.

Second story, and this one's all the way at the other end of the age range. A buddy of mine came to see me one day, told me he was worried about his parents. His father was a master carpenter. His mom was an established efficiency expert—folks hired her to help them clean out their desks, organize their files and closets. (She called herself a *declutterer.*) Things were going great for this guy's parents, who were now in their 60s and looking toward retirement. They did everything right; everything they were supposed to do. They put in their time, and kept moving forward in a by-the-book way to the American Dream. Then the recession happened. In 2008 the last thing people were thinking about was remodeling or decluttering their homes, so business kind of dried up. Between the two of them—his construction work and her consulting work—their income was down about 80 percent, and yet even with that kind of hit my friend's parents might have been okay. They might have been able to ride out the downturn in the economy, the dip in their revenue, but then the value of their home also took a big hit, and they were underwater. Things got so bad, they had to sell their home at a loss, invade their 401(k), and move in with my buddy's grandparents. It was an embarrassing, worrying time—and even if his dad could have signed on as a hired hand with a construction company, it was getting harder and harder for him to climb those ladders and work some of those remodeling jobs. He was getting a little too old for that type of work—hey, he could fall off a ladder and break his hip, and then where would he be?

The solution? Well, it came on the back of a crazy idea. My friend was able to persuade his father to come in with him on this idea . . . before either one of them even knew where it might lead. He went to his dad one day with a set of plans and said, "Build this house."

"Why?" the dad asked.

"Just do me a favor, Dad, and build this house," he said. "I've got a feeling about this."

That's all it was, at first—a feeling. A hunch.

Turned out there was a market for miniature dog homes, which were popular among super-wealthy homeowners looking to set their pets up in style. Makes sense, I guess. If you're spending $4–5 million on a house, if you've got that kind of money, you wouldn't blink at a $50,000 or $75,000 or $100,000 price tag for a doghouse built to look just like your brand-new McMansion. My buddy's father did one of these houses on spec and found that he really liked the work—and that he had a talent for it. There were other pluses too. Each house took about a week to design and build, and the best part was that he could do the whole job in a workshop he set up in his basement. No climbing ladders, no slipping and falling, no dealing with bad weather or driving to the job site.

And then, since my friend's mom was also underemployed, she used her organizational skills to help with the online marketing. She figured out how to target-market pet owners who were also high-end homeowners—*Facebook-targeting, or geo-targeting* as it's called, and this woman became an expert in it before too long.

Last year they sold $2.5 million worth of custom doghouses—not bad for a couple old folks, huh?

The reason I've grouped these two stories together is to make the point that it doesn't matter if you're a digital native like the young artist with the limited-edition T-shirts or digital immigrants like the older couple who kind of stumbled onto the doggie real estate business . . . the *power of broke* can be a real force for change. You don't need a whole lot of resources to change your life. Sometimes everything you need is right there in the smart phone you hold in your hands.

Gotta love technology, right?

FIND BEAUTY IN CHAOS

STEVE AOKI

MUSICIAN, DEEJAY, RECORD PRODUCER, MUSIC EXECUTIVE

Sometimes you come into this world surrounded by success and opportunity, but that doesn't mean you'll have it easy. Doesn't mean you won't have to scratch for it, sweat for it, bleed for it, same as everyone else.

In some cases, you can even make the case that you'll have to scratch a little harder, sweat a little more, bleed another couple buckets, just to prove yourself. Why? Because you might find yourself going against what's expected of you. Because folks might think the good life's been handed to you. Because you have to pick up the pace to step out from your family's shadow.

That's how it was for Steve Aoki, the electro house deejay who's probably done more to define the techno-music scene than any other artist. Electronic dance music—he's made it his brand. He's reshaped, redefined, restamped the genre . . . all of that. To watch him do his thing in front of audiences of 30,000 screaming, sweating, slamming fans, dousing the crowd with blasts of champagne and cakes and pies, whipping an entire arena into a joyful frenzy, is to take in an innovative artist at the very top of his game. Oh, man . . . it's a thrilling thing to watch this guy work the crowd, but underneath all of that is a whole other thrill: here's an entrepreneur who's tapped the heart of a movement in a fundamental way and changed the face of mainstream music, and it's something to see, something to celebrate.

What a lot of people don't know is that Steve stepped into this spot from an unlikely place. He grew up in Newport Beach, California, the son of Rocky Aoki, another entrepreneur who changed the landscape—he was the founder of the ridiculously successful Benihana restaurant chain. What this meant for Steve, growing up, was that he came from a place of privilege. He played badminton on his high school team. He went to college—the University of California at Santa Barbara. Back of everyone's mind, it was generally assumed he'd go into the family business and find a way to build on his father's great success.

Back of everyone's mind, that is, except for Steve Aoki's. Back of his mind, there was something else at play.

By the time Steve was born, his father was already a kind of hip-hop star in his own world. Rocky Aoki went to nightclubs, partied hard, drove fancy-ass cars—he was always making the papers, but not always in a good way. You have to realize, this was a guy who'd scraped and hustled to the top, came over to the States from Japan to make his way. He actually came here on a tour to wrestle for the Japanese national team, ended up staying. Wound up driving an ice cream truck because there weren't a whole lot of opportunities for young Japanese men at the time—not so soon after World War II anyway. Think about that: guy busts his butt wrestling for his country, even earns a spot on the 1960 Olympic team, travels to America on the national dime to represent his country, and the only work he can find is slinging toasted almonds and fudge bars from a truck.

POWER FACT: **In the United States, immigrants are twice as likely to start a business as US citizens....** There's a reason for this: When you're new to American shores, you're hungry to succeed.... If you've been here your whole life, there's less on the line. It doesn't mean you're not hungry, but it's a whole different appetite. When you're trying to make your way in a new place, it has more to do with survival and less to do with getting by.

KNOW YOUR PLACE

Steve felt a different kind of discrimination growing up in the suburbs of California, where there still weren't a whole lot of opportunities for a young Japanese kid. During high school, early 1990s, he remembers feeling like he was always on the outside looking in, somehow different or other than everyone else. He was never sure if it was because everyone knew who his father was, knew he had money, or if it was just because he was Japanese. Whatever it was, he stood out, and he fell in with a group of other marginalized kids and decided to just do his own thing. And how it worked out, he found his own thing by embracing a hard-core punk lifestyle.

"People with money, there are basically two ways they raise their children," Steve says now, looking back on his father's influence. "They either take the attitude, 'I had to work hard for what I have, and I want you to follow the same discipline, so I'm not going to give you anything.' You know, 'Nothing was handed to me, so nothing is handed to you,' that kind of thinking. Or it's more like, 'I've worked hard so you don't have to go through what I had to go through.' And those are the kids who grow up with the best of everything. The best education, the best opportunities, a leg up in business, whatever."

To hear Steve tell it, his father never missed an opportunity to tell Steve and his two older siblings how hard he had to work to get where he was, but that wasn't what left Steve thinking he was on his own. No, that part came from the punk community he'd decided to embrace. "In that world," Steve says, "it's all about what you bring to it on your own. It's all about making things happen. Kids with money, kids with influence, that doesn't cut it. To make it work, it's got to be genuine. You have to make your own way."

So he did—tried to anyway, and at first it was rough going.

Now, it also worked out that Steve's father fell into the category of rich, accomplished dads who expected their kids to go it alone, so even if Steve had put his hand out, it would have come back empty. It was just as well, he says. Creative types on the punk scene at the time—making music, organizing events, writing fanzines—were all about bootstrapping. They dug deep, worked hard, found a way to get things done—on the cheap, on the fly. To go to your rich father with your hand out, that wasn't the way of that world. Wasn't Steve's way either. He wanted to cut his own path, on his own terms, just like his father, so Steve and his crew grabbed at what they could.

Long story short, Steve ended up starting his own record label when he was just nineteen years old—Dim Mak Records. Started it with two other friends, each putting in $400, which was pretty much all they had. Remember, this was a time in the music industry when you could put out a seven-inch single and hope to make some noise with it, only the noise Steve and his buddies made with Dim Mak early on was little more than a whisper.

"It was all about the idea," he tells me. "It was finding a way to get it done. Going to Kinko's, stealing a bunch of copies to get the word out, heading out to shows and selling our seven-inch from the trunk of our car, making maybe seventy-five cents for every record we sold, banking that money until we had enough to put out another. And then, soon as we could, we started putting on our own shows. In my apartment, at the eighty-person-capacity bar down the street, wherever. Same deal as with our records—if we made money on one party, we'd put it right into the next one."

Steve's mind-set was a whole lot like mine, starting out. He did what he had to do to keep his place at the party—but it was all about the party, man. He believed in this music, same way me and my boys believed in our T-shirts and hats. Steve kept putting it out there and putting it out there, and he counted it a success that he was making enough to be able to keep at it—even if he and his friends weren't putting much money in the bank.

MAKE A BEAUTIFUL MESS

The thing with Steve and his friends at the front end of Dim Mak, they weren't thinking about building a business. Their reality was, they couldn't afford to think about building a business. All they could do, really, was scrape and hustle and work like crazy in service of their idea—to put their music out into the world, somehow, some way. The bottom line, for them, was all about keeping it real, keeping it simple. And most of all, keeping it going.

Wasn't a business plan so much as it was a desperation plan—a survival plan. Put out one record and hope like hell you get to put out another. And another. It was a model Steve believed he had no choice but to make work, and with a whole lot of creativity and extra effort, Dim Mak kept going. At some point, Steve started deejaying—small gigs at first, sometimes for the exposure and sometimes for a couple hundred bucks. A lot of times, he'd set up these gigs himself, at local bars and party spaces. It wasn't until Steve signed the British indie band Bloc Party that Dim Mak started to look like it could turn into a real business, but even this success came in a kind of hand-to-hand way. Steve had to max out ten different credit cards just to get the record out. He was over $90,000 in debt, with no idea how to pay it off. He'd moved to New York and started running the entire operation out of his 900-square-foot apartment, which doubled as his office. Oh, and he shared the space with his girlfriend and thirteen interns, so it was a little like living and working in a phone booth. Things were crazy-tight, crazy-basic—just crazy.

"We couldn't afford to hire anyone, so those interns were key," he tells me. "And it was a great experience for them, it was, but I had no idea what some of them were doing. I was like, 'Could you cook something?' I mean, I didn't know what to do with some of these kids, who came to work for us from all over the world. They believed in what we were doing, wanted to be a part of it. Sacrificed a lot, some of them, just to throw in with us. We were kind of a big deal, I guess, but we were a big deal with no money. We were a big deal on paper, in theory. There were records piled everywhere. People were staking out their little pieces of territory. But there was excitement too. Incredible excitement and energy. It really was a kind of beautiful mess.

"I love thinking back on that time in that little apartment. I was broke out of my mind, and the whole time, it would have been nothing for me to reach out to my father and say, 'Hey, can you help me out?' But he would have just told me to run away from what I was doing. He didn't believe in it. He didn't believe in me. Plus, he didn't understand the music business. Not that I understood it either, but I felt it, you know. I believed in it. My father, he wanted me to get a real job. Not at Benihana's, that was his thing. But he would have introduced me to people he knew in business, so I could learn my stuff somewhere else."

CATCH THE WAVE

Steve remembers that those little $100 and $200 deejay gigs really made the difference, kept him going. He was trading on good faith and goodwill just to arrange for all these up-and-coming bands to play at these parties he was putting together, parties where he could sell his Dim Mak records and swag. Parties where he could maybe talk himself into his next deejay gig. He barely had time to worry about things like rent and food and utilities. From the sound of things, he worried more about momentum than money. When things were slow, he threw together another party, put out another record, and over time Dim Mak became like the hipster stamp of approval that spoke to this whole community. Without really realizing it, without really meaning to, Steve had built a kind of movement, a following—and with it, he'd developed a reputation. People came to appreciate that if it was a Dim Mak event, if it was a Steve Aoki event, it would be at a certain level, a certain quality. And if it had been a long time between events, a long time between records, there'd be another one coming along soon enough.

He still wasn't making any money, but he looked up one day and realized he had built this pulsing, thrumming business—all on the back of his sweat and hustle. It was the *power of broke,* man. Don't think it could have happened any other way. Steve doesn't think so either. When I ask him how things would have gone if his father had given him a hundred thousand dollars early on to bankroll his business, Steve smiles, shrugs his shoulders. He says, "I would have squandered it. Spent it on all the wrong things, for all the wrong reasons. No way I could have built the same energy, the same movement. No way the community would have taken me seriously. You have to want it, but it cuts deeper than that. You have to need it. Like a hunger, you know."

Yeah, I know. But it takes an enormous amount of inner strength to see it through. It takes knowing that things will shake out to the good in the end. Because you've left yourself no other option but to succeed.

"You have to eat it," Steve says. "In the end, that's what it comes down to. You have to get knocked off the horse a couple times, and roll around in the dirt, take your lumps, whatever. And then, you've got to find a way to get back on your feet, back on that horse, and go at it again."

That beautiful mess Steve was talking about, when he was ramping up his business from his cramped apartment, with more interns than he knew what to do with? That's the kind of chaos a true entrepreneur needs to survive and thrive, to put his ideas out into the world with the full force of his conviction. Absolutely, you need to max out your credit cards a time or two. You need to go to bed not knowing how you'll keep the lights on tomorrow. You need to bet on yourself, and you need to bet big—almost in an all-or-nothing sort of way.

You need to be resourceful.

You need to catch the wave.

That's how it was with me and my partners, when we were jump-starting FUBU. We emptied our pockets to get it done. I borrowed $100,000 against my mother's house to buy a bunch of sewing machines and enough material to fill our first bunch of orders. That left me with just enough to hire a half-dozen people to sew for us—and a bare-bones operation that had just enough fuel to keep going. But only for a time.

So let's be clear on this: Steve Aoki might have had a little bit more of a safety net than yours truly. He grew up with money. He grew up with opportunities. But it was his father's money, not his. His father's opportunities, not his—his father's safety net too. Far as Steve was concerned, he started from scratch. He was up against it, from day one, and it was because he was up against it that he found a way to succeed. His music, his message, it all came from a genuine place—it wasn't a business venture so much as a business *adventure,* and I have to think the thrill of not knowing what would happen next, not knowing where his next meal was coming from, his next gig . . . that all of that not knowing added up to a kind of dead solid certainty that he was on the right path.

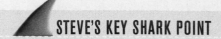

STEVE'S KEY SHARK POINT

SET A GOAL. For Steve, finding a goal meant finding a way to make the music he wanted to hear. That's where it all started for him. The objective each time out was to get to the next time out—meaning, one project needed to make just enough money to fund the next project. Even when he maxed out all those credit cards, Steve just wanted to keep the lights on, to keep going. It wasn't until he'd staged a couple of events that he thought about launching his own record label—and it wasn't until that happened that he was able to start thinking about paying off those credit cards and making some real paper. The great lesson here is that your goals don't have to be life-changing to get you where you want to go—just life-sustaining. Keep the lights on, and good things will happen.

Steve was taking affordable next steps and moving himself closer and closer to where he needed to be. What affordable next steps are you able to start taking today to get you closer to your goals?

For more information and resources, check out
www.DaymondJohn.com/PowerofBroke/Steve

HONOR YOUR TRUTH

ACACIA BRINLEY

SOCIAL MEDIA ICON, FACE OF A GENERATION, "SELFIE" QUEEN

"Broke" is a great equalizer. It levels the playing field, gives the edge to hustle and heart over money and market forces. Best of all, it forces you to dig deep, to invest in yourself and trust in yourself—and maybe to kick yourself in the butt enough times that the full force of your personality has a chance to shine through.

That's how it shook out when we were launching our FUBU clothing line, trying to make some noise at our first trade show in Vegas, competing for orders and shelf space with top designers from all over the world. To a lot of folks, it must have looked like a no-win situation—four street-smart kids from Hollis, Queens, with no business being in business. But to us it was more of a can't-lose situation. Why? Because we were already up against it—because we had no choice but to succeed. We would not be denied, and I think it came across—how much our designs meant to us, what we thought they could mean to our community. Plus, we had a secret weapon. We'd tapped into a disruptive technology that didn't cost us a cent, the same technology that was available to every other designer on the floor of the Las Vegas Convention Center, only they didn't recognize it for what it was.

So here's the thing: When it comes to disruptive technology, there's always something new. For us, it was the reach and power of hip-hop, magnified by the reach and power of music videos and underlined by the unshakable belief that we were on to something. What's that you say, Daymond? Hip-hop—a technology? Disruptive? Well, yeah . . . kinda, sorta. Stay with me on this and you'll see what I mean.

Music has always been a unifying force, a change-agent set to a beat. It's how we talk to each other about our hopes and fears, our wildest dreams, our darkest secrets. It's how we hear about trends and movements. It's how we speak out. In the '60s, it was all about peace and love and war. (Remember? Not me—I'm too young, but I know my history!) Back then, protest music ruled the airwaves. People were against the war in Vietnam, against the establishment, against the machine . . . and these sentiments came out in the music of the day.

Jump ahead a bunch of years and you could hear the same tune set to a different beat. In my neighborhood, in my time, hip-hop was that driving force. It was just a bunch of street kids like me, talking to each other—and absolutely, a lot of what we talked about was rage and "damn the police" nonsense, but a lot of it was about who we were and what we were about. *Hey, man, I like this shirt. Hey, this is what I do. This is the way I walk. This is the way I talk. This is what I stand for.*

The disruptive technology I just mentioned? It was in the marriage of hip-hop and music videos, because that's how we were able to get our shirts on the backs of all these up-and-coming hip-hop artists and make some noise. Getting someone like LL Cool J to wear our gear was like a multimillion-dollar ad campaign for us, and it all came about in an organic way.

BE THE CHANGE

Jump ahead another bunch of years and you'll find a new disruptive technology—social media. For a young girl named Acacia Brinley, growing up in Orange County, California, sites like Tumblr loomed as a great escape. Social media spoke to her the same way hip-hop spoke to me. She didn't look at these sites as tools to grow her brand or build a business—no, for Acacia they were a place to hide, maybe reinvent herself.

And maybe, just maybe, they were a place where she could be herself.

"I was bullied in school," she shares when we sit down to discuss her unlikely rise to becoming one of the top "influencers" on social media today, with over four million followers across all platforms. "All the other girls were wearing Uggs, Abercrombie, Juicy Couture, whatever was new, whatever was hot, and there was me with my fake Uggs from Forever 21, or my jeans from Old Navy, whatever was on sale. I didn't have the right clothes, so the girls didn't like me, and then of course the guys didn't like me because they followed what the girls were doing. Basically, I didn't have any friends. I didn't play sports, didn't play music, didn't participate in any extracurricular activities at school, so it's like I didn't even exist."

POWER FACT: 89 percent of eighteen- to twenty-nine-year-olds use social media.... What does that tell us?... Well, if you're a kid like Acacia, looking for a way to connect with other folks the same age, with the same interests, the same passions, the first place you should look is the smart phone in your hands. And, since 50 percent of the people on this planet are now under thirty years old, social media is

the best, most efficient way to reach this market—no matter what
you're selling.

Okay, so just as being broke can be a great equalizer, feeling
broken can be a great motivator. When you're down on yourself,
when you're feeling boxed in, when your life isn't exactly firing on
all cylinders . . . that's when a lot of innovators reach for that little
extra something and just go for it. Like me and my FUBU partners,
they get it in their head that they won't be denied. They kick things
up a notch and find a way to shine through.

That's basically what happened with Acacia. It'd be easy for me
to suggest that she went out and reinvented herself on social media,
where she's now known as the "selfie queen." (No, she didn't come
up with the practice of snapping and posting pictures of herself
online, but she damn near perfected it—just don't tell my friend
Kim Kardashian that I'm giving Acacia the title here!)

Truth be told, Acacia didn't reinvent herself so much as she
rediscovered herself, at a time in her life when she didn't have a
whole lot going on and her self-esteem was way down low. Alone
in her room, alone with her thoughts, she turned to Tumblr, the
blogging site developed by David Karp that had quickly become
a safe haven and a creative outlet for millions of young, introspec-
tive writers, thinkers, artists, lost souls, and outcasts from all over
the world.

"I was twelve, maybe thirteen," she remembers, "and I made a
Tumblr account just for fun. I wasn't trying to do anything, say anything, become anything big. It was just something to do, a way to
express myself, maybe find some other kids out there just like me.
I had no friends in real life, and I just thought, you know, maybe I
could make some friends online."

Soon enough, sure enough, she did—only they weren't friends
in the traditional sense. Still, when there's no way to fit yourself in at
school, no one to talk to, a follower can be a tremendous validation,

and Acacia found herself cherishing this new community, a place where nobody judged her, where she was accepted for who she was, and it felt to her like home.

STAY TRUE

Now, I've got a confession to make: I'm a fan of pop culture. I try to keep in touch with what's going on in the world—what's going on in my world anyway. It's what I do, how I'm wired, where I find my edge. And for years now, Acacia Brinley has been an important influencer—a person to watch if you want to stay on top of the trends. Does that sound crazy? Me, a forty-something adult-type male following the online doings of a California teenager? Well, maybe it is, maybe it isn't, but those of us who work in fashion, in television, in music, in lifestyle businesses, we've got young people like Acacia on our radar because they're the powerful change-agents of our times, and Acacia's right up there with the best of them. Without even meaning to, without even trying, she's built a meaningful network of sponsors like Drop Dead UK, Brandy Melville, One Piece, and Nasty Gal, who pay Acacia some serious paper just to endorse their products and programs in her own genuine way. Even the folks at Pepsi, McDonald's, and the Olympics have reached out to her for a marketing assist—that's how plugged in she is to the pulse of her generation.

As soon as I hit on the concept for this book I knew I'd have to reach out to this young woman and learn how she got to where she is—and I'm glad I did, because in Acacia's story I saw elements of my own. At some point early on, Acacia started noticing a couple people posting pictures of themselves—pictures they'd clearly taken themselves. Nobody was using the term "selfie" back then, but these mirror-type pictures we take of ourselves were starting to become popular. Acacia thought she could improve on the trend, maybe give it her own spin. Her father was a photographer, and he let her borrow one of his old cameras, which of course did a much better job of capturing sharp images than the primitive cell-phone cameras of the day, so she got in the habit of posting a picture of herself online almost every single day. It became her routine, her thing—and on the back of that thing, people started to pay attention. Folks on Tumblr started blogging and reblogging about Acacia's pics. She developed a following—in the hundreds at first, but then she kept on adding zeroes to the total, and getting other social media platforms like Twitter and Instagram into the mix, and one day she looked up and she was a regular damn phenomenon.

"It felt so good, getting all this attention," she says now. "I started to think all those kids at school didn't know what they were talking about, because these kids on the Internet thought I was cool. They thought I was cute. I was getting all of this great feedback, all these great comments."

This went on for a while, and Acacia was feeling the love, feeling good about herself for the first time in a long time, but eventually the tide started to turn. It happens to everyone on social media: you reach a kind of critical mass, a tipping point, and all of a sudden folks start hating on you—you know, just because they can. It's the way of the Internet, right? Only, when you're thirteen years old, you're not exactly equipped to deal with such mass rejection, such random cruelty. Acacia remembers feeling blindsided by the negative attention that started coming her way.

"At the time, my blog had nothing to do with my personality," she tells me. "It wasn't like it is today, so at first I was able to protect myself a little bit. I could tell myself these people didn't know me, couldn't hurt me, whatever. But at the same time there was an important lesson in there. Even as a little kid, I could see that these people were bullying me just based on my appearance. It was just like in school. People started calling me a slut, a whore, just these awful, awful things, and it's not like I was posting all these provocative pictures or anything. I was just a kid, posting these simple pictures of me in my flannels, me in my bulky sweaters, me in my braces. But even at thirteen, fourteen years old, I knew they were just taking me down to feel better about themselves."

Pretty smart for a kid, don't you think? I had my share of haters back in the day—remember, when I started out, designers were mostly white and gay. That was the stereotype back then, and I cut against it. I wasn't one of those flamboyant designer-types; the crowd in my neighborhood was a little more street, a little rough around the edges. They didn't know what to make of me sewing my own hats, designing my own shirts. I took a lot of heat for it, but if someone stepped to me on this, I usually stepped back. I gave as good as I got—it was the way of the street.

So what did Acacia do when she found herself in her version of the same spot? Nothing. Amazingly, tellingly, she ignored the haters and kept on doing her thing. She knew that if she took the bait and responded to all the negative comments, she'd come off looking just as bad as the haters, so she took the high road. I listen to Acacia share this part of the story and I'm blown away, because what she had to deal with was way bigger than anything I had to face. This was cruelty on a grand scale. With me, the hassle was face-to-face, one-on-one; with Acacia, there were hundreds of people at a time, maybe even thousands, just slinging all this mean nonsense her way. But she didn't react to it. She didn't shrink from it—actually, she grew from it.

Haters like that . . . I call them cheerleaders with dirty pom-poms, because the worst thing in the social media space is when people aren't talking about you at all. If they're talking about you, it means you've gotten to them in some way, and Acacia found a certain strength in that, a certain power.

"I started to see the power in just being me," she explains. "I'd always been this relatable, regular teenage girl. I didn't have any money. I didn't wear Coach. I had my own style, but with me it wasn't about the designer labels. It was about a certain lipstick color I liked, or maybe a certain shoe or accessory. It was about my personality, not taking anything too seriously."

RECOGNIZE OPPORTUNITY

For the longest time, Acacia was too busy just trying to be herself to think about turning her online presence into anything other than a place to escape and be herself. It never even occurred to her that she could find a way to monetize her growing brand. It wasn't until Instagram hit the scene and she'd built her account to over 15,000 followers that she started leaning in this way. When a small clothing company hit her up with a message, saying they wanted to send her some items, Acacia naturally just thought this was a onetime thing.

"I'm like, 'Why are they trying to send me clothes?'" she says. "I thought maybe I was supposed to pay for them. It made no sense. But then they sent me this package and I posted some photos, and right away their numbers went up. There was a nice spike in sales, and after that I heard from other companies, and my followers grew, and it all just kind of took off from there."

Over time, maintaining all these different social media accounts became almost a full-time job—but Acacia's been careful not to think of it that way, because her fans would pick up on that. She'll only endorse items or events that fit with her personality, which is why she's become such a valuable billboard for companies trying to reach the teen market. They know that if Acacia is on board with them—if she likes their clothes, their cause, their movement—then millions of teenage girls are likely to follow.

The bigger her base, the more Acacia keeps reminding herself that folks will keep checking her out online only if she keeps to her core values. Her mom, Melissa, helps to manage her career, and by this point there are other adults on the Acacia Brinley "team," but Acacia has learned to respect the brand that's emerged online. She would never endorse, promote, or otherwise highlight a product or service that doesn't fit with who she is. What folks are "buying" with Acacia is Acacia herself, and she's not for sale.

"It's crazy, right?" she admits. "I mean, I started out just trying to connect with other kids, and it just worked out that I connected with a whole lot of them in this deeply personal way, and out of that all these companies started seeing me as a way to promote what they were doing. But now there's this fine line, you know. I built this up from nothing, and one of the reasons it grew was because it was genuine. Eventually, it was my personality that came through in my pictures and posts. That's what these companies want from me. That's what my followers and fans want from me. But if I'm careless with it, if I promote everything that comes my way, I'll lose the very thing that put me in this spot in the first place."

It's the great tug-and-pull of social media—when to hustle and when to chill, when to reach for it and when to hang back. But Acacia has found the sweet spot—the perfect balance between keeping true to herself and her followers while harnessing that truth to build a business.

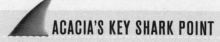

ACACIA'S KEY SHARK POINT

KEEP SWIMMING. This one's probably best summed up by one of Acacia's favorite sayings: "Try, fail, try again, fail better." She's figuring it out as she goes along, and there's a lot to admire in that—a lot to learn from too. And here I'm not just thinking of all those haters who hid behind their laptops and smart phones and trash-talked this kid when she was just starting out. Remember, Acacia didn't let those negative comments keep her from the conversation. No, the most impressive thing about Acacia's growing online presence is the way she's kept at it—day in, day out. To succeed in the social media space, you can never stop feeding the beast—you must be ever-present, all over it, all the time. And she is. Better believe it, she is.

As much as anyone else you'll meet in these pages, Acacia wasn't afraid to embrace failure. That's key. Failure is part of the process. It's an opportunity to start over again more wisely, to paraphrase a line from Benjamin Franklin: Trial, error, test. . . . Become a crash dummy for yourself and you'll understand what will work. So what will you do today and expect to learn from—even if you fail at it?

For more information and resources, check out
www.DaymondJohn.com/PowerofBroke/Acacia

LET IT RIP

ROB DYRDEK

SKATEBOARDER, PRODUCER, REALITY SHOW STAR

First order of business: crush it.

Second order of business: figure out what to do with it.

For Rob Dyrdek, one of the most influential skateboarders on the planet, who found a way to ride his passion to a multimedia platform and a multimillion-dollar brand, "it" was an extreme sport that didn't have a whole lot of household-name-type stars. There was Tony Hawk . . . and that was pretty much it. Rob was an eleven-year-old kid living in Ohio when Tony came on the scene, and he didn't step on a board the first time thinking he would ride it to fame and fortune. No, sir. He was athletic, out for a good time, up for something new. That's all it was at first. All along, he'd been big into soccer, but then he was drawn to skateboarding, and he was big into that soon enough.

He took to it right away. He was good. Damn good. He was fearless. Damn fearless. So damn good and fearless that after a month or two he decided to enter a contest—no big thing looking back, but it was huge at the time, and there's a lesson to be learned in the way he leaned into it. The contest was run by a local skateboard shop, and a lot of pros were going to be there, and Rob got it in his little head that he had to compete. Wasn't hard to see the aggressive, hard-charging personality that would stamp his career later on. But here's the thing: Rob didn't have the money to pay the entrance fee. Wasn't a lot of money, but still. His mom didn't work. His dad sold suits. They lived in a nice-enough house, in a nice-enough neighborhood. It never occurred to Rob growing up that his parents might have been struggling. Like a lot of kids, he thought his father was killing it at work, because they had everything they needed, but the truth was it only seemed that way to Rob—and it only seemed that way because Rob didn't need a whole lot. He played sports, that was his deal—didn't take a whole lot of money to keep him in sneakers and shorts. Once he started skateboarding, he bought his first deck himself, from his sister's boyfriend, for whatever loose change he could scrape together.

This entrance fee, though . . . it was out of reach, so Rob reached in what ways he could. He improvised—an ability that had already served him well on his skateboard, an ability he'd keep calling on throughout his career. Even at eleven years old, he was quick on his feet; he knew to work the angles. He went to the event organizers with a proposal. He said, "Look, if I can get ten people to sign up, would you let me in for free?"

It was a ballsy, brassy move—one that cost him nothing to make and promised him everything he wanted in return.

Now, these event organizers didn't know what to do with a kid like that, a pitch like that; nobody had ever asked for a free ride or a group discount, and it caught them completely by surprise. Plus, Rob was only a kid—eleven years old! So they just kind of laughed it off, didn't really think anything of it, but at the same time they agreed to it, in a "yeah sure what the hell" kind of way.

BE THE BEST

So what happened next? Well, you can probably guess. Rob recruited those ten other entrants, was waived in for free, and then
proceeded to wow the judges and the visiting pros with his fear-
lessness, his style. Right then and there, he started making a name
for himself—at a time in his life when he had no idea he'd need to
draw on that name the rest of the way.

"When I put my mind to something," he says, looking back
on the very first time he skated in front of a crowd, "I'm thinking
I'm going to be the best. Don't know where it comes from in me,
but that's me. Even as a little kid, I was determined. The best and
nothing less. My way and nobody else's. And here's where I put it
together. This was the beginning of my journey."

Starting out, Rob's one and only goal was to ride like a
champion—no small feat, but to him it came easy. Even as a kid,
the skateboard was like an extension of his own two feet, and he
was shot through with the hard-charging mind-set and finesse-
type skills to compete with his role models. Really, the dude had it
going on—and he knew to put it to work. But out of that primary
goal came another: to keep riding, and to find a way to make a living at the sport he loved. This was the hard part, because there
was no money in skateboarding; there were sponsorship deals and
a clear path to free merchandise and sweet gear, but no easy path
to a steady paycheck. Rob tried on a bunch of different business
models. His objective was clear, but at first all he could do was
stumble along on the path.

Rob wasn't out to build a business; that part came later. He
was out to turn a couple heads, strut his stuff on a public stage.
That's all it was at first—but, really, that was everything. Rob
probably didn't realize it at the time, but what he was doing was
building a brand. He sees it now, of course—oh, man, he's all over

it now—and when he connects the dots from the ballsy, brassy skateboarder dude he was back then to the extreme ballsy, brassy brand mogul he is today, it's not hard to see a through-line. It's all connected in a seamless way—like the signature lines he picks out on the ramp when he's riding his skateboard.

He's got a style all his own, and it comes through.

I don't want to focus on Rob's mad skills as an athlete or his long list of accolades and accomplishments, because his success on the circuit has been well documented. Check him out on DaymondJohn.com/PowerofBroke if you want to see what this guy can do when he's doing his thing. (Really—check him out! The man can get it done!) All you need to know, really, is that he could ride like a dream—a fever dream, because he danced on that deck like his feet were on fire! Eventually, he'd set twenty-one world records for skateboarding—including the longest board slide, longest 50-50 rail grind, and highest skateboard ramp jump into water. A lot of his records still stand—and a lot of folks believe they'll keep standing, because Rob has done some crazy-sick stuff that probably won't be matched anytime soon.

So, yeah . . . there's that.

STOKE THE FIRE

What grabs me about Rob's career from a *power of broke* point of view is the way he's monetized his success out of nothing but flat-out relentlessness, passion, and talent, the way he's built on all his crazy-sick heroics to become a key player in his end of the entertainment business. Looking back, it's easy to see how the one kind of followed from the other. That "fire" he skated with? It came from inside. As much as any athlete I've had the privilege to know, Rob Dyrdek competed with a fire in his belly, like he had nothing to lose, and he's taken that same fire into the boardroom. Whatever he does, whatever he sets his mind to, he takes this "nothing to lose" approach. He reminds me of me, in a lot of ways. If I'm the king of product placement, he's the emperor. Or maybe Rob's the king and I'm the emperor—either way is fine by me. The point is, every time you see him, he's wearing his product, sporting his brand, but in a very casual way. It's effortless with him, organic, and people respond to that about him. He's real, to the bone—and that comes through too.

For the purposes of this conversation, about coming at the world from a place of disadvantage, about being hungry, this persistent authenticity is the main takeaway of Rob's life and career—the way he's truly owned his brand. In the beginning, with no money in his pockets and no thought to why this was even an issue, it was all he could afford. "A lot of young people, they don't get that," he observes. "They think it takes some kind of publicity machine, some kind of expertise to build a brand. But your brand is you, plain and simple. It's what you stand for, how you carry yourself, and it doesn't cost a thing. Not a penny. You just need to identify it and start living it and put it out there. You've got YouTube, Twitter, Instagram, all these different platforms, and they're all free. The opportunity is there for the taking, so it's never too early to start building the ideology of what your brand is and start living it."

The secondary takeaway is to be bold enough to make up a plan as you go along. "I'm a bit of a gunslinger when it comes to my business deals," he admits. "I don't think I even met a banker until two or three years ago, so I didn't take a traditional approach. I didn't always think things through. I do now, but when I was starting out, I went by my gut. I learned by watching other people, people I admire. My thing has always been to leverage whatever I can, to barter my way to a deal, just like I smooth-talked my way into that first contest when I was a kid."

His business philosophy would look great on a bumper sticker: "When you grow up with nothing, it's like you've got nothing to lose, so there's this thing in me that tends to roll the dice."

EMBRACE YOUR FAILURES

This "nothing to lose" attitude has been at the heart of Rob's success in television and tech and on the tour—the same *power of broke* mind-set I see in a lot of entrepreneurs who come at their successes in a sidelong way. You look on and start to think maybe success has found them, instead of the other way around. With Rob, it was never about making money so much as it was about making things happen. Mostly, he cared about making noise, shaking things up. The money didn't matter to him in a way it might have mattered to someone else. Why? Because money wasn't what was driving him. No, with Rob it was all about the push to be the best, to stand out—and when you're the best, when you stand out in such a big-time way, the money can't help but follow.

"I'm blessed to have had a lot of failures," Rob tells me, describing how he got to where he is today. "Each time out I learned something new. Each time out I went at it in a new way. Each time out I found someone else to model, some new approach to try."

One of the things he figured out early on was integration—how to layer in all of his projects and prospects across one giant platform. "I was fortunate enough to get my start as an athlete at a powerful time in the evolution of brand integration," he says. "I'd talk to buddies of mine like Bam Margera, back when he was on *Jackass,* and he'd tell me how many boards he was selling through his exposure on that show, how many shoes, how many T-shirts, whatever. So before we launched our own show on MTV, I renegotiated every one of my licensing deals for super-high royalties and way-low minimums. What the hell did I care what they would pay me up-front? I had nothing, so I didn't need anything. So I let it ride. It was all about the back end for me, and then everything just exploded."

What exploded, specifically, was Rob's first show, *Rob and Big*, which debuted on MTV in 2006, featuring Rob and his best friend and bodyguard, Christopher "Big Black" Boykin. That show led to another, *Rob Dyrdek's Fantasy Factory*, which ran for six seasons, and from there it was on to video games and movies and a ton of licensing and sponsorship opportunities.

Rob's latest show is *Ridiculousness*, and it was inspired by a segment he did in one of the *Jackass* movies—and by the long-running success of clip shows like *America's Funniest Home Videos*. "I'd look at shows like that and think, *Man, what if we made a really cool version?*" he says. "*What if I collect all these out there, extreme videos, crazy shots of people doing stupid, dangerous stuff?* There had to be an audience for that, right?"

The folks at MTV certainly thought so—in fact, they were so sold on the idea that they didn't blink when Rob held out for a chunk of the pie. "Again, I didn't care too much about my fees up-front," he explains. "It was the same philosophy I always took. I wanted to own a piece of the show, and they were so desperate to get it on the air, they gave me what I wanted."

Along the way, he also launched the Street League Skateboarding competition series, a line of shoes, a deck manufacturer, a body spray . . . all of this without even finishing high school. (He dropped out at sixteen, before his senior year, and moved to Southern California to pursue his professional skateboarding career full throttle.) And he did it all by being real, being genuine, and being relentless in pursuit of what he wanted.

DEFINE YOURSELF

Really, this guy's all over the place—from skateboarding to movies, music videos to video games, clothing lines to shoes—and I can't help but wonder how he sees himself. That's one of the things I like to ask successful people when we're brainstorming—I want to know how they'd define themselves, in two to five words, because if you can't put it out there in a short, simple, telegraphed way, your message will never come across. We live in a world of first impressions. What do we know about juries? It's often said that a jury will decide whether to ultimately exonerate or convict within the first thirty seconds of seeing a defendant; after that, they're just listening to the lawyers, listening to the testimony, and trying to confirm the things they already think about the person and the decision they've already made.

We do the same thing, every time we walk into a room and meet someone for the first time. That's why I tell people to come up with their own two- to five-word definition of themselves, because if they don't, they leave it to others to do it for them. The rapper Old Dirty Bastard even went so far as to put his two to five words in his name, because he was an old, dirty bastard—that's the image he wanted to put across, and he didn't trust it to others to figure out his personality without a little extra help.

Put another way, if you can't put it on a bumper sticker, the guy behind you will never figure you out.

With FUBU, those words were right there in our name—For Us By Us. (That was really our hashtag—back before the term came to mean what it means today.)

With Nike, it's Just Do It!

White Castle is What You Crave.

Apple is Think Different.

Wheaties is Breakfast of Champions.

The United States of America: Land of the Free.

For a long time, my two to five words were "I'm on a quest!" I was deep into search mode, trying to learn as much as I could and move myself into as many different arenas as possible. I was on a never-ending quest to learn, reach, grow . . . my own personal walkabout! But the great thing about these mantras is that you can change them up, at any time—and, hey, if you want to keep out in front, stay out there on that cutting edge, they better change. Lately I've been thinking of myself more and more as an advocate for aspiring entrepreneurs. That's why I've embraced the "People's Shark" moniker that's been hung on me by fans of our show. I didn't go looking for that bumper sticker, but once it found me I was all over it. So now, when people ask me what I'm about and how I see myself, this is my answer: I'm the "People's Shark," and in those words I put it out there that I've got your back, I've got you covered, and if it works out that our interests are aligned then there's no stopping us. That's me right now.

Rob's personal self-definition? He gave it some thought, then came back to me with this: "Relentlessly living amazing."

He'd never been asked to put it out there in such a straightforward way, but he'd clearly thought along these lines before. Here's how he explained it: "Professionally, I'd have to say it's 'Relentlessly manufacturing amazing,' but the common denominator is the relentless part. There's no letup with me. And whatever it is, it's got to be amazing. To me, 'amazing' is anything that makes your jaw drop, anything that makes you scratch your head and wonder, anything that leaves you gasping, thinking, *Oh, man, that's sick.* It's what ignites you, what inspires you."

Of course, it helps to be relentless at whatever it is you're pursuing—and if that kind of never-ending persistence is keyed in some way to a passion for the pursuit . . . well, then, you're way out in front. But keep in mind—your passion has to make some kind of sense. Your idea for a business has got to be viable. Otherwise, what's the point?

"A lot of people get tripped up on this last part," Rob says, "and usually it's because they aren't clear on what it means to be successful. Everyone's got their own ideas on this, right? But to me it means finding that spot where your passion and talent and interests all meet, where you're able to find a way to sustain yourself while doing the things you love. Look at where all those points connect. That's where you need to be."

Like a lot of successful, passionate, relentless people I've met in business, Rob Dyrdek refused to live his life stuck in a box. He wouldn't be told what to do or when to do it. Instead, he built a whole new box, one that fit him perfectly, and he listened to the ticking of a clock all his own. What advice would he give to other young scraping entrepreneurs looking to do the same?

"It doesn't cost you anything to do a whole bunch of research," he says, "so go ahead and do it. Everything you need to know, it's out there. Tap into it. Learn the business or industry, top to bottom. If you don't have a whole lot of money, reach out to someone in a position to help and ask him or her to mentor you. Maybe get them to help you write your business plan, or think through a plan of action. If you can't pay them, offer them a piece of your business. Make it so there's something in it for them too. It goes back to that whole 'let it ride' philosophy. Believe in yourself, invest in yourself, and maybe you can convince others to throw in with you too."

Okay, so that's job one, really. Know your stuff. Know your customers. Know your competition. You'd think these things would go without saying, but believe me, they need saying. You'd be amazed how many start-ups I see that never really get out of the gate because the starter-uppers have somehow failed to understand the marketplace. (Remember the New Coke fiasco?) So take the time to figure out where you sit at the outset, where you'd like to be in the future, and how the hell you plan to get there. It might not work out the way you picture it going in, but start with some kind of map. Picture it in your head and find a way to make it so.

That picture didn't become clear for Rob Dyrdek until he left high school and moved to California and set about making noise in a determined way. Before that, he was just riding, but he was riding with a purpose soon enough, and what kept him going was his passion for his sport. Really, that's probably been the greatest fuel for a guy like Rob—his passion for what he does. That's the bottom line for almost every successful entrepreneur I've come across: believe in what you do, what you make, what you put out into the world, and good things will come back to you.

"That's how it was with me," Rob agrees. "Definitely. You meet all kinds of people in business. Coming at it from a place of desperation, from having no money, it sets it up so you've got no choice but to succeed. Broke can break you, or it can give you immense energy. If you're someone who's wired in a way that you just refuse to lose, it can give you the fuel you need to push through."

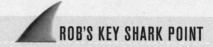

ROB'S KEY SHARK POINT

DO YOUR HOMEWORK. For an athlete, the homework comes in the foundation. It comes in the countless hours of practice, the buckets of sweat and effort, the endless study of the rest of the field. Starting out, this was Rob's focus, but when his supporting business interests kicked in, he was all about the research and development. He learned the ins and outs of the entertainment industry so he could speak the language when he went to meetings, so he could spot a hole in a network's schedule and move to fill it. He knew he needed to walk the walk so he could talk the talk, so he set about it.

Homework these days means analytics. It means looking at others who've succeeded in the same field. But go ahead and also look at all the businesses that failed to connect with your market, and see what you can learn from their missteps. These people failed so you don't have to. Why fail on your own dime and on your own time if you don't have to?

For more information and resources, check out
www.DaymondJohn.com/PowerofBroke/Rob

LOOK UNDER EVERY ROCK FOR EVERY LAST DIME

CHRISTOPHER GRAY

ENTREPRENEUR, APP DEVELOPER, COLLEGE STUDENT

One of the questions I'm asked all the time is how often we make a deal in the Tank at the entrepreneur's exact asking price. The answer: It hardly ever happens. A lot of times the Sharks offer the full price but look to change the terms; often the equity of the deal stays the same, but the investment is reduced. It's rare that a business owner comes in and gets exactly what he or she is looking for.

But that's just what happened when a young man named Christopher Gray came to the studio in June 2014 to pitch us a business he'd come up with to help students tap into the vast marketplace of college scholarship money. According to Chris, who'd developed an app to eliminate a lot of uncertainty around the scholarship application process, more than $100 million in scholarship monies go unclaimed each year, and his idea was to make it so students could better access all of the available information and see at a glance which scholarships might be appropriate for them.

"It took me almost a year to learn about all these different scholarships," Chris says, "so I tell people the app can take that time and shrink it down to just a couple minutes."

I talk all the time about how important it is to have proof of concept for your product or service—a track record you can point to and show that you're able to deliver on your promise, whatever that promise happens to be. Chris was able to deliver the proof in a big-time way, because he was his own success story. In fact, his success came with a jaw-dropping headline: Chris himself earned over $1.3 million in scholarships.

That's right—$1.3 million. So of course the newspapers started calling him "the million-dollar scholar."

But here's the thing: for Chris, the proof of concept went much deeper than the scholarship money that came his way on the back of all that work. As a high school junior, living with his single mom and two younger siblings in Birmingham, Alabama, Chris couldn't even afford the application fees to some of his first-choice schools. A lot of folks don't realize it if they've been away from the college search process for a while, but those fees can run to $50, $75, even $100 per application, so the numbers add up double-quick and make it prohibitive for students on a limited budget to apply to a whole bunch of schools. There are ways around the logjam for certain schools, but for those kids without lots of cash saved up, other schools will remain out of reach.

Making things even tougher for Chris was the fact that he didn't have access to the Internet at home, so he had to grab time at the local library to fill out his applications and search for available scholarships. (Forget the Internet—for a time Chris's family didn't even have a computer.) The way it worked at his library was that he could only use the computer for a half hour or an hour at a time, so he was working with limited resources in almost every sense of the phrase. It wasn't just that he didn't have enough money to apply to some of these schools; he didn't even have the time to check out his options online, so he was feeling the squeeze every which way.

"When I was graduating from high school, it was just after the recession," he tells me. "A lot of cities in the South had been hit really hard, and that's what was going on in Birmingham. My mother's got a good job now, but back then she was trying to find work, so I had to hustle just to get computer time, so I could do all this work."

He applied for every scholarship he could find—didn't matter if it was for $10, $100, $1,000, or $10,000. If he was eligible, Chris sent in an application. If he wasn't sure, he sent one in anyway. That's how it is when you're up against it, with no place to go but up, up, up. You've got to seek out every available opportunity, even if it seems like a long shot. It got to where he was applying to too many scholarships to keep track of, so for the most part, once he sent off his application, he forgot about it and moved on to the next prospect. It was like he was just planting all these seeds, all over Alabama, all over the country, and hoping like crazy some of them would grow.

BE SPECIFICALLY CREATIVE

When you're operating with limited resources—financial or otherwise—you're forced to find creative ways to get the most bang out of every buck. Chris was no exception. One of the ways he tried to maximize his time on the library computer was to write several essays ahead of time and then set it up so he could essentially cut and paste each essay to make it as though each one was being written to answer a specific question on a specific application to a specific organization or institution. It was a solution that came out of necessity, because there weren't enough available slots on the library computer, and the library wasn't even open long enough for him to do all this work during his allotted time.

Chris had strong grades, strong scores on his standardized tests, and thought he had a good shot at getting accepted to a top college—but it wasn't always easy to get the fee waiver he needed to be able to apply to certain schools. The way it works in Alabama is that your school counselor must apply for those waivers on your behalf, but there's a certain pressure put on school administrators to encourage top students to attend state schools, so Chris found himself in a kind of Catch-22 situation.

"It's possible I could have won the scholarship money I needed to be able to afford the tuition at some of these schools," he explains, "but I couldn't even send my application in to the admissions office to see if I could get accepted. So there were all these schools where the doors were just closed to me."

Happily, there were a number of schools outside of Alabama that allowed students to apply for a fee waiver on their own. Also, he was able to save time by applying to a bunch of schools with just one application because some colleges and universities accept the Common Application (though each charges its own application fee).

So he just spread those seeds everywhere he could, then sat back and waited to see if any of them would take. He didn't have to wait long: the very first scholarship he received was a $20,000 award from the Horatio Alger National Scholarship Foundation. Chris was in the school library when he got the call, and he remembers being so excited at the news that he immediately ran over to his AP literature teacher, Tara Tidwell, who'd helped him write his winning essay.

In reality, his teacher did more than just help him with his essay—she'd been down this same road before, advising other students, so she was able to kind of mentor Chris through the entire process. She encouraged him to make his essays personal and to draw on some of the literature he'd read in her class—classics like *Frankenstein, Paradise Lost,* and *The Picture of Dorian Gray.* She pushed Chris to write about his own circumstances and to reflect on human nature and what it means to reach beyond your grasp.

POWER FACT: **23 percent of full-time undergraduates work at a part-time job at least 20 hours each week.** . . . I see a stat like that and it just screams *power of broke*. . . . It tells me that there are always enough hours in the day to do what you have to do . . . that one person's idea of "full-time" is another's idea of "part-time" . . . that students like Chris who make the time to get things done will graduate to become the entrepreneurs and visionaries who make things happen. It tells me that successful, driven, and hungry people don't wait for someone to "give" them a job—they go out and get to work.

One of the things I point out to people when I talk about the themes of this book is the difference between straight-up poverty and poverty of the mind. It's one thing to be hungry, but that doesn't mean you can't feed your head with the insights and information you'll need to take it to the next level. For me, that hunger to learn came from that extra push from my mother, who encouraged me to read, to think big, to look outside my small world of Hollis, Queens, to the big city and beyond. For Chris, that hunger came from those great books Ms. Tidwell had him reading. Yeah, he was busting his butt poring over all those scholarship applications. Yeah, he was busting his butt at his part-time job. Yeah, he was busting his butt logging more than 500 hours of community service before graduation, getting involved in all kinds of extracurricular activities at school. But even with all of that, his teacher was on Chris to realize there was still time for him to enrich his mind and read all those books and learn what it means to go beyond what he ever expected.

"She went over every essay with me," Chris tells me, "making sure I stressed the importance of education in my life, the importance of having this opportunity, making it personal. So of course she was the first person I went to see after I got that first scholarship. If it hadn't been for her, helping me to realize that all these good things were possible, it wouldn't have happened."

LET IT GROW

That Horatio Alger National Scholarship Foundation award was
just the first of many for Chris—by the time he graduated he'd
collected hundreds more, including two "full-ride" scholarships.
That was how he hit that $1.3 million number you see in the head-
lines. Chris couldn't believe it—he was pumped, over the moon.
But at the same time he worried that there were too many blessings
coming his way, that maybe there were other deserving candidates
whose applications were being overlooked. After all, college is ridiculously expensive, but even if he chose the most expensive private universities, he wouldn't come close to needing all the money
he'd been awarded.

So he started looking under more rocks for other ways to make
smart use of all that scholarship money. The way it works with these
independent scholarships is that the money gets sent directly to the
school you decide to attend, where you set up a student account. You
can then draw on that money for books, room and board, travel back
and forth from home, and all related expenses, in addition to your
tuition. If there's money left over when you graduate, you can roll it
over to another institution, where you can go on to graduate school.

"How I looked at it was, all this money, I could afford to go back
to school and get a master's degree, and then a doctorate," Chris
says. "Whatever career I decided to pursue, I'd be covered."

How he looked at it, too, was that he was now duty-bound to
share his blessings with others. Word got around about Chris's success tapping all this scholarship money, and when he got to Philadelphia's Drexel University in September 2011, he started coaching
other students on how to do the same for themselves. In his research, he'd uncovered a lot of scholarships that award money to
current college students, not just graduating high school students, so
he was a popular dude on campus. He was happy to help and share

what he'd learned, only it got to be a time crunch, working with all these folks on a one-on-one basis, so he started thinking of ways he could help a whole mess of students at once. Out of that, he threw in with two other students and developed an easy-to-use app to make the scholarship search process more manageable and efficient.

He called the app Scholly, and it allowed users to plug in eight essential bits of information: state of residence, gender, race, grade point average, year in school, intended course of study, whether they were seeking merit- or need-based grants, and any relevant miscellaneous information, such as sexual preference, religion, disability, or family status. What came back was a personalized list of targeted scholarships.

Like a lot of great ideas, it was simple, elegant, and easy to explain—a streamlined service to help students navigate the clutter and confusion of college scholarships—and it provided tangible results.

Best of all, there wasn't a lot to it in terms of start-up costs. That's how it goes a lot of times when you're first out of the gate with a new idea. You have the field to yourself for a while, so you can limit your marketing efforts to word-of-mouth-type initiatives. You build your proof of concept from the ground up, iron out the kinks as you go, and grow the way your target market tells you to grow.

KNOW YOUR VALUE

By the time Chris Gray came to the *Shark Tank* set, Scholly had been downloaded over 92,000 times, at 99 cents a pop, so Chris knew he was on to something—and the feedback he was getting from his customers was off the charts.

Chris came to the show seeking an investment of $40,000 for a 15 percent stake in his company. He pitched Scholly as a product designed to help students and families deal with the high cost of higher education, and the Sharks were all over it. We'd heard hundreds of pitches by this point, but this kid was right up there with the best of them: his business had a worthwhile objective, and at this early stage Chris pretty much owned the market. (Better believe he owned it—that's one of the benefits of being first in on a new concept.) And Chris himself was an outstanding spokesperson. He was impressive, inspiring . . . all of that. And the app itself, which he demonstrated for the panel, was slick, straightforward. Very quickly, the pitch started to turn into one of those lovefests we all knew would shake out to the good for this kid.

But then it turned in another way. Lori announced that she'd heard enough and offered to meet Chris's asking price. The other Sharks wanted to hear more about the business, do a little due diligence, but Lori was persistent. I was with Lori on this—at $40,000 for a 15 percent stake, I had all the information I needed, so I offered to meet the asking price too, and this set off a heated exchange. The other Sharks started biting, said Lori and I couldn't possibly have Chris's best interests at heart if we didn't hear him out about his long-term plans for the company, his back-office setup, the sustainability of his concept. Seemed to me, this could all be figured out at a later time, off camera. My offer was as much a bet on Chris as it was an investment in his business. That's how it goes a lot of the time on the show. You end up betting on the person.

In the end, Lori and I agreed to partner on the deal, and Chris jumped at our offer. At this point the other Sharks were furious. They still had a lot of questions and didn't like that we'd basically said we weren't interested in the answers. Robert stormed off the set, followed by Mark and Kevin. It made for compelling television, and when the pitch was edited for broadcast the producers really played up the tension on the panel, made it seem like a good old-fashioned dustup, but the reality was, the other Sharks were aced out of a good deal. It was a good deal for Chris—who needed the infusion of cash to hire some support staff while he finished his last year of college—and a good deal for his new partners.

As I write this, some months later, Scholly is firing on all cylinders. They've just signed a deal with the Memphis city council to provide the app to every high school senior in the city school system—over 10,000 downloads. That's a big payday for the company, and it's also a public relations windfall, since every network affiliate and all the local papers came out to the press conference to announce the deal. The way it came about was that some members of the city council are big fans of *Shark Tank,* and they wanted to be the first major metropolitan city to provide this service to students and their families. How cool is that? Even cooler is that Chris is now talking to state governments to offer the same service on an even bigger scale.

Chris has done a great job promoting the app and attracting new users—with over 500,000 downloads and counting—but there's no way to track how successful Scholly has been in helping students with their search. Some write in and share their good news; to date, Scholly has received self-reported notice of over $15 million in scholarships and grants received, so by every available measure Chris is accomplishing what he set out to do. When he graduated in June 2015, he turned Scholly into a full-service operation—and a full-time gig.

Getting folks to sign up for the app is just the beginning. Once they're in the Scholly system, Chris hopes to "up-sell" them with books, application tool kits, seminars, and other related products and services. That's a term Chris probably doesn't like, because he's all about adding value to the lives of students and families, but that commitment to providing service and value can't help but shine through, however he decides to grow the company.

CHRISTOPHER'S KEY SHARK POINT

DO YOUR HOMEWORK. Chris put in the time to research thousands of available scholarships. He did this for himself at first, but he also banked all that work and developed a searchable database. Doing all that extra legwork—looking under every rock for every possible scholarship opportunity—is what eventually made Scholly not just the first app to match students with scholarships, but one of the best pitches we've seen on *Shark Tank*, hands down.

The takeaway for Chris was realizing that the "homework" he was doing on his own could be molded and marketed in a way that could benefit others. What expertise have you developed in your own life that you can put to work in the marketplace?

For more information and resources, check out
www.DaymondJohn.com/PowerofBroke/Christopher

THREE

MONEY CHANGES EVERYTHING

ONE OF THE main reasons businesses go bust? Or never get off the ground in the first place? Overfunding. People hear an answer like that from a guy like me, and they scratch their heads and think, *What the hell is this guy talking about?* I mean, my story's out there—it's become part of my résumé. People know I come from a modest background, and "modest" is probably an overstatement. They know I got my business going with a whole lot of grind and hustle and Scotch tape.

So who am I to talk about the problems of having too much money?

Well, let's break it down: overfunding is what's put this country in a hole. You don't need a degree in economics or in business to see that this is what leaves so many small business owners playing catch-up before they ever really get started. Really, the concept of gaining leverage by using "other people's money" has become so ingrained in our business culture, we tend to lose sight of what it can mean in the extreme. We've been brought up watching shows like *Dallas* and movies like *Wall Street,* and when you remix all those pop-culture influences and take them out for a spin, you're left thinking money, money, money is the answer, answer, answer.

You can't have too much money, right?

Just so you know, this is not a trick question. The answer is an emphatic *no*—but you *can* get yourself into trouble if you get your hands on too much of it, too soon. It's Bootstrapping 101: the more embryonic you are, the more money costs you. I've seen it happen over and over to entrepreneurs who come on *Shark Tank*. When you take in too much funding too early, it sets you on an artificial high that tends to lift you way, way up to where you won't even be able to *see* your bottom line. Really, it's the same concept we looked at earlier when we were talking about relationships. When all the lavish presents are gone, when the fancy dresses run out, and when the bells and whistles stop making noise for you, what are you left with?

Best way to explain this concept is to hit you up with an example: Let's say you're just getting going on a start-up, doing about $50,000 in sales. That's great—you've hit the ground running. Now let's say you decide it's time to grow the business, so you head out looking for investors. You've got a number in mind: $200,000. Off of that, using your current sales figures as a guide, you decide that $200,000 will net your investor a 30 percent stake in your company. It's a pretty big ask, but you've run the numbers and it seems like a good deal for both sides.

So far so good, right? Well, not so fast. See, you now have a partner—a 30 percent partner, but a partner just the same. Next thing that happens, you start to run through all that money, because that's why you went out looking for it, right? At $50,000, you might have been making a profit of $10,000, but now you have a little more money to spend, so of course you start spending a little more freely. But now you have to start feeding back that $200,000 investment, so the business plan has changed. Before you can pay yourself that same $10,000 in profit, you'll have to sell about

$100,000 worth of stuff. That's a pretty big percentage leap, and it won't end there. Now there'll be all this pressure on your nice, sweet, little start-up company to do even *more* business, which means there'll be all this pressure on you to kick things up *another* couple notches. Even if you start to grow, you'll have to grow at a rate your company might not be ready to handle, so it might work out that you need another shot of capital. But what happens then? "Mr. 30 Percent" is not about to give up a piece of his pie, so this next round comes off of your plate, too.

Let's say you have to give up another 30 percent, or 20 percent, or 10 . . . whatever it is. Before you know it, you're working for everybody else—with *all* the risk, and *all* the headaches.

Now, if you hang in there, if you let the business grow organically and take you where it needs to go, you'll be in a better position. Soon your cash flow will be strong enough so you can finance all that extra money instead of giving away all those chunks of your company. Even if you don't get to the point where a bank will lend you money in a conventional way, you can tap outside investors by offering a more attractive rate. If a loan from a bank would cost you, say, 5 percent, but money is tight and you don't qualify, you can offer to pay an investor 10 percent without cutting him in on your deal.

POWER FACT: **52 percent of small businesses are home-based, according to *Forbes* . . .** but just because you're working on your kitchen table, maybe even in your underwear, don't sell yourself short. . . . Make sure potential investors see your business in the best possible light.

And as long as we're talking about financing your business, let's borrow a page from my friend and fellow Shark Mark Cuban, who tells young entrepreneurs to pay down their debt with their first available dollars. "If you've got twenty-five thousand dollars, fifty thousand dollars, one hundred thousand dollars," he says, "you're better off paying off any debt you have because that's a guaranteed return."

Better believe it—debt can knock your business flat if you let it get away from you, so figure out what you need to expand and find a way to get it without giving away a piece of your business. Go this route and there'll be less money bouncing around in the short term—I get that. Your cash flow might look less attractive—I get that too. But over time you'll be way better off, and by the time you get your footing as a business, when you're up and running and good and ready, that big outside investment will cost you a whole lot less.

Bigger money, early on, means bigger mistakes—at a time in your growth when you can't afford to make *any* mistakes.

"EAT LIKE A KING!"

Got time for a story? When I was still in high school, I worked in a co-op program. It was the perfect setup for me—less school work, more *work* work. I'm dyslexic, so school was always a struggle. But I knew even as a kid that I had a head for business, so I got a job through my school working in the mail room at First Boston, in Manhattan. Turned out it was great groundwork for my future *Shark Tank* role because I was thrown into a roomful of Kevin O'Leary–types. For the first time in my life, I was surrounded by vulture-capitalists, so I began to see what that world looks like and how I might fit myself into it. Plus, I got school credit *and* I got paid, so it was a cool deal all around—and it took me to my first in-your-face lesson on what it meant to be successful.

The way it worked, when you were on messenger duty, you'd get $2 if you had to make a delivery beyond a certain radius—say, ten blocks or so. The money was meant to cover your subway fare, only a lot of us chose to pocket it and walk those extra few blocks—because, hey, even then it was all about the hustle.

So there was this one older gentleman named Carlos who worked with us as a messenger. He was like the wise old man of the mail room. He had a family, he had bills to pay, all of that, but this was his gig—and he *never* cashed in that extra $2 bump to ride the subway. Instead, he'd take that extra walking-around money and hit up Gray's Papaya, a legendary midtown hot dog place. In those days, hot dogs were 50 cents, so Carlos would take that $2 and grab three hot dogs and a drink—then he'd bring his "free" lunch with him up to the cafeteria and chow down. Every day he'd be sitting there with his three hot dogs and a drink, with the biggest damn smile on his face. Oh, man . . . I'd never seen such pure contentment. If you stopped to talk to him, he'd lean back in his chair like a man of means and say, "Today, I eat like a king!" With an exaggerated Spanish accent, almost like Al Pacino in *Scarface*, like he was mugging for the cameras.

Today, I eat like a king!

It was such a great, joyful thing to see, especially when you set that picture against all these rich hedge fund guys who used to take their lunch in the same cafeteria. These guys had all the money in the world, but they were miserable. On the surface, they had it all—vacation homes, expensive cars, fine clothes and accessories. And yet they were always stressing about something, their attention pulled in all these different directions. And then there was Carlos, perfectly happy with his three hot dogs and a drink. Whatever little he had, it was more than enough. Whatever those hedge fund guys had, those movers and shakers and titans of industry . . . it was never enough.

Carlos, man . . . he was just a messenger, but he had it all figured out. He had his wife, his kids, his routines. And he even had that $2 bump all figured out. He'd been at it so long, the guys running the mail room knew to send him uptown on his last package run of the day so he could continue on home.

The thing about Carlos was, he knew when it made sense to walk, when to bunch a couple deliveries together on the same $2 ride. He worked it all out: with seven or eight 10-block deliveries each day, he'd only ride the subway four or five times. On average, this meant he would pocket an extra $6 a day, cash.

That's an extra $30 a week, an extra $1,500 a year. Carlos was no hedge fund manager, but he was pretty damn good at investing his money—and thanks to the exponential power of compound interest, in a favorable interest rate environment, after ten years he had enough to buy a house back home in Puerto Rico for when he was ready to retire, even after deducting all those Gray's Papaya hot dogs. And as he sat there each day enjoying his lunch, it was all close enough to taste. Meanwhile, these other dudes in their fine suits and their high-end lifestyles, they were chasing, scrambling, stressing.

I was just seventeen years old, but even as a kid I could see that I was cut more like Carlos than those other guys.

FIND YOUR CRED

Bank on it: too much of a good thing can bring you down.

On an individual basis, we see glaring examples of this all around. Take professional athletes. Did you know that 60 percent of professional basketball players are broke or bankrupt within five years of retirement? That number comes from the National Basketball Players Association. And it's even worse for former professional football players: 78 percent of NFL players are in some type of financial distress within *two years* after leaving the game.

For those of you who can't relate to the struggles of our high-paid athletes, maybe you can relate to another group of folks who find a ridiculous level of financial success in a sudden way—lottery winners. Check out these numbers, and if you're like me, you'll get to wondering what all that money ended up doing for *these* good people:

- About 70 percent of all lottery winners end up broke or bankrupt.
- In a recent study of lottery winners, only 55 percent reported that they were happier after winning all that money.
- Twice as many lottery winners claiming prizes of up to $150,000 went bankrupt as did individuals in the general population.

Too much of a good thing? I'd say so. That's also where a lot of start-ups go wrong, because if you have a bottomless supply of cash before you have a proof of concept for your business, you run into trouble. You're inclined to let the money call the shots, instead of following good business practice; you follow your wallet instead of your gut. I would even take that observation one step further and say that the more money you have at the start-up stage, the more trouble you're bound to buy for yourself and for your business.

POWER FACT: **The odds of winning the Powerball lottery are roughly 1 in 175 million.** . . . If you plan to strike it rich overnight, the Powerball is probably not the way to do it.

Let's look at a hypothetical example to see how a ready supply of cash can sometimes work against you as an entrepreneur. Let's say your grandmother makes great cupcakes. They're not just great, they're world-class, killer cupcakes that melt in your mouth and color your foodie dreams and drive you to distraction. Really, these cupcakes do just about everything for you, that's how crazy

good they are. The recipe for these killer cupcakes has been in
your family for generations, so as you're fishing around for an idea
for a business you decide to go into the cupcake business on the
back of Grandma's recipe. Makes all kinds of sense to you starting out, and even when you take a step back and look at it from an
objective angle, you can't find an argument against. You do your
due diligence, and you look at companies like Baked by Melissa
and Crumbs and decide cupcakes are super-trendy, so that's where
you're headed.

(By the way, you're about to meet a woman from Nashville who
took $33 and launched one of the most successful cupcake fran-
chises in the country, with almost 100 stores in 24 states and $35
million in sales—all while she was working as a cleaning lady to
pay her bills. So you can see why I've got cupcakes on my mind as
I reach to illustrate my point.)

With money to burn, you might get it in your head to open a
super-trendy cupcake shop in a super-trendy neighborhood. Trouble is, you still haven't sold a single cupcake, and yet you're out
there, taking out a $100,000 mortgage on your house, or applying
for an SBA loan, or selling your car and your other worldly possessions to generate some cash, looking to finance this half-baked
pie-in-the-sky idea you have for a business. Worse, you might even
be hitting up your friends and family members to make some small
but meaningful investments—a potentially disastrous move that
will either cost you some serious currency in terms of these relationships if your business tanks or a serious percentage of future
profits if your business takes off.

Somehow you bring in a bunch of money and find a storefront
and put all these wheels in motion. Everything starts to come together. You hire an interior design team to make your cupcake shop
look amazing. You order a custom leather sofa to stand as a kind
of centerpiece, shaped like a giant cupcake. You lay in all of this
beautiful refrigeration equipment and a state-of-the-art kitchen.

You even spend money to hire a first-rate staff and dress them out in snappy, distinctive uniforms featuring your brand-new logo.

> **POWER FACT:** **70 percent of small businesses are owned and operated by a single person....** *Sometimes you've got no choice but to go it alone....* I know I wrote earlier that true sharks rely on pilot fish to help them out, but it doesn't always go that way in the ocean of opportunity, where there might only be room for one vision, for one mouth to feed.

All of this costs money, of course, but you're not too worried about that because you have this little cushion. You're all set and good to go—that is, until you actually open for business and start to realize you're nowhere near ready. What's happened, basically, is the money allowed you to take a whole bunch of shortcuts. It didn't *force* you to take those shortcuts, but if you ever find yourself in this position, you won't be able to help yourself—trust me on this.

Remember, you still haven't sold a single cupcake at this point, and here's where it starts to get real. You've sunk all this money into your business, and just before your grand opening, you find out your store is in a part of the city that's essentially gluten-free. Maybe it's a family-type neighborhood where everyone is ridiculously health-conscious, or a hipster 'hood that's all about the kale and yoga, so cupcakes aren't too, too high on anyone's list. Or maybe you find out that two or three cupcake shops have opened and closed their doors on your block in the past couple years. Why? Because there's a little old lady from the local church slinging her own killer cupcakes in a hand-to-hand way. She sells these suckers like crack—everyone buys from her. Hell, she used to babysit the whole neighborhood, so everyone knows her, everyone's hooked on her crack cupcakes, and you're screwed before you've even started.

Oh, and one more thing: you don't know the first thing about the cupcake business. You set yourself up with software that doesn't really help you manage your inventory, and it turns out, for every cupcake you do manage to sell, there's another cupcake your well-paid, well-uniformed employee is putting in his or her pocket—or stomach. You're also surprised to discover you're dealing with perishables, so half of your inventory goes bad before you have a chance to move it. What now?

DON'T SETTLE FOR "PLAN B"

After just a couple months, that $100,000 you put into your cupcake shop is "gone, baby, gone," and you've got this Frankenstein business on your back you can't unload and you can't possibly turn around. Your rent, your payroll, your material costs . . . it's all adding up, and you're sinking under the weight of it.

Let's say you've taken on an investor, sold a 50 percent stake in your business for $50,000, and now you need even more cash to keep the thing going. You can't go back to your initial investor and ask for an infusion of money. He'll tell you, "Hey, that's *your* problem." And he'll be right. It *is* your problem, and it all flows from the fact that you didn't have proof of concept going in, and you'll either have to scrap the whole deal or raise money by selling off a piece of your own 50 percent share.

Under that scenario, your initial partner will be out in front, and you'll be scrambling to keep ahead of your creditors.

But what if you came at this business a whole other way? What if you had no money? Or maybe just $5,000 or $10,000 to get you started—and no idea how to generate any additional funding?

Well, there's a concept in business school–type discussions these days that suggests some start-ups are better off launching in a ground-up way. Social economists call this concept *bootstrapping*, but let's go the term one better: to give yourself a meaningful shot at meaningful success, *colossal bootstrapping* is the way to go.

That cupcake business you overfunded into the ground? Just think what might have happened if you'd gone at it in a more organic way, if you'd let the business grow as it needed to grow—as it had *earned* the right to grow. All those mistakes you made at the $100,000 level you could have made just as easily at the $5,000 level, and you wouldn't be in such a deep, deep hole. You could have learned from your mistakes instead of being swallowed up by them. And just to be clear, those mistakes would still cost you, but they'd cost you just $5,000 or $10,000, so they'd be less likely to break you.

KEEP IT REAL (REALLY!)

What's the biggest start-up of the last ten years? What company, more than any other, has transformed the ways we interact with each other and the ways we measure success? Facebook, hands down. But Mark Zuckerberg didn't go out and hustle up financing before he knew what he had. He didn't give away huge chunks of his business to investors. He started out in a ground-up sort of way, testing his proof of concept among a few friends at Harvard and then growing from there. Very quickly, he could see he was on to something—only it wasn't exactly the same something he'd had in mind, so he tweaked the concept a little. From his own social circle at Harvard, he expanded his network all across the campus, still getting the kinks out along the way. Then he reached out to other colleges in the Boston area, and then to Ivy League campuses, and after that to college students all over the country, and now the site has over one billion users worldwide.

It's amazing, really, what Facebook has become, especially

when you think back to the initial vision. But here's the great lesson of Facebook: each step along the way, Zuckerberg grew his business incrementally. He figured out what worked, what didn't work, and what could work better. And at some point along the way he hit on a proven formula, a scalable platform. What worked in one market would work in another market. And another. The growth has been exponential, insane, and when Facebook finally went public in 2012 it was the biggest IPO in tech history.

Yeah, I know there's a lot of controversy surrounding the launch of Facebook, so I don't want to get into who wrote the program, who did this, who did that, who was aced out of the deal. Go ahead and watch *The Social Network* if you want to get the gist of how things went down. The point here is that Zuckerberg and company didn't move forward in a big way until they knew what they had. They didn't even move forward in a small way until they knew what they had—and *that's* the way to start a business. It's textbook. It's bootstrapping—on a colossal scale.

Keep in mind, the *concept* behind proof of concept is not to prove something to potential investors, or even to customers. It's to prove something to yourself. Proof of concept is the only way to know if you're truly on to something, and yet you'd be amazed how many entrepreneurs skip over this all-important piece.

With that in mind, here's another lesson learned along the way: your boys will blow smoke your way if you let them.

I always tell people not to go out and give away the store. Go ahead and take care of your people if you want to do them a solid, but don't count on the folks who know you and love you to be a reliable focus group. They're gonna tell you what they think you want to hear—not because they're looking to trip you up, but because they're trying to be supportive. When I was starting FUBU, if I gave away ten shirts to friends and family members who promised to wear them and bring back the reactions they got on the streets and in the clubs, the information would have been useless to me—nice to hear maybe, but not really all that helpful. Out of those ten shirts, maybe I'd get back one or two insights I could incorporate into my next designs, but it'd take a good long while for me to separate the constructive comments from the back-slaps.

POWER FACT: Milton Hershey started three candy companies as a young man, and all of them failed before he found success with the Hershey Company.... *Sometimes you have to learn to fail before you can begin to succeed.*

In the clothing business, the only way to get a real read on the market is to put those items on a rack with a whole bunch of other stuff and let total strangers—who don't care about you, who have to dig into their pockets and pay for these items with their hard-earned money, who have a million distractions and a dozen other manufacturers lining up to catch their attention—weigh in on your designs.

But with market research, just like with anything else, if it isn't organic, it will probably fail. Early on at FUBU, we never hired outside consultants or put a dozen kids in a room with a couple pizzas so we could watch them react to our clothes from the other side of a one-way mirror. That type of setting, all those kids care about is the pizza and the couple dollars you'll throw their way for their time. That said, if we'd had money starting out, we might have been inclined to run those kinds of focus groups, but we didn't have any money, so it wasn't an option, and good thing too.

For my money, the *real* proof of concept was with people who were actually engaging with our clothes. In fact, one of the best reads I'd get on the popularity of this or that design was when I started selling shirts at those Black Expos out of my 15-seat passenger van. The Black Expos, for those of you who don't know, were trade shows made up of a whole bunch of vendors selling clothing, gear, and lifestyle items catered to the African American market. For a while in there, they were like ground zero for the lifestyle trends that would soon shape our community. Wall hangings, incense, hair products, accessories . . . whatever. And clothing of course. So I did my own seat-of-the-pants, *power of broke*–type market research—which basically meant I figured it out as I went along. If I did an expo one month and sold, say, 1,000 shirts, I'd expect to see five or six of those shirts being worn at the next expo. Any variation from that norm, I'd start to notice. I'd even keep a log. I'd pay attention to which designs sold best in each market, and it got to where I'd know how many red shirts to bring to this or that show, how many burgundies, how many blacks. That kind of information was invaluable to me just starting out, because I didn't have the money to keep any kind of meaningful inventory on hand. I could only make what I could sell, and through these expos I could even track the movements of some of the kids going to these shows, seeing how many shirts I'd sold in DC might show up at a show at the Javits Center in New York, and so on.

These shows were my proof of concept. I could see with my own eyes what was working and what wasn't. From Virginia to Washington, from Philadelphia to New York, I could see my clothes on the backs of my customers and get some kind of read. How many embroideries sold versus screen prints? How many hats versus shirts? How many reds versus greens?

It was all right there, in the field, on the fly, and because I was hustling, scraping—because I was broke—I had no choice but to keep close watch.

FAITH AND FLOUR

GIGI BUTLER

ENTREPRENEUR, CUPCAKE BOSS

Okay, so here's that story I promised to share about the Nashville woman who started up a cupcake business with just $33 to her name.

Her name? Gigi Butler—and it turns out her story is even better than her headline. And her cupcakes—turns out they're right up there with the best I've ever tasted. (Her Caramel Sugar Mama and Kentucky Bourbon Pie cupcakes are insane!)

But like a lot of wildly successful businesses, Gigi's start-up almost didn't happen. She'd already chased her dream once and didn't think she had it in her to make a second run at a second goal. True, a lot of us entrepreneurs get derailed, sidetracked, first time out of the gate—but for Gigi, that first dream died hard. Her heart was all the way in it, and when she started out it had all seemed within reach. It was the classic "California girl hits the fork in the road and turns away from expectations" story: she shocked the smiles right off her parents' faces during her first year of college when she announced that she'd taken her second-semester tuition money, made a demo, and was headed off to Nashville to become a country music superstar.

Gigi knew her own mind, as they say in Tennessee—she knew

she wasn't cut out for college, knew she'd always wanted to make it as a singer-songwriter. The move didn't come out of nowhere, so her parents might have seen it coming. In fact, at the ripe young age of seven, Gigi had come home one day from a talent show and announced that she was moving to Nashville to become a country star—so the dream was always there, underneath, all around. She was bound to follow it—it was just a matter of time. By this point, first year of college, Gigi had been singing in a band for a couple years—Gina Butler and the Wild Silver Band. She'd been playing local biker bars, old folks' homes, state fairs, even did a tour of Canada. All through high school, she worked cleaning houses during the week, played music every weekend, tried to fit in a little school in between—the whole time looking ahead to her first big break.

"I had a booking agent at the time," she tells me, "and I was always on him to send me to Las Vegas. For whatever reason, that's where I thought I needed to be. To me, playing Vegas would have meant I'd arrived. But he didn't see it the same way. He didn't think Vegas was such a good idea. He's the one who said I should go to Nashville, become something in Nashville. Vegas was where you ended up, not where you started."

So Gigi listened to that little voice singing inside her head, sold her little cleaning business, paid off all her bills, and headed to Nashville with $500 in cash. She didn't know a soul, didn't have a place to live, didn't have a job. "But I knew God would take care of me," she says.

Oh, I almost forget to mention—Gigi came from a God-centered, hardworking family. Church and faith were a big deal in her house when she was growing up, and so was the spirit of entrepreneurship—and I've come to realize that these hard-won values are tremendous assets when you're looking to go it alone. A faith in something bigger than yourself—it's something to rely on, to help see you through, and here Gigi was able to lean on these influences to give her the strength to make such a major change in her life.

Trouble is, faith alone doesn't put food on the table or a roof over your head, so while Gigi was figuring things out in Music City, she went back to what she knew. She jump-started her cleaning business and took a waitressing job at a local Red Lobster, just to get some money coming in while she chased her dream at nights and on weekends. She sang all over town, at top tourist spots like Tootsie's and The Stage, but that big break never came her way. She was good enough and blessed enough to get these gigs, good enough and blessed enough to keep that dream going for a good long while, but she could never quite make it to a bigger stage.

A little side note on Gigi's Red Lobster job. I worked at Red Lobster, too, before launching FUBU, so she and I have this great piece of common ground. I've written about my time at Red Lobster, talked about it to business groups, school groups, all over. In fact, I'll have a Red Lobster story to share a little later on in the book, but I wanted to put Gigi's story on pause here to reflect on the power of working in an entry-level way for a company with that kind of major footprint—because let's face it, when you're working the floor, hustling between tables, it's just like any other restaurant job. But if you listen up, keep plugged in to what's going on around you, you're bound to pick up a thing or two. A national chain like Red Lobster, there's a chain of command, reaches all the way down from the corporate level to the waitresses, the bus boys, the fry cooks, so without even realizing it, Gigi wasn't just waiting tables—she was getting an education on what it means to work in the food services industry, in a franchise-type setting, for a national brand. Yeah, she was making rent, buying the time she needed to pursue her music, but along with all of that there was this never-ending lesson on what it means to work for a successful, well-run company. In a way, she was getting an education in business, even if she didn't know it at the time.

POWER FACT: **69 percent of successful entrepreneurs have worked over 10 years as employees at other companies....** Get that much-needed experience on someone else's payroll—might as well get paid while you're learning from your mistakes.

Gigi was also making some valuable contacts—this being Nashville, a lot of her customers were country music stars and record industry folks. Somewhere in there, all these little breaks started to add up. It worked out that Gigi's waitressing job kind of fed her housecleaning job. She cleaned for Leanne Rimes, Taylor Swift, and a bunch of other well-known artists she waited on at the restaurant. How those jobs came about—well, she found herself waiting on their tables, and they got to talking. Got to where Gigi built her cleaning business into something bigger than she could handle on her own, so she started hiring people to help her out—the whole time singing at night and on the weekends.

Finally, when she hit thirty, Gigi was ready to give up on her dream. "I knew it wasn't going to happen for me," she says, "and I took it as a huge failure on my part. All I ever wanted was to be a singer-songwriter, but getting off the stage at three o'clock in the morning, working for tips, it started to lose its appeal."

DARE TO GROW

Gigi had always been an avid reader, so she loaded up on business books, self-help books, whatever she could grab to help her get past this trouble spot in her life and grow her game. She expanded her housecleaning business, built it up into a thriving little company. At one point, she had five girls working for her, and they'd each clean two houses a day. Gigi herself would do two or three more—always recognizing the power of doing it herself. She saved enough money to buy a house of her own, pay off all her bills. Life was good. It wasn't what she'd dreamed about all these years, but it was good.

And then the most amazing thing happened. She got a call from her brother, who was visiting New York. He'd just waited on line for a couple hours at a trendy cupcake shop in Manhattan. He said, "I'm eating one of these red velvet cupcakes, and they're not as good as yours. You should open a cupcake shop in Nashville."

Gigi was in somebody else's bathroom when the call came in, cleaning their toilet. It was a tiny little bathroom, with a tiny little mirror over the sink, and when she got off the phone with her brother she found herself staring into that tiny little mirror for the longest time. It was like a scene from a movie, and as it played out Gigi asked herself a bunch of questions, which, taken together, was really one question: why not?

She was wearing old, ratty clothes, a pair of cleaning gloves, she looked a mess, but the face that looked back at her was the face of that seven-year-old girl who wasn't afraid to dream big. So she decided to go for it. Baking was in her blood. Her whole family baked—her mother, her grandmother, her aunts.

Of course, Gigi didn't just look in the mirror and make such an important decision on a whim. Now that the seed was planted, she went back and did a little research. She learned that the recent run of high-end cupcake shops—like Sprinkles in Beverly Hills, Magnolia Bakery in New York, and Georgetown Cupcakes just outside Washington, DC—had all opened up in affluent communities. All signs indicated there was an opportunity in a smaller market like Nashville for a bakery built on her family recipes, featuring fresh cupcakes, made from the finest ingredients, served in a fun, friendly environment.

When Gigi tells her story, I love how it comes down to this simple question: why not? It's a question we should all be asking ourselves as we embark on our new ventures. Really, we spend so much time talking ourselves *out* of things and not nearly enough time talking ourselves *into* things. For my money, the arguments in favor of making a bold, proactive move are way more interesting than the arguments against.

Gigi put together a business plan and went around Nashville looking for a loan. She went to four banks, but everyone she talked to pretty much laughed in her face and showed her the door. "They basically told me I was nuts," she says. "They were like, 'A cupcake shop? Seriously?'"

Now, the good thing about running a successful housecleaning business and owning your own home is that you wind up with great credit, so Gigi decided to loan the money to herself. She maxed out her credit cards and took out $100,000 in cash to ramp up. She drew $35,000 from one card, at 14 percent; $22,000 from another card, at 17 percent. Then she got one card down to 8 percent and took out the rest.

"I just went for it," she says.

Yep, she did.

Now, here's where her rich and famous housecleaning clients and her Red Lobster customers check back in, because Gigi kept working as she ramped up her cupcake business. She had her little safety net and wanted to keep it in place. And they gave her a head start in growing her customer base—in a grassroots way. She kept telling folks what she was up to, and they just kind of smiled sweetly, trying not to be discouraging. "They'd say things like, 'A cupcake shop? Well, bless your little heart,'" she remembers. "Like they thought I was making this huge mistake. They were like all those bankers, but I think they also felt sorry for me, because they kept ordering cupcakes. Leanne Rimes had a dinner party, so I made some cupcakes for her. Every night I was making cupcakes, a dozen here, a dozen there. I was working on my recipes, trying to get everything just right."

What she was doing, really, was market research. This was

Gigi's proof of concept, because after a while she developed a good feel for what her customers liked, what they didn't like.

Meanwhile, she was doing the build-out on her first store and running through that $100,000 cash advance, fast. The day before she planned to open, she was down to $33 in her checking account. It was all she had to her name—and she still had to pay $4,500 in rent, $1,000 in food and supplies, and another $1,000 or so to cover the salaries of the two full-time employees she'd just hired.

HAVE A LITTLE FAITH

The *power of broke*? Gigi couldn't see any "power" in her situation—all she could see was "broke."

Her parents even came in from California to help her get the place ready—it was a full-on family affair—but there was still the matter of all the unsettled bills. Gigi recalls how she approached the shop to give the place a final once-over and was met by the plumber, who wanted to be paid. Gigi wrote him a check, but urged him to please, please, please hold off on depositing it for a couple days. She was honest about it—she said, "If you try to cash it, it'll bounce, but it'll be good on Monday, you have my word."

That was good enough for the plumber, but then the contractor came by. Here Gigi thought the guy was just checking on his work one last time before the open, thought he'd been paid in full, but he said, "There's one bill I forgot to pass on to you."

She said, "Just one bill? That shouldn't be a problem, long as it can wait until next week."

But that one bill turned out to be a $15,000 charge for a new drywall—more money than Gigi could get her head around at just that moment. (And better believe it, more than she could afford to pay—way more.)

"I melted onto the floor," she says. "I went from feeling good about the business to thinking maybe I was making the biggest mistake. I'd already given up on one of my dreams. I didn't think I had it in me to give up on another."

Here again, Gigi's faith helped to see her through. Her mom took her aside, tried to calm her down. She said, "God will take care of you." And in those words, once again, Gigi found the strength to power through.

"When I tell my story to people, I always stop myself at this spot, because I don't want to shove my religion down anyone's throat," she says. "We're all free to believe in our own way. But I mention it because He was an important part of my story. He was. He took a broken-down country singer and helped her to make a beautiful life. At every turn, I knew He had a plan for me. I knew if I believed in Him that He would believe in me."

Strengthened, she got up early the next morning, put on a cute little cupcake-y apron her mother had made for her, and prayed that God would send her some customers. "I had no idea what I was doing," she recalls. "I didn't have a menu. I didn't have a clue how things would go."

POWER FACT: **Did you know there are 9.1 million US businesses owned by women?** ... *And I'm thrilled to say, that number is growing.*

Well, the opening couldn't have gone any better. There were lines out the door at Gigi's Cupcakes that very first day—around the corner even. A local news crew came by to film the crowd, which of course only made the lines grow longer. Word of mouth kicked in—although Gigi's customers couldn't really talk at first because they were so busy feeding their faces with cupcakes.

That was in February 2008—five months after that game-changing phone call from her brother, and in that short time Gigi had managed to read a bunch of books on starting your own business, research the cupcake industry, learn a bunch of new recipes, negotiate a lease, build out her first store, hire staff . . . and she did most of these things on her own.

She wasn't "broke," not by a long stretch—at least, not when she started out. She owned her own home. She had a good line of credit. But once she went and took full advantage of that good line of credit, she was in the hole for a whole lot of money—some of it borrowed at pretty outrageous rates.

So she had to hustle—and I mean hustle—just to stay afloat. And the next five months were even more crazy-making, because Gigi was reluctant to give up her cleaning business. It was her safety net, in case this next dream went the way of the first one. Plus, she worried that the bake shop wouldn't generate enough money for her to start paying off those credit card loans, so she believed she had no choice to keep the cash flowing. Long as there were enough hours in the day for her to clean a couple houses, attend to the business, stay ahead of the paperwork, it would all shake out to the good.

Let's be clear—Gigi still had to work her butt off. She got into a routine where she'd open up Gigi's Cupcakes at four o'clock each morning, get the place going, wait for her staff to arrive, work the counter through the morning rush, then hustle out to clean two houses. She'd be back in the store by late afternoon, work through closing, then race home and start in on paperwork, payroll, all of that. "I was killing myself," she says, "but I couldn't see any other way."

After her first week, she was able to pay off the plumber, pay her rent, make the first payments on her credit card bills, and even put $300 in the bank. That drywall bill had to wait a while, but things were looking up, up, up.

Within three months, she'd paid the contractor in full, added additional staff, taken a big bite out of what she owed to the credit card companies, and saved $26,000—enough to get her to start thinking about opening a second store. And now, six years later, there are almost 100 Gigi's Cupcakes stores, spread across twenty-four states, generating over $35 million in annual sales.

Her secret? Well, it's in the recipe, first and foremost. Gigi's cupcakes are baked fresh daily, with love, with passion. It took her six months to find the perfect vanilla—and now she uses her own extracts to make sure everything's just right. But a lot of businesses launch with the perfect recipe, the perfect formula, without this kind of runaway success, so there's got to be something else at play—and here I think it ties into the *power of broke* mentality that has followed Gigi around her entire life.

It's also in the hard work and passion—Gigi's commitment to serving up the very best cupcakes on the planet. (She's even got a terrific line of gluten-free and sugar-free cupcakes, in response to the changing diets and tastes of her customers.)

But mostly, it's in her to-the-bone appreciation of the value of a dollar.

"I've cleaned 20,000-square-foot homes," she tells me. "I've seen how people live at that level, and what I've seen is that money doesn't buy you passion. I still save every penny. I know what it is to not have, so I appreciate everything. I do. And I don't let anything go to waste. I was raised that way, came up that way with my cleaning business. If we've got a bowl of special frosting, maybe it cost us sixty dollars, and maybe we're done with a certain recipe and there's still some left over, a lot of folks would just throw that extra frosting away. Other people, they don't spend your money the way you spend your money, right? But that's good frosting, so we'll come up with a special, we'll use it on a cake, we'll find a way to make it work."

Sounds to me like a recipe for success, whaddya think?

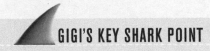

GIGI'S KEY SHARK POINT

REMEMBER, YOU ARE THE BRAND. I don't know that Gigi herself would reach for this particular SHARK Point in highlighting her story, but as I tapped into what she's been through, it's clear she's been about building the "Gigi" brand her entire life. At fifteen, she put her name on her first cleaning business. After that, her first band carried her name. And of course, her cupcake store now does as well. At each step along the way, she's worked hard to ensure that the name would stand for something genuine, something real, something of value. Of course, when you're so closely associated with your product and purpose and when the thing you're putting out into the world is totally reflective of who you are and what you're about, then YOU become your first pitch. You won't be able to make a single sale until you're able to sell yourself, and here it helps to note that Gigi put the same care and dedication into her cleaning business as she puts into her cupcakes. When she was out there making music, her first love, she sang with all her heart. That's one of the things people respond to when they go out of their way to visit a Gigi's Cupcakes shop or buy from the company online. They know that the woman behind the cupcake aims to please. What she's selling is a treat, an escape—and to keep folks coming back, she realizes that she's got to put a whole bunch of "above and beyond" into her business, and that most of that has got to come from her.

It's her name on the store, after all.

For more information and resources, check out
www.DaymondJohn.com/PowerofBroke/Gigi

TURN YOUR PROBLEMS INTO SOLUTIONS

JAY ABRAHAM
EXECUTIVE, CONSULTANT, PUBLIC SPEAKER,
DIRECT-MARKETING GURU

To look today at Jay Abraham—a leading marketing consultant, adviser to Fortune 500 companies, bestselling author, and sought-after growth strategist—you'd never guess he came from modest beginnings. But he'll proudly tell you that his father was a salesman, that he grew up in Indianapolis in a small three-bedroom house with a gravel driveway, no garage. He had to walk twenty blocks to school, and that's where his education ended, right after high school. He was married at eighteen and had two kids by the time he was twenty—so basically he had the needs of a guy twice his age, and none of the tools he needed to meet them.

Only thing he had, really, was drive. Okay, so he was also smart—whip-smart, as you can tell right away if you talk to him or read one of his great books—but that didn't come into play for a while. After all, smart doesn't always get you a job. You just need to put yourself in the right place, at the right time, and maybe pass yourself off as someone with the right skill set. Trouble is, that's sometimes easier said than done.

"The world didn't care," Jay says of his first real job search. "I couldn't get a job. Really, all I could get was a desk and a chair.

Some days, it was just the chair. This one company, they set me up, told me I could sell for them, work on commission. Nothing was guaranteed. And when you only eat if you earn, when your kids only eat if you earn, you figure out very quickly what works and what doesn't, what works better and what doesn't. And that was the beginning of my marketing education."

POWER FACT: Before becoming one of the most beloved figures on television and a pop cultural icon, Oprah Winfrey was fired from her job as a broadcast journalist because she was "unfit for television." ... *Sometimes the folks in the know don't really know—your success is in your hands, not in the whims of others.*

Jay was a quick study—but not quick enough. He was fired from that first (nonpaying!) job, so he had to scramble all over again. He was super-creative, had a knack for getting his foot in the door. One of the ways he did this was to print up a bunch of oversized business cards—they were calling cards, really, because Jay had no business to speak of. He printed a whole bunch of stuff on these cards—like, JAY ABRAHAM, STRUGGLING YOUNG ENTREPRE-NEUR WHO SUFFERS FROM ACUTE SINUS INFECTIONS. You know, whatever he could think to get people to do a double-take, maybe spend a little extra time with him before kicking him to the curb.

And get this—it worked! A lot of the time anyway.

"I was flat broke," he says now of this time in his life when he didn't have a whole lot going on in terms of a career. "I would go to these offices and say, 'Look, I'm trying to learn.' And some of these people would take me in. They didn't give me a job, but they gave me an opportunity. They let me sit in the corner for a couple hours and just listen. They'd have these meetings, and they wouldn't even introduce me. I would just be in the corner, like maybe I was the concierge or something. At the end of every meeting, every transaction, someone would take me aside and explain what just happened. And I soaked it up. My wife thought I was crazy, because sometimes I'd be out all night, 'working' like this, not getting paid. But it paid off."

His great asset, he came to realize, was that he was able to see things no one else could see. He could spot value in opportunities that other folks were likely to ignore. It's a skill he was able to develop when he had nothing else to go on, and one of the first times he put it to use, it paid off—in a big way. It came, of all places, in the eight-track tape business.

LOOK IN WHERE OTHERS LOOK AWAY

Now, I'm betting a lot of folks reading this have never heard of eight-track tapes, but back in the 1970s you could find eight-track players in a lot of cars and home stereo systems. The deal was, you could listen to an album in a never-ending loop on an eight-track tape—unlike audiocassette tapes, which you had to flip over from side A to side B—only, you couldn't record on eight-track tapes, so they never really caught on.

Like the Betamax going up against the VCR, like the Tassimo Coffee Pods going up against the Keurig K-Cups, the eight-track technology was stuck on the second-tier of a game-changing innovation, about to go the way of the dinosaur—but not before Jay was able to squeeze a couple more drops from the well.

"You could already see that eight-tracks were hurting," he tells me, "but there was still an opportunity there. It's something I learned early on—that your problem is the solution to somebody's bigger problem, so here my problem was, I had no money, right? But if you embrace the fact that you have no money, you can learn to think that being without capital can be one of the greatest gifts for a young entrepreneur."

Jay still lived in Indianapolis, and he found a local chain of convenience stores, noticed they weren't selling eight-track tapes. So he went to them with a proposal. He offered to stock their shelves with tapes and cassettes at no cost, no risk, in exchange for a two-thirds cut of each sale. He tried to anticipate the objections of the convenience store owner and found a way to address them before they came up. This was a selling technique he'd learned early on in his commission sales job. One of the ways he did this was to offer to test the concept in a single store before taking it wide to the entire chain of about fifty stores. After a little bit of back-and-forth, agreements were signed and a deal put in place.

Meanwhile, Jay found a Midwest distributor of eight-track tapes that didn't have penetration in Indiana, so he took those agreements to the distributor and arranged for them to send him $200,000 worth of tapes, at no up-front cost. This was the part of the equation where the answer to his problems was the solution to someone else's, because this distributor needed to open up this end of the market—so right away Jay was looking at a win-win-win scenario. There was something in it for the convenience store owner, something in it for the distributor, and—with any luck—something in it for Jay.

Jay put the tapes in his garage—his makeshift warehouse. Then he went out and bought a beat-up 1967 Chevy Biscayne station wagon for $500—his delivery truck, until one of the wheels fell off. He enlisted his brother to help with the deliveries and inventory, and he was in business. Soon he was clearing $4,000 a week—all with no capital.

DISCOVER THE SECRET OF OTHER PEOPLE'S MAGIC

One of the great takeaways from Jay's books is his definition of OPM—which most people use as a shorthand for "other people's money." You'll see that acronym kicked around in business books, in business classes, in business settings—and here the idea behind it was very much in play as Jay ramped up his makeshift eight-track business. Even as a young man just starting out, with nothing in the bank and the household of a much older man to keep afloat, Jay found a way to grow that concept and call upon other people's manpower, other people's marketing, other people's mind-set. Absolutely, he needed money, but he needed all these other resources too.

He'd left himself no choice but to succeed—so he figured out a way to get it done, even if it just meant learning from other people's mistakes.

Out of that, Jay was able to parlay the lessons learned before the wheels fell off of that station wagon into his first big break—and here again, he relied on every possible definition of OPM you can think of. Soon he'd built up enough of a stake to buy a small company out of bankruptcy—a tiny company with about $20,000 in annual revenues that mostly came from a mail-order arthritis cream designed to help people with arthritis. They sold other health-related products too, and at first Jay thought the underlying product line offered more of an opportunity than the arthritis cream.

Now, Jay wasn't going it alone here. He had some partners he was working with, but he was the one out in front, making the deals. "We had no money," he remembers. "We had to go to radio stations, television stations, magazines, newspapers, and persuade them to run our ads on the come. We couldn't pay them, so we offered all the revenue on our first sale instead, but even that was a hard challenge. What I didn't realize at the time was I had no credibility with these people. You had all these other companies out there hustling, same as me, thinking they could trade for that unsold ad time, that unsold ad space."

So Jay found himself having to sweeten an already sweet deal. He sat down and punched all kinds of holes in his pitch, tried to anticipate the negatives he'd hear from each station owner or publisher. The one big negative that kept coming back to him was that mail-order companies weren't always true to their word. They'd take orders and never fulfill them. Or the product wouldn't deliver on the promise, and customers would want their money back. To counter that, Jay offered to give each station owner and publisher a chance to sample his product firsthand. He sent each of them a dozen jars of his arthritis cream and encouraged them to share them with any friends, family members, or employees who happened to have arthritis or joint pain.

Next, he offered an additional 15 percent on each sale—meaning, on a $3 jar of cream, the station owner or publisher would keep the purchase price plus another 45 cents.

And finally, he came up with a bunch of other incentives and promotional items to fold into his pitch.

It was such a crazy deal, and on the face of it there seemed to be nothing in it for Jay and his little company. With these terms, he wasn't just losing out on each $3 sale, but he was also out the 45-cent sweetener and the 45 cents it cost to actually produce and package his product. That's 90 cents out of pocket, on top of the $3 he'd never see from each sale. But he believed in his product. Already, there was a core group of customers who were passionate about it—so much so that when Jay initially shut down production after taking over the company, he started getting letters from little old ladies and older gentlemen, begging him to keep making it. They'd say that without this cream they couldn't walk to church on Sundays, couldn't sit up and watch television, couldn't play with their grandchildren.

Talk about proof of concept!

But there was another concept in play here—lifetime value. Jay knew that until somebody came up with a cure for arthritis, bursitis, rheumatism, joint pain, and every other ache and pain that afflicts folks of all ages, there'd always be a market for his product.

"There was a recurring need," he says. "It's consumptive. It could only grow and grow."

So what do you think happened? Well, with terms like that, Jay was able to get a number of radio syndicators and station owners to sign on to his pitch. Newspaper and magazine publishers too. It was a desperation move, but it paid off in a big way, because out of every ten people who bought a jar of Jay's arthritis cream, eight repurchased the same product within a month—and most of those eight continued to make the same purchase every month going forward. (Also, half of them went on to purchase at least two additional products from the company.) Of course, Jay didn't have to give away the proceeds on those second and subsequent sales, so out of that initial 90 cent loss, he wound up making about $40 each year, on each repeat customer.

That product? Icy Hot—which is now the top-selling topical pain reliever in the country. You've probably heard of it. I'm betting there's even a tube or a jar of the stuff somewhere in your house, but chances are you didn't buy it from Jay. To his great credit, Jay is quick to point out that he was just a part of the "team" that helped to relaunch Icy Hot. He was the strategist, the dealmaker, and he was working alongside some money men and critical operations people.

Back when Jay and his team relaunched the cream, they were filling 50 to 100 orders a day. Then that number doubled—then it doubled again. Before long, they were filling 500,000 orders—all on the back of this *power of broke*-type strategy that Jay and his partners only pursued because he had no other options.

(Oh, and by the way—he eventually sold the brand for $60 million. Not all of that money went to Jay, of course, but his cut was enough to stake him in his other interests for a long, long while.)

What I love about Jay's story is that it reminds me of some of the desperation moves we had to make when we were getting FUBU off the ground. Wherever possible, whenever necessary, we'd take Jay's "other people's manpower" approach and find a way to eliminate almost all of our start-up costs. We didn't know what to call it, hadn't read any business or marketing books, but we were improvising, thinking on our feet, doing what we had to do to make good things happen. For example, I used to go to store owners and say, "Look, do you want to buy these shirts?" I'd take their order. Then I'd go to the screen printer, who wanted to charge me, say, $1.25 per shirt. I'd go back to them and tell them to charge me $2.00 instead, and in exchange I asked them to ship the items directly to the store and arrange for the store owner to pay them directly as well. This way, I could offer assurances to the store owner that the shirts were being made by a reputable company, and in turn I could convince the screen printer that my order was backed by this reputable store, leaving me free to take my cut and essentially finance these orders straight out of the gate—let's call it "street-level leveraging," for lack of a better term.

UP THE ANTE

So what's Jay Abraham been up to since?

- He's spent the last twenty-five years growing the bottom lines of over 10,000 clients in more than 400 industries worldwide.
- He's worked with headline-making, household name–type clients and under-the-radar small business owners.
- He's become known for his concept of "risk reversal"—a strategy that encourages businesses to focus on a lifelong value relationship with their customers and look to make small changes to gain maximum results.

Here's what else you need to know about Jay Abraham: the man is not all about making money. He's committed to adding value in every interaction—whether he's consulting with a client, mentoring a young entrepreneur, or speaking to a group of small business leaders and offering them strategies on how to sidestep the worst of a recession.

It just so happens that making money is a by-product of all that—a happy by-product. But it's not what drives him. You can see it in the way he's lived his life, the choices he's made . . . reaching all the way back to his very first steps in business.

That wife of Jay's who thought he was out of his mind, making himself an unpaid fly-on-the-wall for all those meetings? They ended up divorced. Matter of fact, Jay's been married two other times, and he's still happily married to Christy, wife number three, and I only mention this here because Jay himself points to the lessons learned on the backs of these marriages as a key factor in his success.

"Each time, I was wiped out," he says, "it's like I had to start all over again, and after a couple times I started going to a therapist to figure out the meaning of life. I ran through a couple therapists too, and I finally found one who gave me an answer that's redefined my life. And here it is: most people think that when they acquire wealth, success, getting the biggest house, starting the fastest-growing company, marrying the prettiest wife, making the Forbes list, whatever, they think that's going to transform them. They think the heavens are going to open, the angels are going to sing, euphoria's going to happen, and all their worries will just disappear. But that's not how it goes. It's anticlimactic. All of that, it doesn't change anything. The meaning of life is the process. The meaning of life is in conversations like we're having right now, and you can have the same conversation with a waiter or a janitor or an executive at a top company. It's all in the process, and in my case it's in my commitment to add value anytime I interact with anybody. If you can get that in alignment, find a way to help someone else while you help yourself, then everything else flows."

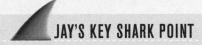

JAY'S KEY SHARK POINT

SET A GOAL. When you've got your hand in so many different companies, when you're working so many different deals, there's a tendency to want to hit your targets along the way. Looking at where Jay has been, and where he's going, I have to think this has become a key aspect of his personality. You can hear it in his voice when he talks about his marriages; each time he was divorced, he had to hit a reset button, so making himself whole became his primary objective. The same goes each time he signs on for a consulting gig—he sets out a bunch of goals and puts the right plan in place, the right people in place, to make sure they're met.

So tell me—what goals are YOU going to set for yourself and your business . . . today?

For more information and resources, check out
www.DaymondJohn.com/PowerofBroke/Jay

PROTECT THIS HOUSE

KEVIN PLANK

FOUNDER AND CHIEF EXECUTIVE OFFICER OF
UNDER ARMOUR

My buddy Kevin Plank was a football player at the University of
Maryland in the mid-1990s when he had a big idea. Actually, it
was a small idea, but it grew and grew. Today that idea has become
Under Armour, one of the dominant players in the sports apparel,
footwear, and accessories business—a business that already had a
couple dominant players before Kevin started out.

Kevin's idea? He wanted a more practical, performance-type
T-shirt to wear beneath his jersey and pads. That's all it was at
first—a way to make his own life a little better, a little easier. Middle of a game, middle of practice, he'd have to pull off his pads, peel
off his soaking wet, gray cotton T-shirt, suit up again, and get back
on the field. It was annoying, time-consuming, unnecessary. "And
it wasn't just me," Kevin says. "Everybody was doing it. A hundred
guys in the locker room, at halftime, ripping off these wet shirts
and putting everything back on. Equipment guys running around,
coaches trying to talk to you about the game. It was just mayhem."

Out of that mayhem came a better way—and a brand with revenues of $3 billion today.

There are a lot of similarities between Kevin's story and mine, the ways we each launched our companies—that's one of the reasons we made such a strong connection when we got together. He recognized a need in his immediate community, and he moved to fill it. At the time, for American football players, the focus on equipment was limited to things you put on your head or your body to keep you safe. Brands were just starting to pay attention to footwear—you know, maybe make a shoe another ounce lighter, give it a slightly different tread, a better look. But that was it. Nobody was thinking about performance in terms of clothing, and yet in locker rooms across the country there were these piles and piles of wet, smelly T-shirts that didn't need to be there.

So Kevin started doing a little research. He learned that the dry weight of most cotton T-shirts is about six ounces—but they have a saturated weight of up to three pounds.

Three pounds! Why would anyone want to carry all that extra weight? Kevin knew he could do better, so he started looking at lighter-weight, stretchy, synthetic materials that would fit the body snugly, like a second skin. And you have to realize, this was a guy with no background in fashion or design. He didn't know the first thing about these synthetic, performance-type materials, but he was out there chasing, hustling . . . all in service of this one idea.

Something else you have to realize: Kevin was still a full-time student-athlete, which didn't leave him a whole lot of free time to pursue this idea. But like all the other scrappy entrepreneurs you've read about in these chapters, Kevin was driven—and creating that better T-shirt became his main focus away from the field. The thing of it is, what seemed like such an obvious, natural idea to Kevin wasn't such a no-brainer to the folks he was pitching. He says, "It wasn't like people were telling me, 'My God, you're right!' Or, 'That's brilliant!' No, it took time."

But Kevin was committed to this idea, locked in. These days, at Under Armour, he tries to motivate his people with the phrase "I Will." It's like a company mantra, a rallying cry, but back in 1995, it was just a phrase Kevin kept muttering to himself. "Ninety-nine times out of a hundred, it comes down to an entrepreneur making up his mind and deciding he's going to find a way," he says. "No matter what, they will make their business happen."

And that's pretty much what happened here.

WILL IT SO

When football season ended his senior year, Kevin only needed a couple credits to graduate, so for the first time since starting college he had a bunch of time on his hands. He filled it with this idea. He drove to New York in his beat-up Ford Bronco, walked into a local fabric store, bought some material that seemed like it might do the trick. Then he found a tailor, showed the guy a tight white Hanes T-shirt, and asked him to make as many T-shirts as he could in the same style out of the new material.

(In those days, I was hanging out in the same neighborhood, trying to get my own fashion thing going—so there's a good chance I was in the tailor shop right next door!)

Kevin's tailor was able to make seven prototype shirts. Kevin drove back to Maryland and handed them out to his teammates, who were just starting their spring season. Looking for that proof of concept, he convinced a lot of them to try out his shirt during practice. He says, "The guys were like, 'Plank, what is this thing?' So I explained it to them. Some of them, they couldn't be bothered. But a bunch of them were curious."

After that first practice, a lot of the guys who initially resisted now wanted to try out the shirts, so Kevin simply washed those seven shirts and handed them out to seven different guys. Day after that, same thing. More and more, people started asking Kevin for a chance to check out one of his shirts, telling him what they liked about it, what they didn't like about it, what worked, what didn't.

Next, he drove back to New York, parked close to what he'd learned was the Garment District, 34th Street and Seventh Avenue, and started walking around. He didn't have any appointments, didn't have a game plan. He was just out to see what he could see. He picked up a copy of *Women's Wear Daily*—the bible of the fashion industry. He wound up at a manufacturer on 11th Avenue, negotiating his first run of 500 shirts.

"What I'd realized with those first seven shirts was that it wasn't just for football players," he says. "I'd passed them out to lacrosse players, baseball players. One of the girlfriends of one of the lacrosse players, she wanted one, too. So it wasn't just this great football undershirt I'd built. There was this whole category I could create, for people who needed a better shirt to wear while they worked out."

When Kevin tells the story of how he got Under Armour off the ground, I get to thinking it's the perfect example of how a business comes to you if you let it. It started out, he was thinking one way, but then his concept took him another way—and his company exploded because Kevin was plugged into all of that. He listened, reacted, switched things up.

So why was Kevin wandering around the Garment District looking for a supplier? Why didn't he just go back to the first tailor with his initial 500-shirt order? Because the guy had charged him $400 for those seven prototype shirts. At those rates, Kevin's inventory would have broken him before he even got going. He had $16,000 to his name, so that became his entire seed money. Out of that, he had to pay for everything, including his first run of shirts, his trips back and forth to New York, and so on. On this budget, renting office space was out of the question, so as soon as he graduated, in the spring of 1996, he set up shop in his grandmother's

Georgetown row house in Washington, DC. He lived upstairs, had an office on the ground floor, kept his inventory in the basement—again, a lot like the way we had things set up when I was in my mother's house in Queens in the early days of FUBU.

POWER FACT: According to a 2011 US census report, over 51 percent of American businesses are operated primarily from the home. . . . That's right: more than half of our going concerns hit the ground in an arm's-length, bare-bones way, so look around and soak it in and know that while you're worrying about how to compete, the playing field has changed.

First year in business, Kevin had $17,000 in revenue—basically a wash.

Second year, he upped that number to $100,000.

The year after that, he came close to $400,000.

I'm giving you the "long story short" version of the Under Armour story: In its first five years, the company went to $5 million in sales. Over the next five years, they got close to $300 million—and then, five years later, they went public and crossed $1 billion.

With each new run, with each new product line, Kevin adapted his designs to the responses he was getting from his first customers, so he collected his proof of concept along the way—together with a bunch of ideas on how to improve his products each time out.

He made his sales through good old-fashioned word of mouth—this being way before the days of social media. People weren't shopping online the way they are today, so a lot of his orders were telephone-based—and that's the reason Kevin came up with that funky, Old English spelling of the word "Armour" in his company name. When he was applying for a toll-free number, 888-4-ARMOUR was available, so he hit on that.

"This is how naive I was at the time," he says. "I thought, 'Who knows how long this Internet thing will last? But I'll have this cool toll-free number, so people will be able to find us.'"

On a lot of the first designs, Kevin even put that phone number on the back of the shirt, along with his Web address—a collector's item now, if you can find one in the back of your closet.

TOUGH IT OUT

Now, I don't mean to race over those first couple years, because like a lot of guys who start out running businesses out of their grandmother's row house, Kevin hit a couple bumps along the way. That first $16,000? "I spent it in about five minutes," he says.

Success doesn't usually find you on your own schedule, and it hardly ever happens as fast as you want it to happen. Sometimes you have to wait for it—but a hard-charger like Kevin didn't have it in him to wait. "I can still remember this one day," he says. "It was a Friday afternoon, and I went to the bank, and I took out the thirty-four hundred dollars I had left in my account. I had six thousand dollars in checks I had to cover, and I didn't know what to do, so I got the idea that I would head to Atlantic City. It was right up Route 40. I would take that thirty-four hundred dollars and hit the blackjack tables."

Wasn't exactly a sound business strategy, but when you're up against it, you're up against it—you'll try anything to keep your idea alive. So that's just what Kevin did, and for a while it looked like his gamble would pay off. The cards were with him when he started out. He turned that $3,400 into $4,000, turned that $4,000 into $5,000. His stack was getting close to $6,000. He could smell it, taste it, started to think he could run it all the way up to $10,000. But then—*poof!*—it was gone. All of it.

"I don't know if you've ever been broke," he says, telling me this story. "Flat broke. Broke broke. But you don't know what broke is until you pull up to the Delaware Memorial Bridge and have to face that two-dollar toll, just to get home. It was the single worst moment of my life, having to face that poor toll booth operator, waiting for her two dollars. I was so broke, I couldn't even check for loose change in the ashtray, in the seat cushions. I'm talking 'can't even stop for a soda' broke."

He'd gassed up the car on the way into Atlantic City, but other than that, Kevin was on empty. All he could do was throw up his hands and beg for mercy, say, "I'm sorry, ma'am, but I just don't have the money."

The woman stepped out of her toll booth and flashed him this scolding, pitiful look, like he was the lowest of the low. Then she took down his license plate number, his registration number, started writing him a summons. He'd never been more embarrassed—he didn't even have $2 to his name, all because he'd gambled away the last of his cash at the blackjack table.

He ended up driving to his mother's house, which was right by the post office where he'd set up a PO box. He figured he could stop in for dinner and check the mail, since he didn't have any money for food anyway. His mother asked how things were going with the company, and Kevin gave her the same answer he always gave. He said, "It's going great, Mom. We're doing fine."

Underneath, though, he was thinking, *I'm totally screwed. I just made the biggest mistake of my life.* For the first time he could remember, he cried. He couldn't think of a way out.

After dinner, he went to the post office—and there in the Under Armour box was a check for $7,500 from Georgia Tech University, one of the first school accounts he opened. He'd been chasing the athletic director for months for payment, and the check just happened to arrive in the middle of this low, low moment—and left Kevin thinking maybe he'd be okay after all.

BE FAMOUS FOR SOMETHING

One of the reasons Kevin was able to grow Under Armour into such a monster global brand was because he never strayed from his commitment to his core concept. "We became famous for making the world's greatest T-shirt for when it's warm outside," he says. "That's how we became known, and that's what I tell people all the time when they're just starting out. Be famous for something. We were famous for our performance T-shirt, which was unlike anything on the market at the time. After that, we set out to make the world's greatest T-shirt for when it's cold outside, so then we became known for that too. It doesn't matter if you're playing football, or bow-hunting, or playing tennis, or skiing, we've got you covered."

As I write this, Under Armour has posted its twentieth consecutive quarter of 20 percent growth or more—one of only two companies in the S&P 500 that can make this claim—and Kevin still runs the business like a football team. Sales and marketing, those guys are on offense. Manufacturing, distribution . . . that's defense. Kevin himself was a special teams guy in college, so that's become his role—he's in the middle of everything. The company's got over 10,000 employees, all over the world, but at the headquarters office in Baltimore you can find these whiteboards in Kevin's office. Kevin writes all these sayings and slogans on the board—words and phrases to inspire his team.

During the financial crisis: "No loser talk!"

He says, "Everywhere you go, you hear people talk about how the world is falling apart. Everybody is an expert. But at Under Armour, I want our people to control what they can control. Leave the pontificating to everyone else. Leave all that negative talk to everyone else."

He's got a whole bunch of them:

"Dictate the tempo."

"Walk with a purpose."

"Protect this house!" That's one of his favorites, and to hear Kevin tell it, a phrase like this, it helps to foster a certain pride of ownership, a sense of teamwork.

"We're very much a 'lean forward' organization," he says. "We're all about what we can do, not what we cannot do."

To illustrate, he points back to those first few months after he graduated from college, running through his $16,000 investment. There were naysayers all around, people telling him he needed more money to launch a business, people telling him he didn't know anybody in the sports apparel business, in the fashion business, in retail. "I didn't have any of that experience or any of those contacts," he admits, "but what I did have was this network of thirty, forty, fifty guys I could reach out to and say, 'Hey, can I just get you to try something?' You could tell me I didn't know anybody in a traditional business sense, but that just didn't apply in this case. I refused to let it apply, because everybody knows somebody, right?"

Really, it drives Kevin up the wall when he hears someone on his team talk about how well the company is doing "in spite of" this or "considering" that. He doesn't want to hear it, so he reminds his team that the same way a rising tide lifts all boats, you have to be prepared for when the tide goes out. He says, "Being the tallest short guy in the room can still be a pretty good thing."

KEVIN'S KEY SHARK POINT

KEEP SWIMMING. Those bumps Kevin hit when he was just starting out? They didn't stop him from chasing this one idea. They didn't even slow him down. Whatever he had to do, he found a way to get it done. He even sat himself down in front of a sewing machine—he didn't have a clue how to sew, but he figured it out because he had no choice but to figure it out. He tells people looking to start their own business to be prepared to change, adapt, grow. To learn every aspect of the business—from the ground up, inside out, top to bottom . . . all of that. "You've got to evolve," he says. "If you try one thing, and it's just not working, figure out why it's not working and address it. There are too many entrepreneurs sitting in their attics and basements right now, saying, 'It's just not right.' Or, 'It's just not ready.' But you've got to make it right. You've got to get it ready. Push yourself to where you need to be."

What do you really want out of life? That's the question that drives Kevin—and for him, just to use a football metaphor since he used to play, the goal line keeps moving. First, it was starting a business. Then it was reaching a certain number in sales, then a certain number after that. And, all along, he kept driving, pushing. The dude is such a hard-charger he makes me feel like a loser who hasn't accomplished anything in life, and I need to do some push-ups.

So keep doing those push-ups, people. Stay sharp. Keep at it. And when you hit your first target, go ahead and pick out another one. And another one after that.

For more information and resources, check out
www.DaymondJohn.com/PowerofBroke/Kevin

FOUR

WHAT IT IS

OKAY, SO BY now you've had a chance to meet some motivated entrepreneurs—each with a *power of broke*–type story to tell. Hopefully, you've found a couple takeaways from their stories you can attach to your own—maybe learn from some of their mistakes and some of their successes. I've also shared a few *Shark Tank* pitches and a couple glimpses behind the scenes at FUBU to show you how broke can make you in business—and how it can *break* you. And we've talked a little bit about what it means to have to struggle when you're just starting out.

But let's not forget—there's all kinds of broke. Sometimes you can have all the money in the world, but you might be disadvantaged in some other way. Maybe you're a minority, looking to open up a business in a mostly white community. Maybe you're a woman, looking to get things going in a male-dominated industry. Maybe you're a young upstart brand like Under Armour, looking to play on the same field with big-budget mega-brands like Nike and Adidas. Maybe you're dyslexic, and you've been able to slog your way through school, but out in the real world it's becoming harder and harder for you to process all the material you need to take in if you want to get and keep an edge in your career.

POWER FACT: **Dyslexia is far more common among entrepreneurs than it is among executives in traditional corporate settings, both in the United States and the United Kingdom....** This is a crazy stat, but you can see these trends across the board.... *More than 35 percent of US entrepreneurs have dyslexic traits,* which tells us folks like me are more comfortable in a start-up environment where we're able to do things our own way.

Let me just finish up on this dyslexia piece, because I've been working to shine some light on the issue for young people today. I've spoken about my own struggles with dyslexia at the Yale Center for Dyslexia and Creativity and worked with the folks at www.Understood.org to develop programming and tools to help dyslexic students achieve in the classroom. (Who knew you could get into Yale by *not* reading? I'm just sayin'.) But what most people don't realize is that being dyslexic is a little like being broke—there can be a silver lining to it. A disability of any kind forces you to compensate—if you're blind, you develop a better sense of smell, that sort of thing. In my case, reading was always difficult for me. I struggled in school—not because I wasn't smart, but because I took in information in a different way, at a different speed. After a while, I figured out all these ways to compensate, different ways to learn. I had to work harder, smarter, more efficiently, more *creatively* . . . just to keep up with everybody else.

For a long time, being dyslexic wasn't the kind of thing you talked about. When I was a kid, nobody even thought to get me diagnosed, to see what might have been holding me back. And now that I've found a level of success, running my own companies, building all these brands, I've come to look on being dyslexic as a kind of asset. Why? Because it forces me to think things through, to assess a situation from all sides, to take my time until a solution becomes clear. These days, all these different learning disabilities, they're all the way out in the open, and what we're finding, as my generation comes of age and starts to make all this noise in the world, is that we're not alone.

Winston Churchill, George Bush, Benjamin Franklin . . . all these great leaders were dyslexic.

Whoopi Goldberg, Jay Leno, George Burns . . . all these great comic minds, also dyslexic.

Great inventors and thinkers like Albert Einstein, Thomas Edison, Alexander Graham Bell . . . dyslexic.

Henry Ford, Richard Branson, Walt Disney . . . aw, you get the idea.

Oh, and as long as we're keeping score—four out of my six fellow Sharks on *Shark Tank* also struggle with dyslexia. I'm not telling tales away from the set here, because they've all spoken publicly about it, but see if you can guess who's with me on this.

(Here's a not-so-subtle hint: Barbara is definitely "one of us.")

Point is, there's *always* something standing in your way. For a lot of us, it's money, but it doesn't end there. There's always a hassle, a struggle. If starting a business was easy, we'd all be moguls, right? If making a fortune and a name for ourselves was such a no-brainer, we'd all be rich and famous. If becoming the best in the world at what we do was a cakewalk, we'd all be Olympic gold medalists and bestselling authors and industry leaders. But that's not how it goes—no, how it goes is that success finds us when we find a way to deal with the stuff that gets in our way. We don't run from it. We don't ignore it. We power past it, make the best of it, look for other ways to make some noise on our own.

In each case, successful folks who've had to deal with any kind of disability are a lot like the entrepreneurs we've been reading about—they have had to find their own way, to push themselves to make up whatever ground they might have been losing. Basically, they had to figure it out—the *power of broke* at its best.

GET THERE ANYWAY (OR: GET THERE *ANY* WAY)

Now let's get back to the idea of disadvantage in general—the idea that being *broken* forces you to take a different path to the same goal, to find another way. So what are those other ways? Well, in my own career, the edge has come from pushing myself to think creatively. Early on, it was about making sure the money I *did* have to invest in my business was spent wisely, powerfully. One way we did that at FUBU was to get our shirts on the backs of some of the background dancers as music videos really started to pop. (Sometimes, if we played it right and got lucky, we'd get the artists themselves to wear our clothes.) That move got us a lot of play—we must've had a dozen shirts in circulation, and we'd run around the city, from set to set, trying to persuade these up-and-coming performers to wear our clothes in their videos. Always, we were careful to seek out performers we felt a deep connection to—someone from our neighborhood, like LL Cool J, who for some reason even let *me* jump into the shot on one of his videos. We couldn't afford to actually *give* these artists the shirts, but we'd have a couple styles to choose from, in a couple sizes, and hope like crazy they'd grab one of our hockey jerseys, or a T-shirt, and pump up the FUBU name on camera.

Remember my buddy Kevin Plank, the CEO of Under Armour, who you met in the last chapter? Turned out, we each got one of these product placement pushes—*in the same movie!* That movie was the great football flick *Any Given Sunday,* directed by Oliver Stone and starring Al Pacino, Cameron Diaz, and a dynamite cast of others. My boy LL was in that movie, it was one of his first big starring roles, and he decided to wear one of our tie-dyed football jerseys in the music video from the soundtrack. (Yeah, I know . . . it looks kind of hideous now, but back in 1999 we all thought it was pretty sweet.) Our FUBU line had been stumbling a little bit, but then LL turns up in the video with this ugly jersey, and in the movie itself in a skull cap with our logo on it, and it totally reinvigorated the brand—it was night and day.

At the same time, Kevin had a bunch of friends from his football playing days who were working as extras in the movie, so he got the name of the costume designer on the set and sent over a bunch of shirts. A couple days later, he got a call from Oliver Stone's office, wanting to see some samples. They loved Under Armour's futuristic, modern look—it fit with the tone and tempo of the piece.

So when that movie came out, the exposure gave both our brands a shot in the arm—the kind of publicity we never could have bought on our own. But here's the thing: over at FUBU, the Hollywood play only pushed us back to where we'd already been. Got to be honest: it pumped us up, but only in a small way, only for a short while. Before *Any Given Sunday,* at our peak, we'd been a $200 million brand; lately, we'd seen those numbers dip, but once the movie and the soundtrack video came out, we shot *all* the way back up to . . . about the $200 million level, right where we'd been before.

The product placement in this film was the spark that fueled the Under Armour fire. It provided the lift in awareness that Kevin needed to be able to drive the brand forward, eventually growing Under Armour into the $3 billion company that it is today.

What's the takeaway here? Over at FUBU, I guess we'd gotten a little fat and lazy. The *power of broke* was no longer running through our veins the way it was when we were just starting out. That urgency we all felt back when we were broke and starting out? Gone.

But over at Under Armour, they were still lean and hungry. There was still that sense of urgency you tend to find in a start-up environment. The *power of broke*? They were still feeling it, in a big-time way. It just goes to show that the breaks that find you when you're hungry and cranking can sometimes make the biggest difference.

LOOK UNDER THE COVERS AND OFF TO THE SIDE

That *Any Given Sunday* plug was a once-in-a-lifetime thing, just kind of fell our way, but those music videos were our bread and butter. Trouble was, the approach only worked for a while. Eventually, these artists got too big, started surrounding themselves with wardrobe people and stylists and managers who were smart enough to treat these types of product placements as a business transaction. When you're "first in" on a trend or strategy, you only have the field to yourself for a short while, so before long we had to start looking for other ways to promote our brand.

A natural extension of our music video push was to get on the channel where these music videos lived. At the time, the BET network was the go-to place for our community. It was our own little safe haven on the dial. Back in 1998, it felt to us like every black kid in America was watching BET—from New York to Detroit to Los Angeles, and everywhere in between. A thirty-second commercial spot on BET ran about $1,500, which was a ridiculous bargain. (Just to give a comparison, a thirty-second spot on *Friends,* one of the top-rated prime-time shows that season, cost $422,000.) One of the reasons the BET rates were so low was because the A. C. Nielsen Company, the folks who measured viewership for the networks and affiliate stations, tended not to put their famous "boxes" in predominantly black communities. I don't know why this was the case, but it definitely was. As a result, the Nielsen ratings for BET programs didn't really reflect the actual ratings, so the advertising was cheap—you got a whole lot of bang for your buck, and when you're *broke,* that's the right kind of equation.

You wouldn't know this unless you knew the market, but we had our eyes open and our ears to the ground. We knew BET shows were watched and talked about, and that BET "influencers" like Ralph McDaniels were helping to set and stamp the latest trends, so we could see that the network would give us a direct hit with our target audience. We ran the numbers and figured we could blast BET with a commercial for about $1 million, and in exchange we'd get wall-to-wall play for about a year. Our spots would run ten, fifteen, twenty times a day, and each time out we made an impression. The numbers weren't huge, but we were target-marketing, reaching our exact demographic.

If we'd spent that same $1 million on, say, two or three thirty-second spots on *Friends,* our message would have been lost. That minute and a half of prime-time advertising, at a million bucks, would have been a waste, a memory. Yeah, we would have been seen by another 10 million sets of eyeballs, but it's not like they would have noticed—*and* they would have been the *wrong* sets of eyeballs for our brand, since a good chunk of that audience was a little outside our demographic. Our spots would have been lost in the clutter. And besides, even if they were paying attention, these coffee-sipping Rachel and Chandler wannabes in the American heartland weren't running out to the mall to buy one of our hockey jerseys, so we would have overspent by a mile. That's the mistake a lot of companies make when they have money to burn. When you're making every dollar count, when it feels to you like it's coming straight out of your own pocket, you *have* to make better, smarter decisions.

Another thing we had going for us, couldn't put a price on, was our cred. We were a black-owned business, and in our community this was like a badge of honor. We wore it proudly—even when we took on our Samsung investors. We made sure that me and my partners—Carlton Brown, Keith Perrin, and J. Alexander Martin—remained the face of the brand, because we remained the heart and soul of the brand. After all, we were selling *our* designs, *our* vision—we just needed a little help from some folks who knew their way around the fashion business, some folks with pockets a little deeper than ours. We set it up so that outside money didn't change who we were, what we were about—and *what we were about,* early on, was damn near broke, so that mind-set couldn't help but carry over into this new partnership.

LOOK UP WHEN THE WORLD LOOKS DOWN

Read a lot of business books and you'll most likely come across a pretty standard piece of advice: telling you to *zig* while your competitors *zag.* It's become a cliché, but it's a cliché for a reason—meaning, there's a lot of truth to it. Often, you'll do well to go against the grain, to look at what the marketplace is doing and to go another way. It's how new trends emerge from the old ways of doing business.

But what happens in an economic downturn? How do you keep from tanking when all around you there's chaos and uncertainty? When the *power of broke* has come to refer to the buying power of your customer, or to a cash flow that threatens to dry up? Well, it helps to be in a kind of recession-proof industry, like restaurant services, office supplies, or low-cost home furnishings—but it still doesn't hurt to keep *zigging.*

During the recession of 2008, for example, Domino's Pizza saw an immediate drop in sales, although the company's internal market research suggested that the drop had more to do with a perceived change in the quality of the product than it did with the economy. So what did they do? They embarked on an ambitious television ad campaign, seeking consumer feedback and promising to change their pizza recipe based on the response. Out of that, they ran a follow-up campaign, featuring the new recipe, which they began to roll out in stores, doubling their profit in the fourth quarter of 2009, with a sales increase to $23.6 million.

Domino's found a way to win by inviting customers into the conversation—a great way to keep them in the mix in uncertain times, because now they can't help but feel a rooting interest in your success. Plus, folks need to eat, right? So they might as well eat with you.

Or remember the Snuggie, the silly backwards blanket-robe that became a late night infomercial sensation? It also became the butt of a bunch of jokes by late-night comedians, but it sold a ton, and what a lot of people forget is that it came on the market late in 2008, during the worst of the recession. It was the perfect product for tough times because it didn't cost a whole lot and because it appealed to customers who were forced to stay home, curled up on the couch, watching a lot of television, since they couldn't afford to go out.

Point is, it's tough to predict when the timing is right for a novelty item such as this one, but if you keep it real, stay true to your brand, and figure out how to tap into the mood of your customers, you'll give yourself an edge—no matter the state of the economy or how much cash you have in the bank.

Look, there's no one way to keep your business humming in a down market—you can even find two competing companies in the same industry with entirely different strategies. Consider the case of Office Depot and Staples, the two giant players in the office products business. During the recession of 2000, each company set out to manage costs—clearly a defensive move in an economic downturn. Office Depot cut 6 percent of its workforce but was unable to substantially reduce its operating costs; perhaps as a result, growth fell from 19 percent to 8 percent. Staples, meanwhile, decided to close underperforming stores, but at the same time increased its workforce by 10 percent; unlike Office Depot, they did manage to put the brakes on operating costs, and as the recession lifted the company was more profitable than it had been going into the crisis.

Why is it that some companies find a way to thrive during tough times while others can only struggle? According to a *Harvard Business Review* study on recession spending, innovative business leaders pushing through an economic downturn can help themselves by cutting costs and investing in growth. When times are "broke," smart companies reduce costs by looking at ways to operate more efficiently, while continuing to spend on marketing and on research and development. (In some industries, it might even be a good time to acquire new assets.) The cost-cutting is necessary and can be looked on as a short-term move, but continued investment is also essential as a company looks ahead to an economic uptick that could set off another period of growth.

Basically, when they're up against it, companies must face the same types of growing pains and worries as individuals—and here again we see the *power of broke* in a full-on way. It helps to remember that.

ASK WITH REASON

Whether it's you who's broke or the times that are broke, it also helps to understand that nothing is going to be handed to you—and you can see this in force when you reach out to someone for an assist or for funding. The "pitch" is probably one of the most misunderstood parts of how business gets done. When you come from a place of broke, when you come from a place of need, it can actually *get in the way* of what you're trying to do.

POWER FACT: According to the University of New Hampshire's Center for Venture Research, 67,000 "angel investor" deals were put together in 2013, totaling $24.8 billion; of that number, only 4 percent involved start-ups run by women and fewer than 1 percent involved

minority-owned ventures.... I learned this alarming statistic from my friend Marc Mathis, managing director of the National Minority Angel Network, and what it tells us is that it's not enough to ask for money.... Too often, people don't take the time to understand how venture capital works.... They might have a great concept, a great idea for a business, *but if they're not positioned to take in financing, if they haven't done their paperwork, their homework, potential investors will look to do a deal elsewhere.*

There's an art to a successful pitch, and the best way for me to demonstrate this is to show you what *not* to do in this situation. What happens a lot of the time is that people let their desire run interference—you know, their back is against the wall, they really need funding or resources or whatever it is, and they can only think about what's in it for them. That's a big mistake. When you're pitching, you should never lose sight of the other person's needs. You should think, *What's in it for them?* and not, *What's in it for me?*

We hear it on *Shark Tank* all the time. We'll be visited on the set by entrepreneurs who need something from us, but they hardly ever think to tell us what they propose to do for us in exchange for our investment of time or money. Instead, they tell us about how their business has changed *their* life, or maybe what *they* expect in terms of future growth. The giveback to *us* is never presented in any terms other than dollars and cents.

Off the show, here's how it usually goes. Someone will reach out to me and say, "Daymond, I have this business. We did a million dollars last year, but I'd like to grow it to twenty million. With your help, I think I can. All I need is access to your Rolodex, five to ten hours a week of your time, and maybe you can let me shadow you a bit so I can learn from you. Whatever we make over that first million, we can split, so that could mean three or four million dollars in your pocket. But there's also a social component to it. Whatever we make, we'll take a certain amount off the top and build wells in this village in Africa, where I've been spending a lot of time. They need clean drinking water. Oh, and while we're at it, I also want to save the seals, because they're endangered."

On the surface, this might seem like a good deal all around—a reasonable pitch. But look closely and you'll see my point. My hopeful partner has only addressed his own needs here, not mine. Four or five million dollars? That's great, but what if I've got plenty of money and my priority is spending more time with my children, who I hardly get to see? Only five or ten hours of my time each week? That's great, but what if I'm already spread pretty thin and looking to cut back on my work time as it is? You want to *shadow* me? That's great, but what if I'm concerned about privacy and keeping my business relationships confidential? And what if I don't care to spend my time or money building wells in a village in Africa where you feel this special connection? What if I'd rather address a crisis in Trinidad, where my family is from? What if that's my priority? And seals? What if I happen to have a fine seal coat hanging in my closet that's one of my prized possessions, and saving muskrats is more my thing?

I know, this is an *extreme* example, but I'm out to emphasize the point, so I want to make sure I'm clear. All of these particulars about me, this person could have easily found them out beforehand. He'd just needed to do a little homework. A quick Google search might turn up a picture of me in that seal coat, a picture of me working with a community in Trinidad, an article talking about how important it is for me to carve out time with my kids.

But that never happens, does it?

So here's my advice to all of you *power-of-brokers* out there: Go ahead and ask for help. Go ahead and seek outside investors. Go ahead and find yourself a mentor. But *broke* shouldn't mean you always have your hand out. Go ahead and extend *your* helping hand to someone else instead—you might be surprised at the good things that come back to you in return.

MO'S BOWS: A PASSION FOR FASHION

MOZIAH BRIDGES AND TRAMICA MORRIS
....
BOW-TIE DESIGNER AND MIDDLE SCHOOL STUDENT;
SINGLE MOM AND TIRELESS SUPPORTER

Oh my goodness, I love this kid. Best *Shark Tank* pitch ever, ever, ever—and the way it played out, I had to convince this young man not to take any money from "Mr. Wonderful," Kevin O'Leary, even though it was the only cash offer on the table.

Here's the story: Moziah Bridges was an eleven-year-old kid from Memphis, Tennessee, who looked like a mini-version of me when he showed up on the set dressed in a full-out suit and bow tie. His mom, Tramica Morris, even reminded me a whole lot of my own mother—just in the way she stood behind her son and tried to make his dreams a reality. It's because of her that Mo's dreams were within reach.

Really, this kid had it going on! We clicked right away; he even called me out as his fashion role model, so that just made him look even better in my eyes—got to be honest. Tramica accompanied Mo on the show, of course, and she told us Mo dressed in a suit and tie just to go riding on his bicycle. So it made sense that Mo's business, Mo's Bows, was a line of handcrafted bow ties he made himself, with a little help from his mother and great-grandmother. It cost him about $6 in materials and other hard costs to make each tie, and once he got good at sewing, measuring, and cutting, he could knock out a tie in about twenty-five minutes. Granny could get it done a little quicker—in about fifteen minutes flat.

Now, what struck me about Mo and his mom and their young business was how organic it was—and how much it reminded me of my own first steps in the fashion industry, sewing my own line of tie-top hats at the kitchen table with my mom. Mo's "business" was also a bare-bones operation. Each tie was lovingly and carefully made—basically because they were making these ties for Mo to wear. It was a full-on family affair more than a full-on business. It started out that Mo was simply looking for something stylish to wear. His mom had a good job, working for a retirement services company, and even though it was just the two of them, there wasn't enough money to spend it on fine clothing. Mo wasn't interested in any rough-and-tumble, cookie-cutter-type threads. He didn't want to look like every other kid in the neighborhood. At nine years old, he was already wearing his church clothes to school, but then he got to where he wanted to switch things up. He wanted to swap out those stuffy neckties for a snappy bow tie—but he couldn't find any kid-friendly styles his mom could afford.

"Imagine me getting him a fifty-dollar tie and then him going out and getting mustard on it," Tramica says.

At the time, in and around Memphis, the only ties Mo could find were single-colored, pre-tied, boring. There was just red, black, blue . . . no fun colors.

"Nothing spoke to me," he says.

LISTEN TO THE WORLD AROUND

Nothing spoke to Moziah Bridges . . . except for a couple of sweet, soft voices, telling him he could make a couple of ties for himself. One of those voices was his great-grandmother's, telling Mo she could help. Granny knew her way around a sewing machine, had been sewing professionally for over fifty years. Plus, she had a stash of loose materials and fabrics, so Mo could go hunting through her treasures and come up with some designs he liked—all without breaking the bank.

The other voice was Tramica's. "I wanted my son to grow up believing that he can do anything," she says. "Whatever his hopes and dreams, I wanted him to know that I would help him find a way to make them come true, so I could only encourage him in this. Whatever the next step, whatever decisions we had to make, I kept telling him we could make it together."

So that's how it all started, just Mo, his granny, and his mother, sitting around the table, sewing up a storm. But Mo would have never even gotten to this point if he hadn't been listening to his own heart. What do I mean by that? Well, let's accept that Moziah Bridges is cut from a pretty unique piece of cloth (sorry, couldn't help it). Far as I know, there aren't too many kids going to school in a suit and tie—unless it happens to be a school uniform and they've got no choice. But Mo liked to look good. I could relate to that. Everybody in town took notice of the way he dressed—folks at church, in the grocery school, at school. His teachers, especially. I could relate to that too. The other kids, they gave him a hard time at first, which was about what you'd expect from a bunch of ten-year-olds. Once, in third grade, one teacher even got the idea to encourage all of the boys in class to wear ties on Wednesdays, just so Mo wouldn't be so alone in this, but that didn't go over so well with the other kids. Nobody wants to be told what to wear, right? Mo understood that better than anybody—I mean, this was a kid who didn't even wear sneakers when he went outside to play with his friends. He had to have a certain boot, a certain dress shoe.

Every day was Wednesday and Sunday for Mo, who always wanted to look his best, and once he started flashing Granny's sporty fabrics around town, other kids began to spark to them. The teasing and razzing began to fall away. Friends, neighbors, cousins . . . people started asking Mo where he got his ties, if he could maybe make one for them, and the "business" just kind of grew from there. I put business in quotes, because it wasn't really a business just yet. Mostly, Mo was just giving these ties away. Sometimes he'd charge just a few dollars—maybe one or two, maybe five or ten. I'm afraid Mo wasn't much of a negotiator back then—he tended to take whatever was offered. Once, he traded a tie for a bag of chips in the lunchroom at school.

Soon, Mo learned his way around a sewing machine—figured if his granny could do it, he could pitch in. "It looked easy enough," he says now, but it took him a while to get it down. His first couple ties were crooked, slightly off, but the great thing about a bow tie is that once it's tied you can kind of mask these mistakes. Plus, it was a pretty easy garment to master—not a lot of difficult lines or unusual cuts, the perfect accessory item for a kid to cut his teeth on as a rookie tailor.

Every night, Mo would find some time to work on a new tie, and he put each and every one in circulation. Every day at school, he'd trot out a different design, a whole new look. Every memorable occasion, he put on something special. This was his thing, his signature style, and after a while someone asked for a very specific white tie—a particular fabric Mo couldn't find in Granny's stash.

POWER FACT: Elon Musk, cofounder of PayPal and founder of Tesla, sold his first computer program for $500 at the age of twelve.... *Everybody has to start somewhere, but it's those running starts that get us where we're going even faster.*

At this point, he sat down with his mother and figured out he would have to charge real money—for this one tie, at least. He would have to sharpen those negotiation skills and know his own value—tough lessons for a kid to master, but Mo wasn't just a sharp dresser, he was sharp where it counted.

"It made no sense to go out and buy specific materials, just to give away the tie or sell it for a few dollars," Tramica says. "It's basic business, but I needed to help Mo figure this out."

Together, they came up with a number—$20. Wasn't exactly the kind of number that would make Mo rich, because if you factored in the time and opportunity cost, he and his great-grandmother would barely be making minimum wage. But at least there was a small profit built into the model.

Mo's first "customer" was happy with his first purchase—and here I put customer in quotes because the transaction started with the dude admiring one of Mo's ties. He wasn't seeking Mo out on-line, or walking into a store looking for something in particular. A particular tie caught his eye, that's all it was, and he asked if Mo could do something similar. This was how most of Mo's first sales came about—he moved up the ladder at school until the older kids started making inquiries, all the way up to teenagers in town who wanted to look good.

"It was great when the older kids started asking about my ties," Mo says. "Adults too. But the sizing got to be a problem. My ties really only fit kid-size necks, which I learned were about fifteen to eighteen inches. Adult-size ties were a little longer, up to about twenty-two inches, so we had to take some special orders."

Then a producer for *The Steve Harvey Show* heard about this little kid in Memphis with the sartorial flair, and next thing Mo knew, he was on television, talking about his ties, his fashion sense, his growing business.

Things were about to pop.

BE READY FOR THE FLOODGATES TO OPEN

Before this first television appearance, Mo and his mom never even thought about advertising. They had as much business as they could handle, thank you very much. But that *Steve Harvey* spot generated a ton of attention. Orders started coming in—and other press inquiries too.

Got to admit, it was a great story: a little kid, itching to become a mini-fashion mogul; his single mom, supporting him every which way.

Next, a reporter from Oprah Winfrey's *O* magazine did a profile, and that generated another batch of attention.

After that, Mo appeared on the *Today* show and by now the phone was ringing off the hook. So Mo and his mom hired two local women to help with the sewing; they'd drop off a bunch of fabrics at the beginning of the week and pick up the finished ties at the end of the week. They developed a website, to help handle orders from around the country. Tramica left her job, and before she went out looking for a new one she decided to devote her full-time attention to helping her son get his bow-tie business off the ground. Mo's Bows was getting bigger and bigger, busier and busier, and the business needed a guiding hand behind the scenes. Mo would be out in front, the face of the company, but Tramica would be watching the books, filling the orders, and handling all the press inquiries and public appearances.

After another while, they decided to bump the price of a standard tie to $25—more for adult sizes or special orders. Soon, Mo started getting some local press as well, and by the time he was ten years old his ties were being sold in a half-dozen specialty shops in and around Memphis.

This was where *Shark Tank* came in. What a lot of folks don't realize is that our producers are always out there, doing the reality-show version of "casting." In the beginning, a lot of the entrepreneurs who pitched us their business ideas were coming to us—and that's still the way it happens for most of our pitches. Folks are lining up for their chance in the Tank with us Sharks, and that's great. But the reality of reality television is that we need to keep people's eyeballs glued to their screens, so from time to time we go off in search of a compelling story that will fit well in our format, and this kid out of Tennessee was basically heaven-sent from Central Casting.

Mo's handmade tie business was just perfect for *Shark Tank*—clearly, our producers knew what they were doing when they booked him on the show. But what the producers didn't know was exactly how Mo's segment would go—and it went off in a wild direction. For the purposes of this book, it offered a valuable lesson in the *power of broke.* The way it shook out, predictably, was that every shark on the panel that week was charmed by this dynamic little kid, wowed by what he'd accomplished. He came on the show looking fine in one of his signature ties, his mom at his side. I was taken in by the whole package—we all were. Mo's ties were sharp, classic, fun. And just as important, he was cute and confident. He even came out and said he was the NBT—the Next Big Thing—which just about blew me away. I mean, for a little kid to talk in such big, bold strokes . . . it was a public relations dream.

And the whole time, Tramica looked on, beaming with pride—and get this, she let her boy run the pitch. I thought that was just tremendous.

Mo and Tramica were asking for an investment of $50,000 in exchange for 15 percent of the business—but I didn't want to see Mo give away such a big stake for funding I didn't think he and his mom really needed. The other sharks seemed to back off on doing a deal for the same reason. They also backed off because it was generally assumed that I was in the best position to help grow this little company—and I guess I was, but I couldn't bring myself to take a bite out of this kid's business the way we normally do on the show. Mark, Robert, and Barbara were all out, but Kevin seemed to want to move in for the kill. (Once a Shark, always a Shark, right?) Kevin said he smelled a royalty deal. He actually held up one of Mo's ties to his nose and started sniffing it, and it got my back up a little bit, the way he was looking to make money off this little mom-and-tot business—a business that looked a whole lot like my business had looked back in the late 1980s.

Kevin offered the full amount Mo and his mom were seeking, and he offered to waive the corresponding piece of the business. He didn't want any equity, he said—making it sound like he was being a good, good guy. Instead, he wanted a royalty of $3 per tie in exchange for his investment—an offer that might have seemed like a sweet deal to an unsophisticated businessperson, but the rest of us could smell it for what it was, so I tried to talk Mo and Tramica out of it.

I didn't just talk—I gave a bit of a hard sell. I tried to persuade Mo that what he really needed was a mentor, someone in his corner to offer guidance and experience—to keep him from going into business with someone like Kevin O'Leary. Nothing against Kevin—even though we clash on the show from time to time, he's a good person with a good heart, but he does tend to see the world through the dollar signs in his eyes. As my first piece of mentoring, I told Mo and Tramica a story from when I was just starting out. I was a little bit older than Mo, but I was still living at home with my mom, still scraping. When I needed a little bit of a financing cushion, somebody offered me $10,000 for 40 percent of my business. At that time, my business was only a couple hats, so of course I was tempted to grab at the deal. But something held me back. Ten years later, FUBU was worth $400 million, which would have made this investor's stake worth $160 million—all for a tiny little infusion of cash I turned out not to really need.

I said, "I'm glad I didn't take that money. I strongly suggest that you don't take on investors at this time." I counted myself in this group, said I didn't think Mo should take money from anyone. I said, "In regards to a deal, I'm out. In regards to mentoring, I'm in. And don't do this deal."

But Kevin kept pressing, and I could see that Mo and his mom were tempted to take his money. I could understand the temptation of course—$50,000 is a lot of money (just like $10,000 was a lot of money back in the day . . . to me), and there was enough of a profit margin in the way Mo and Tramica had priced their ties that they could tell themselves they could afford to pay out $3 each time they made a sale.

So I put it to them plain. I addressed my comments to Mo directly because I wanted to show him the respect he deserved, even though he was just a little kid. I wanted him to know I took him seriously. I told Mo my offer to mentor him was only good if he didn't take Kevin's money. Why? Because as much as I liked this little kid, as much as I liked his mom, as much as I liked their chances for this little business to make some real noise, I didn't think I could work with folks who didn't take the very first piece of advice I offered, when it was clear I had their best interests in mind.

In the end, Mo and his mom passed on Kevin's offer and embraced the opportunity to work with me as Mo's mentor, but even here Kevin would not let it go—he asked Mo to reconsider. He could see that the kid was stuck thinking about all that money Kevin was dangling in front of him, even though the cooler heads in the room were telling him to walk away from the offer.

Finally, Tramica stepped in and put an end to the discussion. She said, "Mo's the CEO of Mo's Bows, but I'm the CEO of Mo."

And that was that.

LET OTHERS GUIDE YOU

Now, we've highlighted some other stories in this book where one of our *power-of-brokers* has benefited from the insights and experiences of a key mentor, but since this was me rolling up my sleeves to help Mo and his mom, I want to spend a little time on the value of these relationships.

In a lot of ways, the mentor-mentee relationship is the single most important relationship you can have in your business career, and it starts from a place of kindness—but it doesn't end there. Let's be clear: I offered to work with Mo for some selfish reasons. For one thing, it would be a way for me to revisit and hopefully correct some of the mistakes I might have made when I was just starting out. For another, it would force me to keep focused on the latest trends in the fashion and accessories industries, which of course would have some carryover benefit for my own business. And just being honest, there'd probably be some publicity that would come my way as a result; Mo's success would in some ways be mine as well.

Ultimately, though, I was blessed to be in a position in my life and career to be able to extend a helping hand to this young man, and I believed it was my obligation (and my honor) to share in that blessing. And so I offered to help—no big thing, but at the same time, a very big deal.

Just how big a deal? Well, take a look at the numbers:

- 75 percent of executives point to mentoring relationships as having played a key role in their careers.
- 71 percent of Fortune 500 companies have a formal mentoring program in place.
- Managerial productivity increases by as much as 88 percent when a mentoring relationship is involved.
- 95 percent of mentoring participants report that the experience motivated them to excellence.

Every entrepreneur needs a mentor. Don't believe me? Check out these findings from a 2012 survey by MicroMentor.org, a matching service that connects aspiring business folks with volunteer mentors in their fields. The study showed that people who participated in a mentoring relationship saw their revenues increase by an average of $47,000—or 106 percent! Those who did not participate saw their revenues go up only $6,600—or 14 percent.

As long as I'm on it, this is why I organize what I call Game Changer Meetings in my office whenever I can fit them into my schedule. It's a chance for me to work one-on-one with folks who reach out to me because they've seen me on the show or come to one of my talks. I'll sit with them for up to an hour and go over whatever it is that's on their mind, on their plate—it's like a micro-mentoring session. I charge a fee for the session, but the money goes to charity, and in exchange this person gets to pick my brain on their business, their goals, their personal finances. Folks are lining up to sit down with me, and I wish there was more room on my calendar to squeeze in some more sessions, but I love the way these entrepreneurs see me as the "People's Shark" and seek out my opinion. It's an honor to be able to help them out, even in this small way.

Another way I interact with aspiring entrepreneurs is through my "Entrepreneur Roll Call" posts I regularly put out on social media. A lot of times, I'll be up at three, four, five o'clock in the morning, sorting through the day just ended, planning the day ahead. It's when I do my most creative thinking, and there are thousands of people just like me. How do I know? Because when I put out the Roll Call, I'll immediately hear back from hundreds and hundreds of night owls just like me. I ask them to tell me what they're up to, what they do, where they live. We get these great conversations going—and a lot of times, folks on the Roll Call get in touch with each other.

Then I'll hit them a couple hours later with one of my "Rise and Grind" posts to start the day—and the conversation continues from there.

HONOR YOUR VISION

It's a little too early to quantify what kind of help I'll be to Mo and Tramica, but I'm committed to helping them realize the full potential of their business—and they are too! As I write this, Mo's Bows is firing on all cylinders. The company has taken in $250,000 worth of business in the past four years, and Mo's bow ties are now being distributed in a small number of boutiques nationwide. They've yet to move into the big-box stores, and I don't know that they ever will, but in the meantime they've expanded their line of products to include pocket squares and T-shirts. Next, they hope to move into other accessory items like socks and belts.

Granny has been "retired" from the business—Mo and his mom now employ several cutters and sewers, full-time. Mo himself has stopped sewing and turned his focus to promoting the Mo's Bows brand, running the business. (Oh, and he's also going to school, and I even bumped into him at the White House.)

Mo's goal these days is to become a fashion mogul by the age of twenty. I love that he's thought this through, love that he's come up with twenty as his make-or-break age, love that his mom is so solidly at his side. But mostly I love that I'll be along for the ride.

MO'S KEY SHARK POINT

ADORE WHAT YOU DO. When Mo talks about not being able to find a bow tie that "speaks" to him, I understand exactly what he means. With me it was about my kicks—I had a sneaker collection you had to see to believe, and the colors had to match up with my shirt, my jacket, some other part of my wardrobe, or the whole look just didn't come together. Mo's cut the same way. The kid likes to look good, and he likes to help others look good. It's what drives him when he picks out his clothes each morning, and it's what drives him when he looks at new fabrics and designs for his business. The money doesn't seem to be all that important to him . . . yet. You can see that in the fact that he used to just give his ties away—or trade them for a bag of chips.

Do you love what you do? Would you do it for free? (Or, for a bag of chips?) If not, then maybe you should think about doing something else. Sure, money and success can be powerful motivators, and for a lot of us our bottom line is our bottom line, but even a little guy like Moziah Bridges knows that out of his joy in making these great ties, good things will come.

For more information and resources, check out
www.DaymondJohn.com/PowerofBroke/Mo

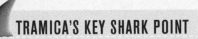

TRAMICA'S KEY SHARK POINT

KEEP SWIMMING. It's tough to say how motivated Mo would have been without a constant push from his mother on this. But to her great credit, it was a gentle push. She tried to let Mo set the pace, to follow his lead on how much time and energy to put into their business, but she never lost sight of the fact that Mo was just a kid. He had other things on his mind. The business was important to him, but he also wanted time with his friends, time to play video games, time to just chill. In all the start-up scenarios I've encountered, I imagine this one—a mother and young son setting off on an exciting partnership—was one of the toughest for the adult in the relationship.

And so, Tramica's filling in some of those spaces where an adult partner might be in this relationship. She's made this business her focus, because her son is her focus—just like my mother turned her full attention to me, at some point.

Who's standing behind you and alongside you as you go about your business?

For more information and resources, check out
www.DaymondJohn.com/PowerofBroke/Tramica

THE POWER OF HUMILITY

TIM FERRISS

AUTHOR, MOTIVATIONAL SPEAKER, ENTREPRENEUR,
ANGEL INVESTOR

The *power of broke* doesn't recognize class or station or circumstance. It has nothing to do with privilege or access or resources. You can grow up in the Hamptons, go to a school like Princeton, make a bunch of solid connections, maybe even have a little money behind you . . . and still get stuck at the starting gate.

That's the situation my friend Tim Ferriss found himself in when he was trying to publish his first book, *The 4-Hour Workweek*.

Now, I should probably mention here that Tim grew up on the wrong side of the Hamptons tracks—in a nice enough neighborhood, but nothing like the swanky summer homes of the summer beach crowd. So don't go getting any ideas about any kind of cushy childhood. These days, folks know Tim as a successful entrepreneur, an angel investor, and one of the most influential bloggers on the Internet, but in 2006 he was struggling. Back of his mind, he knew he was destined to make some kind of noise, and he was ready to crank up the volume. He had his hand in on any number of deals, including his own start-up. He was also a guest lecturer teaching a course on effective career strategies. It was a sideline pursuit, but in his lectures were the seeds of the four-hour workweek concept—seeds that were destined to grow and grow.

Trouble was, Tim couldn't figure out how to plant those suckers.

"People heard me speak, heard what I was doing, and they kept telling me I should write a book," he shares when we sit down to discuss the theme of this book. "It was the most ridiculous thing I'd ever heard. I couldn't write, couldn't think how to begin. I didn't want to write anything longer than an email. But then the class started to take on new shape, the notes started to come together, and I had all these ideas about lifestyle design, and breaking free of all the outdated assumptions that were coloring our working lives. I started to see there might be an opportunity here."

It took a while for him to chase it down, though. And in the chasing, without even thinking about it, Tim harnessed the *power of broke* and put it to work for him—just by treating people with the courtesy and curiosity that came naturally to him.

His book was a mega-mega smash, but it came together in a "back against the wall" kind of way. Initially, it took reaching out to a contact he'd made a couple years earlier, after Tim had just moved to Silicon Valley to work on his Internet start-up—an online nutritional supplements company.

"I didn't know anyone," Tim recalls, "didn't have any money, was driving my mom's hand-me-down minivan. It was horrible."

Like a lot of entrepreneurs and outside-the-box thinkers, Tim had a restless energy and a boundless enthusiasm for new people, new ideas. Yeah, he was busting his ass on his start-up, but he was also hedging his bets, working a lot of different angles. He still made time to volunteer for a local nonprofit that staged some big-time promotions. He believed the one fed the other, so he found the time, and he busted his ass as a volunteer as well. He kept taking on more responsibility, showing more initiative, and it got to where he was asked to attend one of the organization's board meetings and take on a lead role in an upcoming event. One of his jobs was to put together a panel of A-list speakers, so he reached out to a group of folks he really, really wanted to meet—the guy who created the Pet Rock, the guy behind the hundred-million-selling *Chicken Soup for the Soul* publishing franchise, the cofounder of Electronic Arts, the man behind the Cliff Bar, and on and on.

"I had no money, no connections, no way to meet these people and figure out how they got to where they were," he tells me. "Those kinds of connections, they're invaluable. The chance to talk to these people, to learn something from them, even just to breathe the same air, it's huge. But on my own there was no way I could get them to sit down and talk to me. The only thing I had to offer was time, and an invitation to a pretty cool event that promised a ton of media coverage, so I made an investment. I'd spend all my time on this, take full advantage of the organization's name, the access it was giving me, and make things happen."

Tim wanted to organize a killer event, set up a killer panel of speakers, but he also wanted to meet these good people and soak up what he could from them. I totally get that—I was the same way when I was just starting out: hungry for inside insights, eager to soak up what I could from folks who knew their stuff . . . whatever that stuff happened to be.

WALK THAT TWO-WAY STREET

Tim's a smart guy; he could see that, on his own, he had nothing to trade on other than his keen interest and enthusiasm. That's how it goes in most mentor-mentee relationships. When you're on the way up, it's all about what you need, what you want out of the deal, but my thing is, it's got to be a two-way street. I tell young people all the time, when they're reaching out for advice, guidance, whatever, that in order for me to help them, to be available to them, to take them under my wing, I've got to sleep less, or maybe take myself away from something else I need to be doing. There are only so many hours in the day, right? In the story of Moziah Bridges that I just shared, what was in it for me was personal. He came on the *Shark Tank* set like a little Mini-Me, and it was so clear to me that he and his mom were on to something that could be life-changing for them—life-affirming even. It felt to me like I had no choice but to help him power up his bow-tie business.

But that's not how it usually goes. No, usually, there's a cost to me when I mentor someone, and it's on the prospective mentee to recognize this cost in the transaction. That doesn't mean that I'm not happy to help, just that there's got to be something in it for me as well. Usually, the takeaway comes in the chance to see how these young people think, how they interact with a product, how they move about in the marketplace . . . but you've got to give to get, man. It's how business gets done, and Tim recognized this early on. He knew, for example, that if he abused this up-close relationship with Jack Canfield, the Chicken Soup author, it wouldn't serve him in the long run, so he made an effort to nurture this connection over the years without really asking for anything in return.

"I never asked Jack to mentor me," Tim says, "even though I could have benefited from his advice, but from time to time I'd reach back out to him with a question or comment. You know, whatever I could think to keep the conversation going, as long as he didn't come away thinking I had my hand out. This went on for years, until finally I mentioned that I was thinking of doing a book, and at that point Jack was all over it and introduced me to an agent. He wanted to help. It's like I didn't even have to ask. We'd hit it off on that first pass, and he'd seen that I wasn't just out for myself, so he went out of his way for me."

The story doesn't end there, of course. Publishers kept turning Tim down, and some of the rejections were just about violent. Sure, there were a couple of polite turndowns, but for the most part publishers had an intensely negative reaction to Tim's pitch. The worst of these tended to focus on Tim's age, with comments like, "Who is this kid to tell me I'm working too hard?" Or, "How old is this author again? And he knows the secret to creating work-life balance?"

POWER FACT: Before publishing his first book, Stephen King was ready to give up on a writing career. After getting thirty rejections, he threw his first novel in the trash, but his wife retrieved it and urged him to keep going. He has since gone on to sell over 350 million copies of his books, most of which have been made into major motion pictures.... It's tough to believe in yourself when the rest of the word lines up against you, so be sure to have someone on your side to help you see things more clearly.... *Mentors are great, but sometimes a cheerleader is even better.* And as far as strategic partnerships are concerned, sometimes you find your best support at home.

The response was mystifying, frustrating, soul-sucking . . . but Tim kept at it. I think that's one of the reasons I was drawn to him—and him to me. He was turned down by twenty-seven publishers. I'd been turned down by twenty-seven banks when I was out looking to finance our first FUBU orders. Twenty-seven rejections! And yet neither one of us was willing to take *no* for an answer, so we kept pounding on doors. Tim had a respected literary agent to help with the pounding—a superstar editor who'd recently switched to the agency side of the business and was determined to do right by his first clients. So that helped, obviously—but in the end, all the agent could do was get Tim to the door. It was up to Tim to power his way through.

POWER FACT: Walt Disney was turned down 302 times before getting financing for Walt Disney World; today the resort attracts over 25 million visitors each year.... A stat like that, it tell you two things:

> *(1) there are a whole lot of people and institutions you can hit up for a*
> *loan, and (2) when those people and institutions hit back, you've got to*
> *hang in there.* . . . . Believe in yourself, believe in your business, believe
> in your dream, and the money will come—maybe not right away, but
> soon enough.

That kind of determination, it comes from a place of nothing to lose; it comes from throwing all of your heart, all of your energy, into this one big project. It's your one big opportunity, so you give it your all. Finally, after that twenty-seventh rejection, Tim was down to his last shot—a meeting in New York with a team from Crown Publishing, a division of Random House. (Full disclosure: Crown happens to be my publisher as well.) Going in, Tim knew he'd have to crush this meeting in order to get a deal, so he figured he'd just go for it. Put himself out there. Do his thing in a big-time way. At the head of the table sat the guy with the power to say *yes* or *no,* so Tim focused in on him—always a good strategy in a make-or-break moment.

"It was one of those Death Star meetings," Tim remembers, "the way they do it at a lot of the big media companies. They bring in like thirty people, from marketing, sales, publicity. Everybody sits around a giant conference table. There was no way I could re- member everyone's name, or what their role was in the company, so I kept trying to steer things back to the main guy at the head of the table. The room would go on his gut, so that's where I put my focus."

SEIZE THE DAY

That meeting with the publisher went well enough, and when it was about to wrap, Tim made his final pitch. He truly believed that the ideas he'd been discussing in his classes could transform the ways we live and work, and by telling these folks at Crown that he was prepared to fight like crazy to make this book a hit, to make sure his message resonated with the widest possible audience, they could move forward knowing they weren't just buying a book—they were buying a brand, with a pit bull–type marketing machine behind it.

You have to realize, this whole thing went down just before Christmas 2006—prehistoric times in terms of social media. Facebook was still in its infancy, just kind of creeping from college campuses into the mainstream, and Twitter was only a couple months old. Tim took a look at the Internet landscape and realized he'd have to find a way to make some electronic noise, to call attention to his book, because Crown wasn't about to throw a whole lot of money at promotion—especially now that he'd all but told them he'd generate a ton of publicity on his own. The way it works in the book business, like in other businesses, is that publishers tend to put money behind books they've already put money into—and they hadn't really sunk any money into *The 4-Hour Workweek*. So Tim was on his own here.

"I realized that online was really the only sandbox I could play in," Tim tells me. "Everyone was talking about bloggers, so I thought, *That could be interesting. Who are these blogger people? I should probably figure all of that out.* So I did. And it's embarrassing to admit, but I went online, the day after Christmas, I started reading all these different blogs, and I just tried to soak in as much as I could. You know, see where I could fit myself into that conversation."

FOLLOW YOUR GUT, FOLLOW YOUR NOSE

It turned out Tim's research took him to the Consumer Electronics Show (CES) in Las Vegas, where he learned he could find a group of bloggers all in one place. It turned out, too, that the first job he'd had out of college was selling mass data storage systems, so he knew the landscape a little bit, knew the language. He realized that if he wanted to connect with bloggers, maybe find a way to get them excited about his work-life concept, the easiest way to do that would be to reach out to them in person—to as many of them as possible, all at once. He figured any successful blogger was already getting a ton of email, so there was no way his message would stand out in a crowded in-box. And he could just forget about contacting them by phone, so he had to find a way to put himself in the same room with them and make his pitch face-to-face, one-by-one.

The Consumer Electronics Show . . . that was his answer.

Once in Vegas, Tim did some more investigating, more net-working, and was able to talk himself into a convention lounge called the Bloghaus, where there was free booze and free wi-fi for bloggers—basically, a good place to see and be seen. He skulked around for a bit, looking for a way in, and ended up at the check-in table, making small talk with the woman who was handing out wristbands to the bloggers who had been invited to the event. Without an invite, Tim could only hope to snake past this check-point—or he could turn on the charm and see where that got him.

"That's always been a key for me," he says. "Being nice. If you're nice to people, if you go out of your way to be helpful, then good things tend to happen."

So Tim kind of lurked around the check-in table, and whenever he saw that the woman was free, he would tell her a bit of his story, tell her this was his first time at the convention, tell her he didn't really know anybody, didn't really know how things worked. He would have offered to buy the woman a drink, but the drinks were free, so instead he offered to make a drink run for everyone at the table. He did this a couple times, and in between bartending trips he sat and listened, soaked up what he could, offered to help where he could—just generally tried to be nice and make himself useful.

MAKE YOUR MOMENT HAPPEN

One of Tim's goals for the day was to meet an influential blogger named Robert Scoble. He was like "the guy" at this CES conference, as far as Tim was concerned. And Tim wasn't the only one who wanted to get to him—there was a scrum of people trying to get Scoble's attention. This presented a problem, because Tim didn't want to be just a face in the crowd if he got a chance to talk to Scoble. He didn't want to have to scream or wave or tug on his shirt to get him to talk to him—that's no way to start a meaningful conversation—but every time Tim saw a potential opening another scrum of people would materialize at this guy's feet, like he was a rock star.

At some point, Tim mentioned his frustration to his new friends at the check-in table—specifically, to the woman who seemed to be in charge. Her name was Maryam, and she just happened to be married to Robert Scoble.

She said, "No problem, I'll introduce you."

"That's how being nice can pay off," he explains. Of course, he had no way of knowing, going in, that Maryam was married to Scoble, but because he moved about that convention lounge like he wanted to earn his keep, because he made no bones about being a little out of his element, because he wasn't shy about asking for help and guidance, because he'd gone out of his way to be helpful and to make sure he didn't come across as a pain-in-the-ass, this one piece of good karma came his way. His positive energy brought back a positive result.

Sure enough, he got some time with Scoble later that day, and Scoble found enough to like in Tim's concept to write about it in his blog—and Tim credits that one small mention with getting the ball rolling. The book still hadn't come out, but now there was this buzz attached to it, and from there he managed to beg, borrow, and sweet-talk an invitation to South by Southwest, another influential conference and multimedia music festival—this one held annually in Austin, Texas.

Here it was the same story all over again. Tim didn't have a real presence at the conference—he had no idea what he was doing there, really. But he knew enough to connect with Hugh Forrest, who runs the show down there. Tim introduced himself, told Hugh Forrest about his book, told him about the buzz it was generating, told him he'd love to land some kind of speaking slot at the conference. Tim had no idea what to expect when he flew to Austin—hadn't even thought to book a room in advance, and since the hotels in the city were all sold out, he ended up crashing at a friend's place.

Whenever possible, whenever he saw an opening, he pressed his case to Hugh Forrest—he was treading that line between being persistent and being a pest, between ingratiating and irritating. And on about the third or fourth pass, something amazing happened—there was a sudden opening in the conference schedule. One of the speakers had to drop out at the last minute, and Hugh Forrest needed someone to fill the slot.

Timing is everything, right? So there was Tim Ferriss, in exactly the right place, at exactly the right time, happy to step in. He had a day to prepare—not a whole lot of time, really, but this dude knew his stuff. He'd be speaking in one of the sponsored rooms, away from the main stage, which meant people would be eating and drinking and milling about—not exactly an ideal gig, but he was happy for it just the same.

MAKE NOISE WHERE YOU CAN, WHEN YOU CAN

"I tear up when I think back on that moment," Tim says when he walks me through what happened next. "I was really nervous about my presentation, and the friend I was staying with, he had three Chihuahuas. Great dogs, all three of them, each a different size, each with a different personality. So I was kind of pacing around my friend's house, and I went out into the garage, and the three dogs all followed, I guess because they thought I was going to get food, and as I turned around and saw them sitting there, looking at me expectantly, I thought, *What the hell*.

"So I went right into my pitch. Right there in front of these three Chihuahuas. I knew they couldn't understand a word I was saying, of course. But I also knew they could tell by my energy, by my body language, that what I was saying was interesting, important. It sounds crazy, I know, but I told myself that if I wasn't engaging, the dogs would just wander off. If I could keep them interested, then I would be okay."

Somehow, my boy Tim held the dogs' attention—he "went all Tony Robbins on them," he says—and if anyone had been looking on, they would have thought he'd gone completely Looney Tunes, but out of that weird moment in his friend's garage, doing his thing in front of those three dogs, he found his way.

Here it would be great to be able to write that Tim went out the next day and nailed his presentation, but it didn't exactly go down that way. The tech support failed on him. He had a whole PowerPoint-type thing set up with his laptop, but the wi-fi went dead, and the sound was all messed up, and he had to scramble. But he knew his material cold by this point, he'd rehearsed it so much, top to bottom, even played it to an audience of dogs. (Talk about a tough room!) So he did okay—better than okay, actually.

However it came about, that South by Southwest conference was where he made his bones. Robert Scoble might have put him on the map, but it was this next push from Hugh Forrest that made people start to think that spot on the map was a place they had to visit.

TURN EACH OPPORTUNITY INTO THE NEXT OPPORTUNITY

Out of all that, good things started to happen, and the great lesson here is that Tim put himself in a position to succeed. Over and over again, he found ways to position himself for a strong selling opportunity. Yeah, it helped that he had a kick-ass concept that he'd field-tested in his classroom and fine-tuned as he set it all down on paper. But it also helped that he put himself out into the world, looking for a way to make some noise for his book. It helped that he went out of his way to be nice to people—and that he was honest enough in his dealings with the movers and shakers he was trying to reach that he didn't try to pass himself off as something he was not. He was genuine, and people responded to that. He believed in himself, and he believed in his message, and people responded to that too.

And here's another thing: one of the biggest assists Tim got in his prepublication push came from Robert Scoble's wife, Maryam. This didn't come about in a scheming way. It was real. It was serendipitous. But it was all-important. Without that connection to this woman at the CES show in Vegas, he might have been dead in the water; with it, he was on his way.

A lot of times, with a *Shark Tank* pitch or another business idea I'm pursuing, the real test comes about in a behind-the-scenes kind of way. I'll call my go-to guys and try to drum up financing, but it can take a gentle nudge from someone completely outside the transaction to seal the deal. Here's what I mean: Let's say one of my guys is in bed, watching television with his wife, eating potato chips or ice cream or whatever, and there's a spot featuring a product my guy is considering. If his wife leans over to him and says, "Oh my God, I would totally use that!" . . . well, it's a done deal.

Think about it: Our most trusted advisers are the people closest to us. They might not know our business, but they give it to us straight, and here it worked out that Tim Ferriss had just happened to make a connection with the wife of an influential blogger uniquely positioned to shine some light on his upcoming book. If Tim had been pushy or arrogant or full of himself, she wouldn't have offered to introduce him, but because he was nice, because he was transparent and forthcoming and helpful, she went out of her way for him. Jack Canfield, the Chicken Soup author, went out of his way for Tim too—because Tim didn't try to trade on their friendship. And Hugh Forrest at South by Southwest ended up needing something from Tim, the same way Tim needed something from Hugh, and it worked out that they could fit their needs together in a mutually beneficial way.

I'll leave it to Tim to tell the rest of the story behind his amazing book—a book that was on the *New York Times* bestseller list for nearly five years. But know this: Even with all of that runaway success, he's still out there hustling and scraping.

"There's that great Wayne Gretzky line," he explains, "about skating to where the puck is going, not where it is. That's been my approach. I want to be able to anticipate all these different trends, anticipate all these changes in the marketplace, and sometimes that means you have to take some risks. You take a lot of arrows. But if there's a wave no one's surfed before, that's the wave I want to be on."

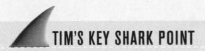

TIM'S KEY SHARK POINT

ADORE WHAT YOU DO. All along, the *4-Hour Workweek* concept was close to Tim's heart. He practiced it, preached it, lived it, loved it. Mostly, he loved the way it could transform lives, once people bought into it, and this became his passion, his fuel—only, the irony of making that happen for others could have been easily lost on a hard-charger like Tim. He was too busy working his tail off and loving every minute of it to realize that his *4-Hour Workweek* concept was only connecting with so many people because he was putting in 100-hour workweeks himself.

Here again, we see a great example of a successful entrepreneur who started out with a message, a mission. And out of that, he was able to build a business and a brand.

So what are you trying to get across?

For more information and resources, check out
www.DaymondJohn.com/PowerofBroke/Tim

"THIS IS WHERE I NEED TO BE"

JOSH PECK

ACTOR, COMEDIAN, SOCIAL MEDIA INFLUENCER

If you grew up at a certain time, in a certain way, you know the Nickelodeon tween sitcom *Drake and Josh,* which came out in 2004. For a lot of millennials, this was one of those defining shows that stamped their childhoods—and now one of the show's stars, Josh Peck, is continuing to influence their young adulthoods, but in a whole new way.

Josh has continued to act in the years since *Drake and Josh* ended. He's been in movies like *The Wedding Ringer, Red Dawn,* and *The Wackness* and guest-starred on hit television shows like *The Big Bang Theory* and *The Mindy Project.* Probably his best-known post-Nickelodeon gig has been as the voice of Eddie in those great *Ice Age* animated movies. He's also been kicking it as a stand-up comedian. (If you've never seen him perform, you should check him out—this is one funny dude.)

A lot of actors have a hard time transitioning from childhood stardom to adult roles, and here Josh has been blessed with a "second act" in his career—he might not be cranking at the same level as when he was a kid, but he's working. A lot. But that's not the reason I wanted to talk to Josh for this book; I sought him out for the work he's doing in social media, where he's become a phenomenally successful influencer, with millions of followers on Facebook, Instagram, Twitter, Vine, and YouTube. This alone is not so unusual—there are dozens of important taste-makers and opinion-setters helping to shape public opinion and shine a light on the shifts and trends that define our popular culture. (Actually, "dozens" seems like a lowball estimate—there are probably hundreds of people who fill this role in a meaningful way, maybe even thousands.) No, what's interesting to me about Josh, and the reason he needs to be a part of this conversation, is how he's done such a swift 180 in his acting career and found a way to build on his fame that doesn't leave him at the mercy of casting directors and producers who may or may not want to hire him for this or that role.

It's easy to look on and think this transformation came about on its own—a happy accident of the information age—but that's not the case. As we'll see, Josh set out to adapt his television personality to an entirely new medium as a way to take control of his life and career, and he did it in a way that was completely genuine—and a great example of the *power of broke*.

"I grew up as a pretty chubby kid," Josh says. "My sense of humor came out of that. I didn't want to be the sad chubby guy, so comedy was like my defense mechanism. I figured, if I can make you laugh first, you wouldn't be inclined to maybe poke fun or for me to be the butt of the joke."

His comedy is at the heart of his social media presence. He regularly posts short funny videos that seem to share the silly Nickelodeon-type sensibility that made him famous, but in an adult, turbo-charged way—he's no longer the chubby kid out to deflect any negative attention. These days Josh is a toned, slimmed-down poster boy for healthy living—you can barely recognize him from his *Drake and Josh* days, and yet his loyal fans have followed him from the small screen to the even-smaller screens in their pockets. And they don't just follow him: They're devoted to him, sharing his posts and tweets and videos in the kind of viral way that can't help but catch the attention of major advertisers.

One of the reasons I sparked to Josh's story was because, like many of the stories you've read about in these pages, it reminded me so much of my own. An only child, raised in New York City by a single mom, he didn't always have it easy. There weren't a lot of positive male role models in his life, so he got himself a "big brother" through the Big Brother Big Sister Foundation, and he's still close to that person today. (That's a great reminder that even "influencers" need influences.) His mom worked out of the apartment as a career coach, so the income wasn't always steady. "There were tough times," Josh says now. "Some months were better than others, but mostly we were doing okay."

FIND YOUR FIRST BIG BREAK

Josh's *power of broke* story has more to do with his passion for performing than it does with a lack of resources. Starting out, there was money for head shots and lessons and all the stuff that goes along with pursuing a show business career—not a lot of money, but just enough. Also, Josh was surrounded by supportive, talented mentors from the moment he decided he wanted to pursue an acting career. He went to school at the Professional Performing Arts School, so the idea of acting was in the air and all around. There were mentors and coaches and role models up and down the hallways of that school. There was a clear path to follow. His mom's schedule was flexible enough that she was able to take him on auditions around town. "Those were real cattle calls," he remembers. "You look around the room, and there's literally two hundred kids who look just like you, and everybody's trying to get the gig, selling Oreos, or whatever it was. And my mom would sit there for hours, trying to be supportive, but after a while she'd want to just get out of there. She was so over it. But for some reason I had this drive. I said, 'No, this is where I need to be.'"

Trouble is, in the acting business, your success is tied to the whims of others—basically, to forces beyond your control. Even our most successful performers talk about their "first big break," and how so many things had to fall in just the right way for them to land their breakout role. So, for a while in there, Josh was riding high, but as *Drake and Josh* ran its course he was finding it tougher and tougher to get his next gig.

That clear path he set out on when he was just starting out? It was no longer taking him where he wanted to go. But instead of throwing up his hands in frustration, Josh grabbed his cell phone and turned on the camera. He was a performer at heart, so he worked the room, in whatever way he could.

Without even thinking about it, Josh started making these short, quirky videos—mostly to amuse himself and keep busy. His videos made him laugh, then they made his friends and family members laugh, and soon they were making a lot of people laugh, people Josh didn't even know. He had a small base of Twitter followers from his Nickelodeon days, so there was a ready group of fans who had access to these videos once he posted them on Vine, and before he knew it he was getting an enormous number of hits, likes, retweets, whatever. He'd tapped into something way bigger than anything he'd ever experienced on television—not because the raw numbers were bigger, necessarily, but there was a deeper, more personal connection.

"This wasn't a business maneuver," Josh explains. "This wasn't a strategy, or anything I'd thought through. This was just me trying to find new ways to express myself. This was me, putting my energy into something new, because it's easy to have a dream when you're a kid, when you're a teenager. Back then, it doesn't cost you anything to follow your dreams. But then you get a little older and life takes hold. All of a sudden, you have bills and responsibilities, and it's easy to say, 'Okay, let me make a little money first and I can worry about the dreams later.' And then, inevitably, that voice gets softer and softer until it almost disappears."

SURVEY THE SCENE

The way it worked out for Josh the Actor was that the voice started to fade around the time Josh the Social Media Magnate was emerging. He had a couple friends who encouraged him to bolster his online presence in a systematic way—one, a school friend who went on to work in social media, the other his "big brother," who'd become a savvy businessperson. Josh studied how others had grown their platforms to where they could turn them into viable, sustainable engines of promotion, grow them into something even bigger than he could have ever imagined. He started hearing from big companies like McDonald's and Citibank, which saw a way to tap into the young adult market by aligning Josh with their products and services, and soon there was an income stream coming in on the back of all those loopy videos. That stream went from a trickle to a torrent in just a couple years.

"The biggest key was consistency," Josh reflects on his social media roll-out. "People get accustomed to seeing something on a daily basis, or some kind of regular basis. They know that at a certain time each day, a certain time each week, they can find a new video from me, maybe something that will take them out of their routines for just a few minutes, maybe make them smile. They know there'll be some cool new trend being talked about by this person, or a stunning photo posted by that person. It becomes like clockwork, and people start to know they can rely on you. That's the way to build a devoted following. You have to deliver, and you have to keep delivering."

When you listen to Josh talk about how he found his way online, he sounds like he's got a doctorate in social media, but that wasn't always the case. The dude did a lot of research, spent a lot of time figuring out the lay of the land, and that bumps right into one of my key SHARK Points—H, for do your Homework.

"You have to become a student of the game," he explains. "Study what you're passionate about. See what other people are doing. Learn what works, learn what doesn't work, and then figure out how you can improve on that, do things slightly differently, make it true to your own voice."

This right here is one of the keys to Josh's online persona—it feels completely natural, unforced, and that's because it *is* completely natural, unforced. Take a look at Josh's Twitter or Vine feed and you'll see what I mean; if you follow him, it's probably because you get the sense like you're being invited along on this giant roller coaster of a party. He's fun, and funny, and sometimes downright silly, and occasionally he sprinkles in a product endorsement, if it's something he believes in, if it's consistent with his personality. He's definitely true to his own voice—so much so that his millions of followers are never made to feel like they're being sold. His "business" doesn't feel like a business, and that's one of the key reasons he's been so successful.

Here's Josh's work-life advice to young people looking to make some noise in their own fields, in their own way: "I would say, 'be in the efforts business, not the results business.' It's hard to know exactly how things are going to turn out when you put something into the ether. You hope that people like it, have some kind of positive reaction to it, maybe want to share it with their friends. And that reaction can be immediate, or it can come over time. You just never know. So the point, really, is to take that first step. Put something out there. Put yourself out there. Because, really, there's nothing new here. Advertising and promotion, these are not new concepts. What's new is that companies are figuring out that there are all these great new ways to reach their customers, and to have that interaction be more natural, more personal."

He's right, you know. There is nothing new under the sun. The more things change, the more they stay the same. Even a transforming social media platform like Twitter isn't such a radically new idea. Like I wrote back earlier in this book, Twitter was a note strapped to the leg of a homing pigeon. It's just a new form of delivery. So the game comes in how to figure out all these new variations on these old ideas, and to find a way to get out in front of them—and right now, my friend Josh Peck has got it figured out just about as well as anyone.

JOSH'S KEY SHARK POINT

ADORE WHAT YOU DO. Look back at Josh's impact in social media and what do you see? You see a young performer who loves to make people laugh, loves to be in the spotlight, loves to call his own shots. It comes down to passion—the dude's a performer at heart. But when you're an actor, you find yourself working at the whims of others. You might be really good at your craft, but unless you're writing, producing, and directing your own material, you still have to go after each gig with your hand out. Josh just kind of stumbled on a way to eliminate that part of the hustle. He started making these short videos as a way to keep his creative juices flowing, never once thinking they would turn into anything other than a way to amuse himself and maybe make a couple people smile. That's the key reason they took off the way they did—because he didn't have his hand out. Because he was genuine. Because his enthusiasm was all over the damn place. He was just out there having a big old time, and folks couldn't help but pick up on that.

What makes you happy? What are you passionate about? Figure it out and embrace it. Once you make joy your biggest asset, you're way ahead of the game.

For more information and resources, check out
www.DaymondJohn.com/PowerofBroke/Josh

FIVE

BROKE ISN'T JUST PERSONAL

THERE WAS A great moment during the 2012 presidential campaign when Mitt Romney famously said, "Corporations are people, my friend."

He caught a lot of flak for that comment—remember?—but he said it in the context of a 2010 Supreme Court decision that found that businesses have rights to religious freedoms and other forms of personal expression, same as you and me. Still, it sounded a little weird, a little *out there*, to hear all these politicians and lawmakers talking about corporations in human terms—and yet I'm about to do the same thing here.

Kind of.

Sort of.

See, when I'm on the road doing my thing, speaking to people about the benefits of staying lean and hungry in business, I'm always quick to point out that our *power of broke* mind-set can be applied to companies as well as to individuals. Even big corporations with huge budgets can keep thriving if they find a way to honor their homespun roots and stick to the same principles and strategies that drove their initial growth. In other words, if they had to scrape and scramble when they were just starting out, they should continue to scrape and scramble—continue to act hungry—even if they now have the resources to throw a bunch of money at a problem.

POWER FACT: 62 percent of Fortune 500 companies maintain an active Twitter account.... A stat like that, I can only shake my head and wonder what the other 38 percent are thinking.

Case in point: A while back I was invited to speak at General Mills. The guy who arranged for my visit wanted me to talk to his brand managers, who kept telling him they couldn't launch this or that product with "just" a $20 million or $30 million marketing budget. This was frustrating, he said, because General Mills was well known in the cereal and snack food industry for its guerrilla-type relaunch of its top-selling line of granola bars, Nature Valley. These days, Nature Valley is one of the top-performing brands at General Mills—in 2014 the product line made the largest contribution to the company's growth in absolute terms, across all categories.

The story behind Nature Valley, my General Mills contact told me, was that it used to be an underperforming brand. It was started in 1975, but it never really took off. "We couldn't give the thing away," he said. You'll see this type of thing at a lot of companies—there'll be a drag on the bottom line the bigwigs just can't shake for trying. But that doesn't mean you stop trying, so the company assigned the product line to a young brand manager, gave him a small budget, and told him to do the best he could with it. And that's exactly what that young guy did.

GET OUT THERE

Instead of going the traditional route to boost Nature Valley sales—buying up expensive commercial time on television, hustling for shelf space and promotional placement in supermarkets, taking out ads in major national magazines—the brand manager took an "off the beaten path" approach. Literally. (Remember, this was *way* before the explosion in social media, well before the time when our biggest companies regularly promote their products and services on Facebook, Twitter, etc., at little to no cost.) He reached out to ski resorts, outdoor adventure centers, and other places where active, health-minded young people and families tended to congregate. He plastered the lodges and common areas at these resorts with posters and signs featuring the Nature Valley logo. And then he gave away a whole bunch of granola bars—as many as these hungry outdoor enthusiasts could grab. He also handed out stickers and encouraged folks to find places to display them—although I'm afraid this tactic might have backfired on the resort owners, because soon there were stickers plastered all over the chairlifts, the locker room areas, the parking lot signs.

Still, it turned out to be a genius move, and it cost next to nothing—just the cost of the goods, basically. Despite the sticker-graffiti, the resort operators were happy to have the brand representatives on-site, because they were able to offer this free benefit to their guests, so it was a win-win all around, and most agreed to stage Nature Valley giveaway promotions again and again. After a couple seasons targeting this narrow, affluent market, the product line began to show some serious signs of life.

For a public company like General Mills, with over 43,000 employees, to be agile enough to embark on this kind of ground-up campaign . . . it basically means that no company is too big to think small. It puts me in mind of a concept I covered in my second book,

The Brand Within, where I talked about the four stages of product evolution. I'm reinforcing it here because it ties into our discussion about growth. Point is, our biggest global brands don't just *become* global brands. After all, there are no overnight successes in businesses—at least, there are no *sustainable* overnight successes.

POWER FACT: **Coca-Cola sold just twenty-five bottles in its first year of operation....** It helps to know even the big boys started out small....Go ahead and dream big, but keep it real out of the gate. And, know that your proof of concept can be found in just twenty-five bottles of soda—as long as you keep moving the needle on sales.

No, brands emerge over time—and they must pass through four different stages before they become huge, ubiquitous, unstoppable. You can apply these same stages to every entrepreneur as well—and what I've learned in studying the pop culture marketplace is that *most times* you have to get past each stage in order to reach the next one:

1. Item
2. Label
3. Brand
4. Lifestyle

An item is just that—an item. It's plain, basic, no-frills, with nothing to distinguish it. Think of a plain brown tote bag, with no markings on it. A plastic bowl, with no special Tupperware-type features. A paperweight. It is what it is, and it does what it does, and if you misplace it, you'll find it's so readily available you can replace it with no effort at all. It fills a need, that's all.

A label has got a little more to it. Maybe it's a flannel shirt you pick up on the sale rack at Walmart, or a cheap pocket calculator you find at Rite Aid. There's a name on the product, but it's not a name you know, it's not a name you reach for—and even if you're happy with the purchase, it's not a name you'll necessarily remember when you're in the market for another flannel shirt, another pocket calculator. That Nature Valley granola bar you picked up on the mountain that day? Maybe it made an impression, maybe it didn't. Maybe you'd heard the name before, or maybe you hadn't. Maybe you'll buy another one someday, if you're in the store and you recognize the package, but you'll be buying it because it fills a need. You'll be buying it because of the price, the look, the feel, the timing of the transaction. It shows up in the right place at the right time, so you take it home with you—and here you would have gladly taken it home with you even if you couldn't find the General Mills name on the package.

A brand is a label on steroids. It might have started out as one of those nothing-special names on the back of a flannel shirt, a distinctive green package on a granola bar you didn't even know you wanted, but it's become something else, something more—and usually that's because the company behind the label has pumped a lot of advertising or promotional dollars into the product. It's got an identifiable logo, an identifiable style. This is where quality comes into the equation, because now you've been conditioned to expect a certain type of experience, and in this context experience can also mean price. If it's a low-end brand, that's one type of experience. If you're at the high end, that's something else entirely. Either way, it's something you can count on. In our Nature Valley illustration, this is what happens when you've made enough trips to that same ski resort, when you've sampled enough of those granola bars to develop a taste for them, an appreciation for them, and you start to go looking for them in the store. Over time, the Nature Valley name has become a name you can trust for all your granola bar needs. You've started to associate it with being active, being outdoors, paying attention to the food you put into your body—and once you start to think in this way, once you take yourself into a store with the express intent of purchasing a granola bar, you'll more than likely pick up the one you already know.

The next step up from the brand stage is when you start to buy into a lifestyle. At this level, there's still the same promise of quality you've been conditioned to expect from a brand, only more so. There's a predictable experience awaiting you, only more so. But now that name has extended its reach into a number of products, goods, and services. Now it's like a seal of approval that cuts across a broad spectrum. Nike, Apple, Club Med . . . FUBU. It gets to where you're so comfortable with the quality and service of a company in one area that you seek out that same seal of approval in other areas. At General Mills, the Nature Valley brand became so successful that you can now find it on cereals, snack foods, nutrition bars—it's even become "the official natural energy source" of the US ski and snowboard teams. Clearly, General Mills has built that initial, ground-level push into something much, much bigger—something much, much broader.

Over at FUBU, we went through these same stages, one by one, starting when I was slinging generic tie-top hats and T-shirts from a duffel bag outside the New York Coliseum, to where we'd moved into dozens of different clothing lines, shoes, fragrances, and accessories. Folks came to know that they could hit us up at FUBU for almost anything they could wear or carry that would help them make a little noise when they walked into a club, when they hit the gym, when they sat down in a meeting or walked down to the corner to chill with friends.

Along the way, we came up with our own "viral" marketing campaign back in those prehistoric days before social media. We didn't have an unlimited budget—or even a limited one—but we had an idea. We were just starting out, flush with a bunch of cash from our new partnership with Samsung, but the money was meant to cover production, not promotion. We had just enough in the budget to meet our first batch of orders—to do more than that, we were still on our own.

Over time, our deal with Samsung was supposed to include marketing costs and help us ramp up our advertising efforts in a traditional way, but while we were waiting on that piece of the partnership to kick in, I hit on an idea for a guerrilla-type advertising campaign we could do on our own.

Here's how it shook out: I got it in my head that we needed to do some billboard advertising—only, billboard advertising in a city like New York can be one of the most expensive and least efficient ways to get the word out. You wind up paying ridiculous rates, for eyeballs that don't necessarily have any interest in your product—so there was no way to justify the cost, even if we could afford it. Instead, I tried to think creatively. One night I was coming out of a meeting downtown, and I noticed a shop owner pulling down the security gate in front of his store. You've all seen these ugly, reinforced-steel gates, right? You roll them down and they cover the entire storefront. They're a part of the landscape in our big cities, and in Manhattan they're usually covered in grime and graffiti. They can be a real eyesore.

But one man's eyesore is another man's eye candy, right?

So I had this thought. What if I could convince a bunch of store owners to let me pretty up those security gates for them? I could give the gates a good power wash, spray-paint the FUBU logo on these clean canvases, done up in vibrant, attention-getting colors. It would be a way to get our name out there on the fly, on the down low—in full view of every pedestrian, every bus, every taxi that happened to pass by. Next morning, I started knocking on doors, making my pitch. And do you know what? Every single store owner I reached out to on this was happy to give me a shot. Why not? It didn't cost them anything. They could see I was passionate about what I was trying to do and would take the time to make sure my "billboard" looked good, which would of course make their store-front look good too. And if they didn't like it, they could paint it over and start fresh.

In just a couple weeks, I put together a network of fifty to seventy-five stores, all over the city, so that at six, seven, eight o'clock at night, as these stores started to close up for the evening, our billboards would be rolled down and we'd be on full display—all night long—until these stores opened up the next morning. It cost me about $200 to redo each gate, most of that going to the young graffiti artists I hired to do the makeover. They were happy for the gig—and no two gates looked alike. Some of them were real works of art.

Yeah, it was a desperation move, but all these years later I look back and realize it was a perfect example of the *power of broke*-type strategies at the heart of this book. Matter of fact, it was so successful, we eventually moved the campaign all the way down to Philadelphia, where we were starting to make some noise. And here's the great kicker to this story: To this day, you can still see some of those FUBU logos every here and there—a little worse for wear, a little worn down by the elements, but a gritty reminder that there are ways to get the word out on the cheap.

FLEX THOSE *POWER OF BROKE* MUSCLES

Sometimes an entire industry is up against it and these same *power of broke* principles kick in across the board. Just look at what happened to the tobacco industry. Some of you might be old enough to remember a time when cigarette ads ruled the airwaves. There were "Joe Camel" and "Marlboro Man" and "You've come a long way, baby!" billboards all over—across the street from schools even. Television ads ran with the same frequency we see beer and car commercials today. But that all changed in the 1970s, and before the tobacco lobby caved to public sentiment, in an interesting sidebar-type story, American tobacco companies had one last chance to put the *power of broke* to work before the advertising restrictions kicked in.

You see, around this time the Chinese tobacco companies were looking to make a push into the US market. This was a big deal, because the state-owned Chinese manufacturer alone already controlled about 30 percent of the world's cigarette sales. The last thing the American tobacco companies wanted was that kind of stiff competition here at home—just look at how the Japanese electronics firms have effectively crushed their American competition, outside of Apple.

So what happened? Representatives of US tobacco companies agreed not to fight government restrictions here—because they effectively eliminated competition from abroad. Camel, Marlboro, Virginia Slims . . . they already had a chokehold on the market, so they allegedly got together and found a way to keep the market to themselves—by agreeing to support a bill that would severely limit their advertising options. Understand, there was nothing preventing these Asian tobacco companies from selling their cigarettes in the United States, but without the ability to advertise on television, the move made no sense.

Tough to make the case that these billion-dollar companies were "broke"—but they were definitely up against it, and here they had to find a way to scramble to hold on to their business.

THINK LIKE YOUR CUSTOMER

One of the best ways I can think to illustrate how much more swiftly a lean, hungry, relatively "broke" company can respond to shifts in the marketplace than a well-financed corporate giant and market leader is to look at how the Girl Scouts of America have managed to compete with the big boys at, say, Nabisco, the division of Mondalez International that makes and markets the Oreo cookie.

Thin Mints, Samoas, Tagalongs . . . they're a not-so-secret vice for a lot of us. But then, so are Oreos. Still, while Oreos are a $2 billion global brand, Girl Scout Cookies pulls in more than a third of that, or $700 million in annual sales (based on an average of 200 million boxes sold each year, at $3.50 a box). Think about that for a minute. It's amazing, really, that a sales force made up of little girls, with a selling season that lasts just six to twelve weeks and a mission statement that says the organization's primary goal is to teach Scouts about goal-setting, money management, organizational skill, and decision-making strategies, can even get close in revenues to the corporate giant. But they do, every year—in fact, in the first quarter of 2012, for the first time, the Thin Mint line actually passed the Oreo to become the number one–selling cookie in the United States, with $200 million in sales.

How do the Girl Scouts do it? Well, first of all, they have a great product, so that certainly helps. They've also got a great mission, and that helps too. Their customers feel a certain obligation to buy from the Girl Scouts, because each sale comes with the promise that some of the proceeds will flow to the organization and to local scouting programs. That makes it a *feel-good* purchase, whereas for a lot of folks, when they go in to buy a pack of Oreos, it becomes a *feel-guilty* purchase.

All of these factors go into the plus column for the Girl Scouts and help to erase the clear advantage enjoyed by the Nabisco folks in terms of advertising dollars and brand recognition.

Here's another edge: because Girl Scout Cookies are only sold at certain times during the year, the American public has become conditioned to jump on them when they're available. The seasonal selling cycle creates a sense of urgency among customers—setting it up so that folks start to think they better get them while they can.

So, yeah, there are all these contributing factors that help the Girl Scouts move a whole bunch of cookies, but I have to believe that the organization's biggest asset is the passion and commitment of its sales force. Think about it: these girls become eligible for all kinds of prizes and scholarships if they manage to outsell their friends. You've got situations where an entire troop is out there trying to ring up the most sales in the country—an incentive-laden selling program like that, it's a powerful motivational tool. It encourages these kids to think outside the cookie box and set up shop in places where they can maximize their limited selling window. In one famous story, a Girl Scout in San Francisco sold 117 boxes of cookies in just two hours outside a medical marijuana clinic, where someone must have told her she'd find a bunch of folks with the munchies—easy marks for her not-so-hard sell. In another move that got a lot of media attention, a girl in New York set up a table on the corner of Park Avenue and 51st Street, right outside the headquarter offices of some of the biggest financial institutions in the city, including JP Morgan Chase, UBS, and the Blackstone Group. She sold through her entire inventory of 240 boxes in less than an hour.

Can't imagine that a big company like Nabisco, with its corporate infrastructure and ingrained selling strategies, would have ever been nimble enough to sell in such a targeted way, but this is just one example of how you can remain competitive *without* a big budget.

HEAR WHAT YOUR CUSTOMER HEARS

The Girls Scouts aren't the only ones thinking like their customers. One of the best examples of this type of approach came from the King of Pop—Michael Jackson. It came to me through my friend Hype Williams, one of the most successful music video directors on the planet. He told me a story one day that really struck me and stayed with me. He was working with Michael Jackson at the height of Michael's fame, and one day the King of Pop, at this point one of the most famous and successful musicians in the business, showed up on the set with a dinky little transistor radio. Hype took one look at Michael, listening to his song through this tiny little radio, with a tiny little sound, and Hype wondered what was up. So he asked Michael.

Michael's explanation hit home. He said, "Hype, most of the people listening to my music will be listening through a radio just like this one. I want to hear what they hear."

This was Michael Jackson's thinking, and he had everybody working with him keep this in mind. I found this fascinating because I was close to the music industry and all I knew of the business was that music always sounded great in a high-end studio. I don't care if you're recording a version of "Old MacDonald Had a Farm," if you dress it up the right way, with state-of-the-art sound and production, it can blow you away. It sounds amazing, and all these producers and executives are nodding their heads, really digging what they're hearing.

And then, on the other side of the room, there's the great Michael Jackson with a crappy little transistor radio pressed to his ear, listening to how the music really sounds.

Something to think about, wouldn't you agree?

KEEP ONE SHRIMP FOR YOURSELF

When big companies think small, they harness the *power of broke* that helped them grow in the first place.

Here's an example I took in firsthand, back when I was a teenager hustling my tail off at Red Lobster. I'd worked there for a couple years by this point—all through high school and continuing on after I graduated. It's where I learned my first lessons in marketing, customer service, and going above and beyond. (It's also where I learned how to stretch my paycheck and find my own way to "eat like a king," once I learned to appreciate the great windfall of an untouched plate of food being sent back to the kitchen—but that's a whole other story.)

One of the things I learned at Red Lobster, just to give you an idea, was that you didn't make your money on the entrée alone. You made money on the appetizer, the desserts, and the liquor. Basically that meant we had to concentrate on "up-selling" the customers. Of course, the company was concerned with getting people in the door, but once they were in the door, we weren't content with just getting that basic $25 average check per customer. We had to squeeze as much as we could out of that customer—that's how the company made its money.

The takeaway here is, don't just spend your time looking for new customers—spend time looking at ways to keep selling to the customers you already have.

Red Lobster management used to meet with the staff on a regular basis to go over the specials and other programs the company was putting in place, and we got word one day that there was a directive from corporate to cut back on the size of our portions. They didn't want to raise their menu prices, or put it out there that the customer was getting less bang for the buck, so they'd come up with a plan to kind of mask what they were doing. What it came down to was a single shrimp. Up until this time, our shrimp scampi entrées would come with eleven or twelve shrimp, and from this point forward they would be served with just ten or eleven.

It might have been a small shift—one stupid shrimp—but across the entire Red Lobster chain, it potentially meant an enormous savings in food costs. It was a great strategy, even I could see that, but it was not without a possible downside. A customer could notice and complain that he was being shortchanged—but nobody ever noticed, at least not in our restaurant, so the great lesson for me was that the little things can mean a lot. Even in big business, the little things add up.

Once I started making my own way in business, I would think back on this little shrimp cutback whenever I read about pricing strategies and other initiatives to squeeze an extra few pennies from a transaction. There was one famous story I came across out of Pocket Books, the paperback publishing division of Simon & Schuster. It used to be that the default price point for all Pocket paperbacks was $2.95, $3.95, $4.95 . . . whatever. The 95-cent piece was the kicker, and it was pretty standard across the industry. But then some finance whiz got Pocket Books to shift its strategy to a 99-cent price point—meaning that titles would now sell for $2.99, $3.99, $4.99 . . . and so on.

Again, it was a small thing that barely registered on customers' radar, but those extra few pennies added up to millions of dollars at the end of the year—another great example of the stealth approach to business we're embracing in this book. Find a way to grow your business without changing your business model, without alienating your core customers, without taking a big bite out of your advertising or promotional budgets . . . and you'll find a way to win.

One shrimp at a time.

BIG THINGS IN LITTLE PACKAGES

LINDA JOHANSEN-JAMES
SERIAL ENTREPRENEUR, SPECIALTY RETAIL LEADER

Remember how earlier in the book I wrote about my mother always encouraging me to think big? She was constantly on me to imagine the unimaginable, to think just beyond my grasp. Well, Linda Johansen-James is out there doing the same thing—but she's found a way to flip that thinking on its head. Linda runs American Kiosk Management, the largest "specialty retail" outfit in the country. If you don't know the term, it refers to a relatively new segment of the retail economy, covering all those carts and kiosks we're starting to see more and more often in our shopping malls. The smallest carts take up about sixty square feet of space—but merchants are able to pack a powerful punch on that small patch of real estate.

Together with her husband, Max, she's been able to accomplish big things by thinking small—a winning concept that fits well with our *power of broke* theme. No, she doesn't have the same hard-scrabble backstory as some of the other *power-of-brokers* featured here, but she's been following an entrepreneurial path from the moment she got out of high school—managing health and weight-loss centers, working as a body-building judge, working in the nonprofit sector, launching her own promotional products business, and trying her hand in any number of multilevel marketing programs. But

I wanted to highlight her work here for the example it offers other entrepreneurs who are just starting out—and for the lightbulb-over-the-head that just might shine down on a wannabe retailer who can't quite afford to open up shop in a traditional store.

On that note, get this: sixty square feet doesn't sound like a whole lot of space, but it can be all you need to test out your proof of concept on your product or service. (In one location, Linda was able do over $1 million in annual sales, so size doesn't *always* matter.) But even those sixty-square-foot spots are now hard to come by. It used to be a local merchant could test out a new concept by renting a table in one of the common areas of the mall, without having to make a major investment in a traditional in-line store. It was one step up from setting up at the local flea market. Typically, you could rent space for a weekend or a month, maybe for a couple hundred bucks in a cash-under-the-table way, and at the other end you'd have some idea if your business might be viable.

But that's no longer the case. These days, you can expect to spend between $2,000 and $15,000 for a monthly rental depending on the size and stripe of the mall and the location of your cart or kiosk—still a small amount compared to the hard costs of opening a traditional retail space with a long-term lease, but a big nut for some mom-and-pop operators to carry. And you can just forget about grabbing one of these spots for a weekend. Most likely, you'll have to rent for at least three to six months—the shorter the term, the less say you'll have on where you'll be setting up shop, which means you could find yourself shoved into some remote corner of the mall basement, nestled between a shuttered Radio Shack and a specialty sock store.

POWER FACT: In 2011, there were 5.68 million employer firms in the United States; 99.7 percent of businesses had fewer than 500 employees; 89.9 percent had fewer than twenty.... *The days of the giant corporation* *and the big-box giants are coming to an end, and entrepreneurs are finding more and more opportunities in outside-the-lines ways of doing business.*

The need for affordable, temporary retail space presented a tremendous opportunity for Linda. At the end of 2015, Linda's company was managing over 1,000 of these specialty retail locations in malls all across the United States and Canada. They're the largest player in the market—earning them a spot in the Specialty Retail Hall of Fame. (Yep, there's a Specialty Retail Hall of Fame—so, clearly, these small shops have become a big deal.) In addition to managing their own locations, they also offer a full slate of services for small businesses looking to open their first location. "We provide everything," Linda says. "If you want us to help you develop an employee manual, we can do that. If you need help with development, design, HR, IT, operations, we can help you with that. We can give you the full boat, or we can just give you the oars if you already have the boat."

Over 800 of these locations are "owned and operated" by Linda's company, and from these outposts she sells Proactiv, the number-one acne product on the market. It's a concept American Kiosk Management started in just a couple stores, trying to see if the business model worked before adding locations—a *power of broke* strategy that came about after a hard lesson. See, when Linda's husband, Max, started out in specialty retail, he was selling Metabolife, a weight-loss product. He very quickly expanded from one location to seventy-eight locations, but then he lost the business—Linda says because he took on too much, too soon.

"That's why we looked to do that slow roll-out when we started selling Proactiv," she explains. "Whatever we're selling, the idea is to test it out, put your foot in the water. Specialty retail is the perfect environment for that sort of thing. If it's not working, there are things you can figure out, maybe some things you can change.

Maybe it's your staff, or your location. Maybe it's the product, in that particular market. Whatever it is, you can make some corrections."

PUT YOURSELF IN THE MIDDLE OF THINGS

Thirty years ago, the common areas in shopping malls were mostly given over to fountains and displays, maybe some parklike seating areas, maybe a food court. But that all started to change once mall developers realized there was an army of hungry young entrepreneurs looking for a low-cost entry point into the retail market. Back then, the rent from these pop-up shops was like found money for these malls, because these common areas were essentially treated as open spaces designed to give each mall a certain look or feel. Today, however, the rents from specialty retail outlets account for as much as 20 percent of top-line mall revenue, so you can bet these landlords are taking full advantage of the windfall.

As a result, specialty retail merchants have gone from being treated as second-class tenants in the shopping mall hierarchy to commanding the same respect as traditional brick-and-mortar merchants.

Let's be sure we have our terminology straight: a "cart" is just what it sounds like—a portable selling station, usually on wheels, like a pushcart. A "kiosk" is a little more permanent: it's a stand-alone storefront with free-standing walls, and it's usually set up in a common area in the center of the mall. Imagine a Sunglass Hut, Cinnabon, or Auntie Anne's location in your own local mall, and you'll get the picture. A "pop-up store" might be a short-term or seasonal rental in a traditional in-line setting, perhaps with a Christmas or Halloween theme; it will only occupy its location for a short stretch, so the store won't be listed in the mall directory, and the build-out of the space will leave it with a bare-bones, no-frills look.

But the key to Linda's business is not just scouting out prime pop-up locations—it's developing a line of products that move well in such a tight space. She's tried selling everything over the years, from handbags to sunglasses to Furgles—little furry monster-animals that looked a little more creepy than cute. "You don't hit them all out of the ballpark," she says, "but you learn as much from your misses as you do from your hits."

What she learned from her first few Proactiv locations was that acne isn't going away anytime soon. And even though the product works, it's not going away for Proactiv customers either. "It's a 'one of' business," she explains, using another term you hear frequently in the specialty retail space—as in, "I'll take just 'one of' this and 'one of' that." "But acne's not curable," she explains, "so if you buy 'one of' on one visit, you'll be back thirty days later to buy another 'one of.'"

(By the way, those Proactiv kiosks have proven so successful that the company now has several "automated" selling stations—high-end vending machines placed in key areas in malls, at airports, on military bases, and in targeted store-within-a-store locations.)

It's a tough business. Most shopping malls are open every day of the year, so there's no chance to hit the pause button. But Linda doesn't mind the hard work, the long hours, the relentless schedule. In fact, she's turned that 365-day schedule into a kind of joke—a twist on the TGIF mantra you sometimes hear in other workplaces. "When Fridays come around, we have our own saying," she tells me. "We say, 'Only two more workdays until Monday!'"

In the fifteen years she's been in the business, Linda estimates she's sold to over 50 million customers and that she currently serves over 3.2 million customers annually. "What I love about our common-area locations is that we're in the middle of all the action," she says. "Thousands of people walk by each one of our carts and kiosks every day. With a traditional in-line store, they have to be looking for something in particular, they have to seek you out.

But with us, they walk by and we have three seconds to make an impression. If we're lucky, we get another few seconds to try and make a sale. That's the part I love about the business."

Linda says the key to a successful cart or kiosk specialty store is to feature products that you can't find anywhere else in the mall and to staff her locations with knowledgeable, personable salespeople. "We look for products that are demonstrable," she says, "products that someone needs another 'one of' and we can have our people demonstrate. Because, let's face it, the customers who buy from you once are the ones who help you build your business when you're just starting out, but it's those repeat customers who help you grow over time."

LINDA'S KEY SHARK POINT

DO YOUR HOMEWORK. Listen to Linda and she'll be the first to tell you one of her biggest assets as a manager is her ability to troubleshoot a problem—and to find selling opportunities where she'd never thought to look. One of her latest initiatives offers a great case in point. She's partnered with a company called SolarCity—the largest residential solar company in the country. "The thing about our SolarCity locations is, we're not selling anything," she says. "It's a lead-generating business. We're setting up in the middle of the mall, where there's a captive audience, and we're offering all this useful information, getting people excited about solar. We're also collecting names, phone numbers, talking about ways to save money, and then we sell them solar outside the mall setting." I love that her business plan is flexible enough to make room in her company for this kind of creative approach to retail, and it only came about because she studied the market and saw an opportunity. That's what I call outside-the-box thinking in an inside-the-box setting.

Another thing Linda learned as she did her due diligence was that more and more mall operators were reporting an uptick in the number of teenager visits. Trouble was that the kids were in the mall, in the food court, in the common areas, but they weren't necessarily in the stores. So one of the great lessons behind Linda's business is that she's found a way to bring the retail experience to the customer. It's like a version of that old adage that says you can bring a horse to water but you can't make him drink. Here, you can bring kids into the mall, but you can't make them shop, so it made all kinds of sense to push the retail experience beyond the confines of the brick-and-mortar stores and into the middle of the action.

Can you think of ways to bring your product or business closer to your target market?

For more information and resources, check out
www.DaymondJohn.com/PowerofBroke/Linda

GETTING BACK TO ZERO

RYAN DEISS

ENTREPRENEUR, DIGITAL MARKETER, CONSULTANT

When you've got your fingers into everything, it's usually because you've been grabbing at everything. That's how things started out for my friend Ryan Deiss, the founder and CEO of Digital Marketing—one of the world's leading digital marketers. His company pretty much owns the Internet when it comes to offering cutting-edge strategies and elegant solutions to help brands get attention online.

If that sounds like a tough concept to get your head around, that's okay, because Ryan himself is still figuring it out. When he started the company, just a couple years out of college, he was determined to build a viable, sustainable business, but he had no idea what that business might look like. All he knew was that there had to be ways to make money online—somewhere along what he used to call "this newfangled thing called 'the information superhighway.'"

As a student at the University of Texas at Austin, Ryan was throwing darts against his dorm room wall, trying everything he could think of to get and keep ahead of his expenses. He was putting himself through school, with a little boost from scholarships and loans, but he realized early on he'd have to put in more time hustling to make money than he would making good grades in his classes. Academically, he was a little all over the place. For a time he thought he'd go to seminary, maybe become a pastor. He actually studied classical Greek for a semester, but that didn't go too well.

"My Greek professor told me I'd made a D in the class," he remembers, "only by D she meant an F, but she said she'd give me a C if I promised not to go on to the next level. So that's when I figured out I should probably study something else."

Remember, there was a lot of excitement over Internet start-ups in the late 1990s. It was the height of the dot-com explosion, and as Ryan sat in his dorm room, trying to figure things out, he couldn't help but want in. "There were all these people getting rich," he says. "Even the janitors at some of these companies were exiting with million-dollar stock options."

One of the ways Ryan thought to grab at that kind of money was to design websites. The problem with this thought was that he didn't have the first idea how to design websites, so he got his hands on some Web design software and tried to teach himself a thing or two.

He started reaching out to every dot-com company he could find, in and around Austin, offering to work for free. His thinking was, if he did a good job, maybe they'd throw some stock options his way. "I was completely naive," he says now. "The very first interview I went out on, the guy asked me what I could do, what my strengths were, and I didn't have an answer. I hadn't even thought that far, never occurred to me they would ask a question like that. I just thought, you know, if I was willing to work for free, they'd let me hang around."

His answer: "I don't know."

It wasn't a very good answer, didn't exactly help Ryan make an impression, so he prepped before his next interview, decided he would start telling people he was a website designer. It wasn't entirely true, but he did have that software program, so he thought that gave him some kind of edge. He thought he could teach himself how to do it once he got the job.

Somehow, he convinced an email marketing company to take him on, and he spent the next weekend trying to get up to speed before reporting to work the following Monday. Basically, the company would harvest email addresses from forms and databases and then send out these massive spam-type emails to try to sell a product or service offered by one of its clients. At the time, the company was an industry leader in email marketing best practices, which basically meant that they had an "unsubscribe" button that actually took folks off the company's mailing lists.

"Other companies, when you tried to unsubscribe, that just told them it was a real email address, so they'd spam you even harder," Ryan says.

Eventually, the company went out of business, but not before Ryan learned a thing or two about Web design—but there was only so much he could learn on his own. "I could build a text-based page," he tells me. "I could maybe drop an image in, but the state of the art back then were these fancy flash introductions, there was stuff flying around. I didn't know how to do that, so I was extremely limited."

Years later, Internet marketers would make a science out of conversion rate optimization and online selling. Studies would show that you get a better response from a simple site, so Ryan's first designs were surprisingly effective. In this way, he kind of backed into his first success. "It's the *power of broke*," he says. "This was what I could manage, what I could afford, but I just got lucky in being naive. Not knowing what I didn't know wound up being the best thing."

Soon, he was designing a website for a lactation consultant and starting to get discouraged. His roommate thought he was strange, with all these images of breast pumps on his computer. Plus, Ryan was realizing his dot-com dreams weren't likely to come true. The tech bubble was about to pop, so Ryan knew he wasn't going to get rich just by being in the right place at the right time.

This was a concern for him, because all he ever wanted was to be rich. That was the extent of his ambitions. As a kid, his favorite superhero was Bruce Wayne—not Batman, but Bruce Wayne. "I wanted to be a millionaire," he says. "I thought that was a job."

RISE TO MEET IT

Around this same time, Ryan met a girl, Emily, and within a couple weeks he knew she was the girl he was probably going to marry. He didn't tell Emily that, of course, because it would have been a little creepy, but he filed it away, started thinking what that might mean. First thing it meant was he'd need to buy an engagement ring, so he did a little research and realized it would cost him about $10,000 just to get something halfway decent.

"That's when I started to get really serious about making money," he says. "Before that, it was just a way to get a little something extra to pay for expenses, but now I had this big number sitting out there in front of me. Ten grand. It might as well have been a million, that's how out of reach it felt to me."

Ryan knew he would never get to that number unless he took a different approach, so he started thinking of ways to maximize his efforts online. He had no real idea what he was doing, but he somehow stumbled across the concept of "bundling," back before it even had a name. Through his own crudely designed website, he started offering low-cost domain names and Web hosting solutions, which he packaged together with other tools to help do-it-yourselfers like himself create and manage their own sites.

"Everyone was selling Web designs," he explains, "but I started offering all these other services too. Hosting, tools, countdown timers. And all of this stuff was available for free, but you had to know where to find it. I had to do something to differentiate myself, and

I just wasn't talented as a Web designer, so this was a way to plus my offering."

He called his website SiteSightings.com—and like his other efforts, it was bare-bones, basic. The service he provided was right there in its name—the same way it is today, with his Digital Marketing brand. The site proved popular among other Web designers, and as Ryan started to track the clicks, which told him how many subscribers followed his recommendations on all these other tools and services, he had his first real "Aha!" moment.

He says, "I started to think, instead of directing these people to other sites, other companies, I could direct them to a product or service that was actually mine, and I could maybe make some money."

So he set about it. He came across a simple pop-up builder product in need of a face-lift. It had a terrible name, wasn't being sold very well, but Ryan used it himself and found it to be an effective tool, so he reached out to the developer. He didn't know what it meant to license a product, didn't know how difficult that could be. But he made the ask. All Ryan wanted was to sell the product on his website. The developer thought he was trying to buy the product outright, so at first he resisted, so Ryan tried another approach.

"Essentially, it was a private label deal," he explains—although at the time he didn't know what that term meant either. "The developer could continue to sell it. I just wanted to sell it too."

Ryan offered the guy $500. Ryan didn't have the money, but his father had just given him an emergency credit card, with a $600 limit. He left himself a little cushion, in case he had to negotiate, but the developer didn't counter and Ryan was in business.

Next, he stayed up all night and built a website to promote his new product. He called it the Opt-In Automater, because that's what it did—it automated the process to allow people to opt in to an email newsletter, which had very quickly become a key component of permission-based email marketing. He priced it at $14 and earned enough money in the first thirty days that he was able to pay off that emergency credit card without his father even knowing about the transaction.

From there, the product sold steadily enough to allow Ryan to start saving toward that engagement ring.

"I didn't have any context for generating that type of money," he says now. "There was no way I could have worked and saved enough to get there. I had this part-time job with a financial services company, but it wouldn't get me close to that kind of money. I had to introduce a different paradigm."

KNOW WHAT YOU DON'T KNOW

By the time he graduated from college, Ryan had about 500 little businesses and products he was marketing online. He was big into ebooks—way before Amazon changed the publishing industry with its Kindle. His thing was to figure out what people were searching for on Google—like, information on how to make sushi, or how to make baby food—then go out and produce an ebook on the subject. Either he'd hire a ghostwriter to create original content or license existing material and repackage it in his format.

He was generating over $100,000 in sales, but he had no idea that this was a lot of money for a college student to be making in his spare time. This, too, is what happens when you look out at the world from a place of broke—you don't know what you don't know. You associate the money with a specific purchase, a specific need, and you don't think of it as a way to fund your life going forward.

Ryan says now he had no financial intelligence whatsoever. Money wasn't talked about in his house when he was growing up, not in a practical way, so Ryan was still treating these online businesses as a kind of hobby. "I was so naive, I thought all adults made like half a million dollars a year," he admits. "Out of that hundred thousand, I was probably keeping about thirty thousand. I was spending money on advertising, on products, on ghostwriters and editors, but it never occurred to me that this could be a career. No way. All it was, at first, was a way to get that engagement ring. After that, a way to buy a car. And I knew I was getting married, so I put the rest away in savings."

He got married a week after he graduated and immediately went to work at the financial services company where he'd been working part-time. Ryan likes to tell people now that he realized the first day on the job he wasn't cut out for it, but he stuck it out until he started learning what other folks in the office were making. "That's when it hit me," he says. "I could make more money messing around with these stupid websites than a lot of the people who'd been working there for five years, so I walked in and quit."

Trouble was, he'd been neglecting his online businesses. He still had those 500 or so different Web properties, but that meant 500 different businesses, 500 different ad campaigns, 500 different markets. In the six months he'd been working full-time, Google had made some changes to its advertising program, but Ryan's focus had been elsewhere. Now he looked up and realized he'd made about $250,000 in auto-draft payments—$250,000 he didn't have, by the way.

"I'd authorized those payments," Ryan says, "but I wasn't really paying attention. I thought I was just entitled to all this success, but I was spending more money than I was making. It was stupid, and when you're in a spot like that, you're the guy at the blackjack table who's lost four hands in a row and decides to go all in. When you're down, the best way to get back up is to bet more, right? That's the thinking. But of course that doesn't work, and the hole you've dug just gets bigger and bigger."

Eventually, Ryan learned that the way out was to bet small, not big. He pulled back on those 500 sites, cutting his online businesses to the four or five that were actually making money. Within months, he got to a place where he was able to pay down that $250,000 debt and start earning a living, but he wasn't out of the hole just yet.

See, Ryan was so focused on paying off that debt, staying out of bankruptcy, and keeping his family afloat that he neglected to pay his taxes. He was so unsophisticated in this area, he thought that since he wasn't actually keeping any of the money he was making he didn't owe anything to the government. Growing up, he had no idea what it meant to pay quarterly tax estimates, to set money aside for the government, so when his accountant called him on a Sunday night in April, four days before his taxes were due, Ryan kinda freaked.

"I now know it's a bad thing when your accountant calls you on the Sunday night before tax day," he says. "At the time, I just thought he must've had a last-minute question. But then I also learned that a phrase you don't want to hear just then is 'Wow, you sure did have a good year.' I now know this is not a compliment, not from your accountant on a Sunday night in April."

This was where Ryan's lack of financial intelligence kicked back in—and now he was looking at another $250,000 obligation, this time to the federal government. "I hung up the phone and I started crying," he says when he shares this story. "It's the only time in my adult life I can remember crying. It was late at night. I thought, *I can't do it again.* I'd just finished paying off that last $250,000, and I'd been beaten down by that, and I couldn't see any way out of this. And it's not like I'd been spending all this money on Lamborghinis, hookers, and blow. I wasn't living the life of a rock star. I just wasn't paying attention. I was putting the money back into the business, paying off that debt, there was next to nothing in the bank. I didn't know you had to pay taxes if you spend all the money, but apparently you do."

It took a reality check from his wife, Emily, to set him straight.

He told her what had happened, and she said, "I don't know why you're freaking out so much. You'll figure it out. You always do."

End of the story? Ryan gave himself twenty-four hours to mope, then he pulled another all-nighter that Monday and created promotional campaigns for the six primary businesses he had going at the time. In some, he was transparent about his situation, told his customers he owed a bunch of money to the IRS and could really use their support. Then he woke up late the next morning and saw he'd generated about $80,000 in revenue, just from these desperation appeals. That figured doubled by the end of the day—and two days later, on April 15, he was able to cut a check for the full amount he owed to the government.

But that's not really the end of the story, is it? No, because it was out of this low moment that Ryan finally harnessed the *power of broke* and put it to work in a long-term way. He'd seen that when his back was against the wall, he could use that wall to prop himself up; he could push off that wall and start moving forward. It took a couple times for the lesson to register, but once he was able to meet this surprise tax obligation that shouldn't have taken him by surprise, he had a whole new outlook.

In fact, a couple days later, Ryan cut another check to the government—this one to cover the money he'd just generated to pay off his tax bill.

"I was finally at zero," he says. "And zero felt really, really good."

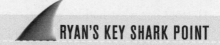

RYAN'S KEY SHARK POINT

SET A GOAL. With Ryan, the front end of his career was all about setting incremental goals. First, he needed to scratch his way to $10,000, so he could buy his girlfriend an engagement ring. Next, he needed $250,000 to pay off those advertising fees that had kind of run away from him. After that, he needed another $250,000 to dig himself out of the hole he'd jumped into with the IRS. Each time, he was out to hit a very specific target, and as he grew his line of products and services, those targets kept moving, but once he trusted that he could hit those targets, he freed himself to start thinking about actually building a business.

The thing about goals is this: You can't hit a target you don't see. At each step on his journey, Ryan was able to keep his targets in sight. Yeah, they kept changing on him, but he was able to keep his focus. That's something we'll all do well to keep in mind as we move our businesses forward.

So tell me, what's your next target?

For more information and resources, check out
www.DaymondJohn.com/PowerofBroke/Ryan

OWN YOUR OWN STYLE

LOREN RIDINGER

FASHION TRENDSETTER, INTERNET RETAILER

The thing that struck me about Loren Ridinger's story when I met her was how she and her husband worked in service of one big idea when they were first starting out. They didn't have any money—in fact, Loren's husband, JR, was just coming out of bankruptcy when they first met—but together they had an idea that the Internet was going to change the way America shopped.

Now, this might not seem like such a big idea today, but you have to remember that these two started their company, Market America, all the way back in 1991, when most people didn't have computers. That was the Stone Age, right? Sites like Amazon and eBay were still a couple years away, and the only way for most people to get online was through dial-up services like AOL and Prodigy, so the concept of people shopping online was all the way out there.

Really, it was a game-changer—but it was a game Loren believed she was destined to play. Why? Because she could close her eyes and picture it. Because she could see into the future and imagine a completely different type of shopping experience. Her determination reminds me of one of my favorite quotes: "If people aren't laughing at your dreams, then you're not dreaming big enough." It's a great line, don't you think? I wish I knew who came up with that line, so I could give credit where credit is due, but I use it all the time. Here Loren must have felt like she was walking into a wind machine. Even the people closest to her thought she was nuts, pursuing this wild idea. Maybe they weren't laughing at her, but they were certainly scratching their heads—but Loren and JR saw something the rest of us weren't seeing just yet, and they were committed to bringing other people in on their vision.

See, JR had been an Amway distributor, so he had experience with multilevel marketing. That's a controversial phrase to some people—it refers to a selling model that pays salespeople not only for the sales they generate, but also for sales generated by the people they recruit. That's how it works at some companies like Amway and Avon, and while Loren and JR saw some positive characteristics of this time-tested business model, they knew that it could be improved upon. They set out to create their own business model that incorporated networking aspects of the direct-sales industry into the then-untapped world of online shopping—an industry where they saw limitless potential. They trusted the Internet to provide an unprecedented selling opportunity, but they didn't trust the American public to get online and start shopping without some kind of push. Basically, they believed they needed an army of individual entrepreneurs to supplement the reach and power of this new global marketing machine—a machine most people didn't have, back when personal computers were still coming on the scene.

"People were already shopping at home," Loren explains. "The Home Shopping Network, QVC, they'd been around for a while by this point, so it wasn't such a big leap. That whole home-shopping phenomenon was a big deal, but it hadn't gone electronic, not yet. So the only leap, really, was how much time people would be spending online."

The big idea behind Market America was that it would offer more than a simple listing of available products. To Loren's thinking, this much was a given. The plan was for customers to hear directly from local sales reps with testimonials, demonstrations, and special offers. The local reps would take a hefty commission cut, but Loren hoped to recruit thousands of reps to help her get the word out in a traditional way, and then maybe drive customers to make their first online purchases.

"We knew we'd have to rely on word-of-mouth to get our products out there," Loren says. "Today it's so much easier to do that through social media, and so many other forms of advertising that don't really cost any money, but back then we didn't have all that. It took blood, sweat, and tears to build a brand. We didn't have that amplifier. We had to get out there and tell people what we were about, almost in a hand-selling way."

Market America didn't even have a product to sell at first—that's what folks used to call putting the cart before the horse. All they had was a primitive website, and even that took some doing. Loren had no background in Web design, and neither did her husband. So she reached out to a few high school friends who knew something about computers and invited them over. "We had two people in the kitchen," she says, "five people in the living room. We set up shop all over the house. It took forever, because for a long time they were working off of just one computer."

For their first product, Loren found a topical cream to help you quit smoking. The only problem? She wasn't sure it worked—and as it turned out, it didn't. "It supposedly had all these magic ingredients," she remembers. "And the manufacturer had all this research to back up his claims, and people really wanted it to work. Psychologically, the world was ready for a nonsmoking cream. People were willing to try anything. But this cream wasn't the answer."

POWER FACT: **For almost all retailers, inventory is the single-largest asset on their balance sheet, but in most cases it's also the least productive asset.** That's why it was so important for Loren and

her Market America team to bring in their first products at the lowest
possible cost, and why it's so important for you to find a way to do
the same.

The good news here was that Market America had been able
to license the product at no cost, because it was the manufacturer's first product too, so Loren and JR weren't really out any
money—just a bit of momentum and credibility, two things they
didn't really have to spare, but Loren felt they could get them back
in time. And they got their first failure out of the way—always a
silver lining when you're just starting out. "It was an important
stepping-stone for us," Loren says. "Failing is a part of succeeding."

HIRE FROM WITHIN

Early on, the only people Loren and JR could afford to hire were
friends and family members. Both of Loren's brothers came to work
for her before the website launched, and all she could afford to pay
them was $50 a week for gas money. They slept on Loren's couch,
grabbed what they could find in Loren's fridge, earned themselves
a ton of goodwill and good karma and not much else . . . all because
they believed in the concept of Internet selling.

Essentially, Market America brought people in on the
come—the default move for a lot of start-ups that can't afford to
bring people on at full salary.

"It was a leap of faith for everybody," Loren says now. "I couldn't
even show them my ideas for the company on a computer. I had to
sketch it out for them on a notepad, but once they got it, they got it.
People loved the concept. They could see there was an opportunity
here. And they were willing to work for it."

The great takeaway for Loren and JR after that first failure was
to look beyond the manufacturer's claims. They knew their next

product had to really deliver on its promise if they hoped to gain back some of what they'd lost. Happily, they came across a weight-loss supplement called Thermochrome, which continues to be one of their bestselling products. Loren had a deep interest in nutritional and wellness products, and she was thrilled to have a chance to bring this supplement to market.

"It was such a win-win for us," she says, "because it was a way to really serve our customers, and at the same time get our people in the field excited about working with us."

Those people in the field? Loren and her team were hitting the road almost every weekend, driving up and down the East Coast, hoping to attract like-minded folks with a computer and a decent dial-up connection. There was no money in the budget for airline tickets, so they gassed up the car in North Carolina and pointed themselves to any metropolitan area within a day's drive. Some weekends, they made it all the way up to Boston and back.

"It was exhausting," Loren says now. "We were always tired, but everybody's tired when they're trying to succeed. That's when most people quit. But we knew success was just around the corner."

Their Thermochrome launch was a big hit—Market America ended up selling $60 million of the stuff in the first eighteen months, so I guess maybe "big" is an understatement. Really, it was huge, and by the time the manufacturer and the reps had been paid, there was a foundation left on which the business could grow.

"That $60 million, we were afraid of it," Loren says. "We were afraid to spend it, didn't know what to do with it. All we did was put it back into the business, which of course is what you have to do when you're just starting out, but in our case it was because we didn't trust it, all that money. We found new products and invested in them. We found new salespeople and invested in them. And the more we found good products and good people to help sell them, the more our customer base grew."

That goes back to the proof of concept we talked about earlier, only here Market America was a business of so many moving parts that the company needed to build on a bunch of different successes. Not only that, each rep had to build up his or her brand, with his or her own customer base, and since Loren envisioned a sales force of thousands, these building block elements were key.

After Thermochrome, Market America's next big hit was Isotonix, which is still the number-one vitamin on the market. The cool differentiator with this product is that it comes in a powdered form you can mix in water, kind of like Alka-Seltzer. It delivers the vitamin directly to the bloodstream—a revolutionary product at the time.

Product by product, the company was able to build its brand—and this, too, is what happens when you operate from a place of "broke." One success leads to another, and if you trip up along the way, one failure is not about to break you. If anything, it forces you to work even harder to make sure you don't follow up one misstep with another stumble.

KNOW WHERE YOU'RE GOING

Now, jump ahead to today and you'll see a whole different enterprise, built on this same foundation. The company acquired the domain name SHOP.COM a couple years back, so now the Market America brand has sort of migrated over to this new name, which really shines a powerful light on what the company is and what it does—deliver the most complete, the most compelling shopping experience for its customers.

Along the way, Loren has transformed her own personal brand to become one of the world's most respected fashion consultants. She's created an award-winning cosmetics business, a luxurious skin-care line, and a collection of fine jewelry, and she continues to seek out innovative products with the goal of improving the lives of her loyal customers. She's also built up a star-studded network of celebrity friends, who regularly endorse SHOP.COM products on their social media posts. And on the back of all that, she counts more than three million repeat customers in the SHOP.COM database.

Those sales reps Loren worked so hard to recruit on all those road trips? There are now over 180,000 "Shop Consultants" beating the drums on the company's behalf, generating over $6.5 billion estimated accumulated in retail sales. And get this—more than $3.4 billion has been earned by top consultants and more than 400 of these individuals have become millionaires! So clearly Loren and JR were on to something with this weird concept they had all those years ago.

"I love that you're talking to people about this concept," she tells me when we sit down to talk about the theme of this book, "because I don't think we would have made it if we didn't have to struggle in the beginning. It helped us to refine our pitch. It helped us to think carefully about the products we selected and developed. And it helped us to stick to our business plan, even when other people were telling us it just wouldn't work."

This right here is a great example of the *power of broke,* because Loren and JR found the freedom to pursue their vision in their empty pockets. They had nothing to lose, everything to gain, and a long line of folks they were determined to prove wrong.

Powerful motivation, don't you think?

LOREN'S KEY SHARK POINT

DO YOUR HOMEWORK. In the early days of Market America, Loren devoted most of her time to researching and developing new products. "I loved learning what people spent their money on, what was important to them," she says. What she found was that her customers were eager to spend on products and services that would make them feel better and look better. The same is true today, which is why SHOP.COM devotes most of its attention to health, wellness, and beauty products, and why Loren has emerged as an impeccable style leader. Absolutely, the idea behind Market America's online business model might have been a gut instinct, but the company's runaway success flows directly from Loren's research in this area. She knows her stuff, she knows her customers, and she knows what works.

Do you trust your own instincts enough to move your ideas forward?

For more information and resources, check out
www.DaymondJohn.com/PowerofBroke/Loren

SIX

BE THE CHANGE

THIS HAPPENED: I was at the South by Southwest conference in Austin, Texas, in March 2015. I was there for the vibe, the excitement, to pump up some of my businesses. If you've never been, the conference is a killer mash-up of music festival, movie festival, and think tank. Austin's a great city to begin with, and when you add South by Southwest on top of that, there's an electrifying amount of energy. There were a lot of events going on all over the city, and I was drinking it all in, meeting some interesting people, connecting with this dynamic group of artists and entrepreneurs and critical thinkers.

The highlight of the conference, for me, came about in an after-hours way, away from the main event—how it usually goes at these types of things, right? I was invited by my friend Gary Vaynerchuk to attend one of his famous "jam" sessions. Gary's a well-known social media visionary and one of the most creative, forward-thinking entrepreneurs I know, and every year he puts together this wonderful collection of people who gather in a private setting and exchange ideas. That's all it is, really—and it's the most amazing thing. There's no agenda, no objective, no set guest list from one year to the next—just a chance for Gary to reach out to all these interesting folks from all these interesting fields and get them together in one place to talk about interesting things.

I was thrilled to be invited, so I raced up to this private suite at the W, where the jam was supposed to take place. It was late on a Saturday night, around 10 o'clock, maybe 11. Gary wasn't there yet, but I went with my head of business development, Ted Kingsbery, to see what we could see. When we got to the suite, there were maybe a half-dozen guys just waiting around. Then, a half-dozen more. For a couple beats in there, it felt to me like we were being punked, because this didn't look like any kind of powerful get-together or meeting of the minds. Soon, the place started to fill with top executives from companies like Uber, Yik Yak, Twitter, Product Hunt, and Meerkat, a bunch of angel investors, some venture capital folks, my buddy Tim Ferriss, who you had a chance to meet a little earlier in these pages—in all, a couple dozen game-changers, just kind of hanging around this one suite, anxious to gaze into the future together, to get the benefit of our shared perspectives.

Sounds like a pretty cool gathering, huh?

Anyway, I was all over it. The way these things work, there are no cell phones, no computers. Nobody's taking notes. The rule is, there's only one conversation going on at a time—no cross-talk, no interruptions. And for the most part, what we share in terms of ideas, forecasts, whatever it is we're talking about, is meant to stay in that suite. Matter of fact, I'm breaking ranks a little bit just by writing about it here in this book, but I cleared it with Gary beforehand, so we're good. I told him I wanted to let my readers peek behind the curtain to see how big ideas get kicked around in this kind of setting, and he was down with that, agreed with me that it could maybe get an even bigger conversation going.

Meanwhile, we were still waiting on Gary—the guy who'd brought all these folks together in the first place. There was a lot of confusion over who else was coming, where we were supposed to be, all of that. Somebody mentioned that the night before the neighbors had complained to hotel security about the noise level, so as soon as our group reached a kind of critical mass we got a call telling us to keep it down. At first, I caught myself wishing I'd been invited to *that* party, but this one was also off the hook, in a different way. And it's not like we were making any real noise, wasn't any kind of wild gathering. There was no music, no crowd of people, but I got it in my head that we'd be better off meeting in a conference room downstairs, so I raced down to the lobby to see if I could arrange something. I told the manager what was happening, but for some reason he wasn't able to hook us up right away.

Around midnight, I finally got this guy to set aside a room for us, but when I went back upstairs to tell the group, I couldn't find anybody. I'd been downstairs a while, but I couldn't think where the group would have gone. Then I heard them, almost whispering, all the way in the back of the suite. Gary had arrived by now and gotten things started, and they'd moved the conversation . . . to the *bathroom.* Yep, people were sitting on the tile floor, on the sink, on the closed toilet seat, in the tub. It was a strange scene. Granted, it was a *giant* bathroom, the kind you'd expect to find in a luxury suite . . . but it was still a bathroom. I took a look around, and it just seemed crazy to me, all these visionaries, all these influencers, all these fearless, mega-wealthy entrepreneurs, huddled in this supersized bathroom, trying to keep the noise down on this informal jam session. Why the bathroom? Simply because it was about as far as our group could get from the wall we shared with the complaining neighbors in the next room, so these guys were just trying to be considerate.

So there I was in the middle of this unlikely scene, like

something out of a Marx Brothers movie, all of us crammed into the bathroom like that. But what was really remarkable about this moment was what these remarkable people had to say. Gary started working his way around the room, asking each of us to weigh in on the future of technology, commerce, communication . . . whatever it was that was lighting our imaginations. He'd put out a question or pose a problem, and we'd take turns answering it, addressing it.

The basic theme of our time together in that bathroom was that the world was changing. Faster than any of us could have imagined—but at the same time, not fast enough to keep up with our imaginations. If that sounds like a contradiction, it's not. Here's why. At one point, Gary polled the room and asked us to reflect on what the future might look like in five years. When I had the floor, I talked about the rise of e-commerce and the fall of conventional retail outlets—the "brick-and-mortar" stores that have controlled the way we shop for goods and services for generations. To my thinking, it's one of the biggest revolutions we're facing as a society, but even as I put it out there it sounded like an old-fashioned idea. I mean, we're already seeing this shift—we're deep into it, on a global level. The space between online and offline purchases gets smaller every day, so these geniuses and visionaries didn't need to hear from me on this.

And then the guy next to me said something that blew me away. He said that in fifteen years there'll be a way for us to "drink" data and knowledge—the same way we can now download information from a flash drive onto our computers. And by "drink" he meant there'll be a special formula or cocktail or additive you can put into your drink to help you, say, learn Spanish. Or maybe US history, or how to change a flat tire. I heard that and thought, *Damn, I'm a little out of my element here.*

We were a roomful of tech nerds, entrepreneurs, and visionaries, and as I sat there on that bathroom floor it became clear to me that everything we were talking about, everything we were imagining, every innovation we were anticipating . . . they all came down to one basic element, one commodity we were all in the business of selling: time.

(Actually, this only became clear to me once Gary Vaynerchuk summed it up for us in this way—*that's* how out of my element I was with this group!)

Think about it: Time is the one thing money can't buy, and yet we're *all* out there selling it, one way or another. And if they're not helping us maximize our time, or save it, or spend it wisely, companies are selling us a good time, an easy time, a memorable time. Financial service companies are helping us avoid an uncertain time. And Miller Beer tells us it's five o'clock somewhere—Miller time!

Time—you can't give it away and you can't take it back, but at the same time we've got all these brilliant, brilliant people spending their days trying to find a way to monetize it. What is Uber, after all? It's a ride service designed to save you time and money. Apple Pay—a way to help merchants and customers make seamless, cashless, *frictionless* transactions, ultimately saving them time. GrubHub—a way to order food and get it delivered to your home faster. Every innovation Jeff Bezos is trotting out over at Amazon . . . they're *all* about time. Our economy has become a race to deliver goods and services faster, more efficiently.

Just look at how time has been compressed and repackaged in the evolution of social media. Facebook took all of our friends and all of our friends of friends and put them in one place, so we could reach out to them and keep tabs on them more easily; not only that, they started telling us who we might want to add to our circle, saving us the trouble of going out and actually making new friends ourselves. After that, Twitter came on the scene and shortened our interactions to little sound-bite comments of 140 characters or less. Then along came Instagram, and now we didn't even have to bother writing out those few words—we could just post a picture instead. Next, Snapchat made it so that we could only look at those pictures for a few seconds.

Who knows, by the time this book comes out, there'll be some new form of interaction that will save us even more time. And that idea just might have been born that day in that luxury bathroom. After all, *these* were the innovators changing the ways we communicate with each other, conduct business with each other, connect to each other. They'd turned our cell phones into remote control devices of the wide, wide world, allowing us to start our cars, monitor our homes, transfer funds, transmit documents, watch the State of the Union address, and track the locations of our teenage children . . . and pretty much everything else besides. Thanks to them, we can point this little device at whatever we want, whenever we want, and it connects us to anyone, anything . . . right away.

Really, there was more energy and excitement in that one hotel bathroom than I'd ever experienced under one roof, and we stayed there talking until four o'clock the next morning. We all had someplace we needed to be in the morning, but nobody wanted to leave. The conversation was like this living, breathing organism—it had taken on a life of its own. At one point, we started talking about self-driving cars, but the talk wasn't so much about *how* or *when* we'll see this type of innovation, but how long it'll be before it's illegal for human beings to drive at all—that's how close we are to seeing this type of change transform the way we work and live.

GET WITH THE PROGRAM

We want what we want when we want it, right? And these are the people, sitting on the bathroom floor, in the tub, who are going to see that we get it in five years, ten years, whatever the case may be.

All of this is basically a drumroll as we reach the end of the book—my way of telling you the world is changing and urging you to get on board with these changes if you don't want to be left behind. After all, the *power of broke* is about working harder, faster, smarter, and more efficiently, so let's take a look at one of the ways we can *all* be doing that—no matter where we live, who we know, or what industry or business we're trying to disrupt. And let's be clear: You don't have to be a tech-visionary like my friend Gary Vaynerchuk. You don't have to be Jeff Bezos. You don't have to have millions of dollars in the bank or a bunch of seed money behind you. No, you just have to have the passion, ingenuity, hustle, and drive . . . an entrepreneurial heart. You have to have tapped the *power of broke* and found a way to put it out into the world.

What did they used to say about Michael Dell? Word was that he couldn't operate a computer, so he told his engineers to come up with a product that even he could find a way to use. Me, I can't draw. I can sew a straight line, but that's about it, and somehow I was able to start my own clothing line. So don't tell me you can't do something or move into an area where you don't have any expertise. Just because you can't do it doesn't mean you can't do it. If basketball is your thing, and maybe you're a little short, a little slow, or can't cut it on the floor, there are still tons of ways for you to stay in the game, either as a coach, manager, front office guy, marketing guy, or whatever.

Hard to believe how the world works these days, compared to how things were when we launched FUBU. Back then, if we wanted to get our shirts into the stores and onto the backs of our customers, we had to work through the major retailers. We had to get on the racks at Macy's, or wherever, because they had the distribution. Oh, we hit some of the smaller boutiques, especially in and around New York, but those numbers were never all that big. The problem was, to make any kind of profit we had to get our line placed in these national chains—but for that to happen we had to give up a bit of our "street cred," which weakened our relationship

with our customer. Forget what it did to our profit margins, because that was a part of the trade-off too, but the *real* cost to us
over time was our authenticity. It pushed us further and further
from the kid on the corner who was wearing our clothes because
they spoke to him—because they were a reflection of who he was.

National distribution . . . it came at a price.

Cut to today, when it's now possible for brand owners and manufacturers to get the same kind of mass distribution without giving
away the store and still keep those all-important customer relationships in force. Today pretty much anyone can create a billion-dollar
business sitting in her basement in the middle of nowhere, selling
T-shirts or sneakers or socks . . . whatever she can stuff into a shipping box and send out into the world. In a relatively short stretch
of time, the reach and power of the Internet has turned start-up
businesses—and in fact, *all* businesses—on their head, to where
now the only real commodity you need to start a business is not
capital, it's *creativity.*

That's a massive shift. You don't need to be born with a silver
spoon in your mouth. You don't need to sweet-talk your way into
stores, or cultivate important contacts. You don't need to spend big
money on advertising to drive sales. You don't need to dig deep to
bankroll a three-month cart rental at your local mall. And you don't
need to finance beyond your simple production costs. No, money
is no longer the catalyst—*you* are the catalyst. Your *ideas* are the
catalyst. And putting yourself and your ideas out into the marketplace has never been easier.

Of course, by the same token, that marketplace has never been
more competitive. Now that all those barriers to entry have come
tumbling down, everybody and their mother is out there trying
to make a sale, but I choose to look on this as a great good thing.
Why? Because it pushes us entrepreneurs to be the best we can be,
to make sure our product or service stands apart, to strive to be the
best of the best at whatever it is we've chosen to do.

Let's face it, people—the moment we stopped asking, "Where can I buy it?" or, "When will it be made available in *my* community?" was the moment we started asking smarter, more relevant questions:

"What's your product like?"

"What inspired you to make it?"

"What are you passionate about?"

"What's next?"

Really, this *democratization of retail*—that's a phrase I first heard from my friend Harley Finkelstein, the chief platform officer of Shopify—is probably the biggest thing to happen to retail since the invention of the credit card. It's changing the way we shop—and for our purposes here, it's changing the way we do business.

This is another area where the power has shifted back to the people—to the customer and the small business owner alike. Because of companies like Square, you no longer have to go to the bank. You don't have to deal with stockbrokers or traders because you can execute your transactions online, at little to no cost. And on and on.

So what is Shopify? It's an online platform that enables merchants to sell their products directly to consumers, without having to work with traditional retailers like Walmart, Sears, and Best Buy. They're not the only players in this space, but they represent one of the most exciting new developments in merchandising, and it comes at a time when our shopping malls are shutting down. Our big-box chains are closing stores left and right. The business landscape is being transformed, and the consumer is driving that transformation. Think about it: We don't *just* want to buy online. We don't *just* want to buy in-store. We want what we want when we want it—I repeat myself, I know, but it's an important point. *This* is the world those folks in that bathtub have made for us. *This* is the world we live in today. And just as consumers are learning to adapt to this new world, the business community is adapting as well, through platforms like Shopify, which now hosts over 165,000 online "stores," with aggregate sales of over $8 billion. That's a big, big number. How big? More than *half* the countries of the world have a gross national product of less than $8 billion . . . *that's* how big. And that number is growing every year, so clearly Shopify has tapped into something.

As my friend Harley Finkelstein puts it, the future of selling is "retail everywhere." For example, if Best Buy wants to sell to you, they should have a wonderful online store, because that's how you want to buy. If they want to sell to your father, he might want to go into a store, pick up a camera, play with it, feel the weight of it, and then maybe go home and buy it from his iPad while he's sitting on his couch. He wants a little bit of a combined experience. And then, all the way at the other end of the spectrum, you might have your grandfather, and if Best Buy wants to sell to him, they'll have to have knowledgeable salespeople on the floor to help him understand the product, and they need to be set up so your grandfather can pay for the item in cash and walk out the door with it.

The point is, for the first time in history, it's *the consumer* who dictates to the retailer how he or she wants to buy. "A lot of people, they have this debate," Harley says. "They think it's a question of online versus offline, but that's not what we're seeing. What we're seeing is retail everywhere. It's the customer calling the shots."

It's all so exciting to hear this type of thinking from someone on the front lines of this change—really, I could listen to this guy talk about the future of retail for hours. In fact, I direct my *Shark Tank* partners to Harley's platform all the time—and I steer my Game Changer Meetings clients his way as well.

More and more, the merchants who pitch us on the show are using online platforms like Shopify to reach their customers and make their first sales—or maybe they're taking a page from Linda

Johansen-James's playbook and setting up a short-term cart rental in a nearby shopping mall. However they choose to sell their products, it's clear to them that the power has shifted back to the *people* in today's economy.

These days, there are even bar-code scanning apps that let you check in an instant if a product is available at a better price at a nearby store—and if you twist their arms, buyers for Best Buy, just to give you an example, are so mindful of this transfer of power, they won't even stock a single item in a category. What do I mean by that? If you sell electronic scooters, say, and you have the very best electronic scooter on the market, Best Buy won't carry your product unless they also carry two other brands. Why? Because their research shows that customers will just wind up checking out your scooter and hoofing it on home to buy it online.

Make no mistake, *we* call the shots as customers—more than ever before—and the businesses that get out in front of this shift are the ones that'll prosper.

SEEK NEW SOURCES OF REVENUE, NEW METHODS OF DELIVERY

For those practicing the *power of broke,* the incredibly low cost of today's technology offers incredible opportunities to get your business off the ground or your foot in the door. By now I'm betting most of you have heard the term *crowdfunding*—a relatively new term that refers to the way folks are now funding their new products or ventures with an assist from a global community of investors, through websites like Kickstarter, Indiegogo, GoFundMe, and SeedInvest. According to Wikipedia, monies generated through crowdfunding sites for projects based in the United States alone topped $5 billion in 2013.

That's a lot of paper, but what gets me excited is the way these sites help to generate interest in a product when it's still in development. Typically, one of these online appeals is built around some kind of pitch video, which gives a brief background on the project and shows why the money is needed and how it will be spent.

Some sites allow investors to give as little as $1, and some try to get you to give in round-number chunks like $100, $500, or $1,000. Most times, the entrepreneur behind the pitch will offer some kind of creative incentive to generate donations. For example, a writer I know was out to raise $5,000 to fund a self-published young adult novel, and he offered to name a character in his book after you if you gave at a certain level. Another entrepreneur who sought $30,000 to design a new type of performance pouch that would allow runners and outdoor enthusiasts to easily hold their wallet, their keys, and their cell phone while they were out for a run or a hike offered to send a finished prototype to anybody who donated $20 or more to her campaign.

POWER FACT: Since the end of the recession in 2009, small firms have accounted for 60 percent of new jobs.... Doesn't matter if your sales figures are in the hundreds, the thousands, or the millions—*small business is big business.*

This last type of pitch has been a particularly effective way for merchants to presell an item and bypass the conventional retail model—not only do you make your first sale, but you've generated real engagement by inviting your first customers into the process. Back in the day, we didn't know the first thing about our FUBU customers. All we knew was what we could see on the streets, in the clubs—who was wearing our clothes—and how they were wearing them. But nowadays we know everything about our customers. We've got their whole profile online. And when we engage with crowdfunding sites like Kickstarter, we're harnessing a new type of sales power. We're not only creating "investors," we're building our customer base. The people who participate in these campaigns are more than just customers, they've become fans, with a rooting interest in your success. And now you've collected their names and email addresses and set it up so they want to keep hearing from you as you develop and refine new products and services.

The whole process of crowdfunding is proof of concept at its best. How it works is, you come up with a prototype version of your product, market-test it, and find a way to get it into the hands of a core group of "vested" investors, all before you release it to the general public. In this way, you're able to get a good handle on inventory and keep your costs down, while at the same time seeding the marketplace.

While I was writing this part of the book, I went looking online for an example of a project that really took off via crowdfunding—*way* beyond the entrepreneur's wildest dreams. One success story in particular pretty much blew me away. Have you heard of Honey Flow? It's a clever innovation in the beekeeping, honey-extracting business—"honey on tap"—and it was developed by a father-son team in Australia.

In March 2015, Honey Flow launched a fundraising campaign on the Indiegogo site, looking to raise $70,000. This was the amount they thought they needed to grow their business to the next level—an *affordable next step*, a goal within reach. When the campaign closed a month later, they'd earned over $12 million in pledges from more than 36,000 customers all over the world, making it the largest, most successful campaign in Indiegogo history at the time.

Those are astonishing numbers, especially when you consider the expectations going in. And what's interesting here is that these guys didn't just come out of nowhere. They'd been testing their special hives for years with beekeepers, so they'd been fine-tuning and market-testing their product along the way, but in less than a month they were able to make the kind of splash it would have cost millions to make a decade earlier—and they now had a way to get the product directly into the backyards and gardens of thousands of customers who'd essentially prepaid for the privilege of receiving one of the first hives once the company began full production.

But here's the best part: they did this at virtually no cost, beyond the cost of producing an informative five-minute video to explain their product and introduce potential investors to the wonders of beekeeping and the pleasures of harvesting your own honey. But that doesn't mean these guys didn't work hard to get to where they are. Quite the opposite. If you've never conducted one of these crowdfunding campaigns before, it might seem like easy pickings—but that's hardly the case. You can't just slap a video together, pass around the hat, and expect folks to donate. That's not how it works. You've only got one shot here, so it pays to take some time with it. After all, the more you put into any initiative, the more you'll get back in return, and these Honey Flow guys are a great illustration of that. They busted their butts, refining their product, testing it in the field, collecting feedback from farmers and beekeepers at every step. And at the other end, when they finally got around to passing the hat, the Indiegogo community rewarded them like crazy—all because they'd taken the time to do it right.

Because they *needed* to do it right—and as a result, they found success way sweeter than any honey they're likely to harvest.

HAVE A GOAL IN MIND (ACTUALLY, HAVE SEVERAL)

I'm a firm believer in setting goals. The thing of it is, too often a lot of us let *others* set negative goals for us. What do I mean by that? Well, we let ourselves become convinced that we *can't* get the girl, we *won't* get the job, we'll *never* get rich. We take in all those negatives, and that becomes our baseline. There was even an interesting study, conducted by a linguistics and anthropology professor at Penn State, that determined the seven most common words to describe human emotions—in English and Spanish. Those words were *joy, fear, anger, sadness, disgust, shame,* and *guilt.* Think about that for a moment: seven words, and only one of them describes a positive emotion, so that tells us we've been conditioned to think in the negative.

Goal-setting—*positive* goal-setting—is one way to change that. I've been doing it since I was fourteen years old—around the time I first read Napoleon Hill's great book *Think and Grow Rich.* That book was a game-changer for me, especially since it was such a challenge for me to get through it. Remember, nobody had any idea that I was dyslexic when I was a kid; we just knew that I struggled in school, struggled to keep up with my reading. But for some reason I was drawn to this book, and I could never figure out why I kept reaching for it. I liked it so much that every year or so, I decided to reread it—but I realize now that this was probably because I wasn't retaining everything from the previous time.

Every time I opened that book, there was something new, but the goal-setting piece came through the very first time. Once I started setting positive goals instead of negative ones, my life changed completely—don't know how exactly, but there was definitely a connection. I would write something down, think about it, visualize it, and work my way toward it. And over the years, I've kept at it—only, I've since come up with my own style. The visualization piece was a real key for me. I'd start by picturing whatever I was trying to achieve.

When you've got a tangible, accessible goal, you've put it within reach.

POWER FACT: According to a Harvard Business School study, 83 percent of the population does not take the time to set professional goals; 14 percent have goals in mind, but they don't write them down;

3 percent set down their goals on paper and commit to them.... Right away, you can see that if you simply make a record of your goals, you'll be ahead of the game. But get this—*the 14 percent with goals in mind are ten times more successful than those with no goals at all, while the 3 percent who write down their goals are three times more successful than the ones with unwritten goals....* What's the takeaway?...It's a no-brainer—write down those goals, people.

So that's one kind of goal-setting—you close your eyes and picture it. But these days, I'm all about writing down my goals on a piece of paper. At any given time, I'll have about seven goals that I spend some time with about five days each week—I try to give myself two days in there where I can just relax, refresh. I'll read over these goals at night, so they're the last things I think about before I go to sleep. Sometimes this helps me to dream about them—that's the idea. Then I'll read them again in the morning, first thing—and the idea here is that I can hopefully make a small step forward in each of these areas if I set everything in motion before the rest of the day runs away from me.

Also, I put an expiration date on my goals, a clock. Some of them expire in a couple weeks, some of them in a couple months. Some I give myself years to see all the way through. When I write the goal down, I say what I want, the date I want it by, and a couple lines on how I'm going to get there and what kinds of things I'm prepared to give up or give back in order to do so.

At age twenty, I might have written down that I wanted to go from selling hats to selling T-shirts, to selling hockey jerseys, on a certain timetable. Or maybe that I wanted to be in a certain number of stores by the following Christmas. Right now, I have a health-related goal to get down to 170 pounds by July 4. How do I plan to do that? I'm drinking eight glasses of water a day, avoiding food after seven o'clock at night, and cutting down on fried foods, meats, and alcohol. The folks who study this type of thing will tell you this is *not* the way to state your objectives. You're not supposed to say what you're planning to avoid—the focus is meant to be on what you *will* do and not on what you *won't* do. So, to be clear, I plan to reach my goal by only eating fish, drinking only iced tea and water, and exercising two times a day.

With me, I always have a health goal, a family goal, a business goal, a relationship goal, and a philanthropy goal. Sometimes there'll be a goal about achieving a certain type of work-life balance, or maybe a secondary business goal, especially now that I'm in *Shark Tank* mode and I've got all these different projects occupying my attention. Sometimes there'll be a goal about financial security, or setting aside money for my kids.

Whatever it is, I keep it specific. And I try to keep in mind the visualization techniques I learned when I got started on the habit—because, after all, you can't hit a target you don't see.

GET WITH THE PROGRAM

These days, one of my biggest areas of concern is the so-called digital gap in the workplace. The term refers to the way certain workers are left behind if they don't have the digital skills to compete—it's a problem for a lot of our older workers especially, and I mention it here because broke is no excuse for getting left behind in this area. The same way you're never too broke to find a way around a roadblock in your business, you're never too old to get past any digital roadblocks you might find in your path.

POWER FACT: **People between the ages of fifty-five and sixty-four have the highest rate of entrepreneurship in America. . . .** It's never too late (or too early) to follow your dreams and start a business—but do yourself a favor and get started on it right away.

Consider these trends, which I've pulled from a recent study funded by Capital One as part of its Future Edge program to help folks succeed in a digitally driven economy:

- Eight out of ten middle-skill jobs require some form of digital skills.
- Middle-skill jobs requiring a level of digital expertise are growing at a faster rate than other middle-skill jobs.
- Jobs requiring digital skills pay higher wages—an average of 18 percent higher.
- Middle-skill jobs requiring *no* level of digital expertise are growing at the slowest rate of all—slower even than low-skill jobs.

Now, I'm not suggesting that we all need to be able to code, but we all do need to get with the program. I'm thinking here of someone in my parents' generation—a smart, creative older person who would be an asset to any office environment. But because he or she might have trouble doing even simple things on a computer, they'll be boxed out of certain opportunities.

And what about those diligent blue-collar workers who suddenly find themselves out of work after thirty years? Factory workers, shipping clerks, cabdrivers, bartenders . . . if they can't use QuickBooks or conduct a simple search online, they're in trouble.

Plain talk: you'll never make manager if you don't know how to use an accounting program like QuickBooks. You'll always be on the cash register; you'll always be on fries. And forget about *just* lifting yourself up from a minimum-wage job onto a management track. Without the most basic digital skills, a college degree and years of management experience can't help you out. You leave yourself at the mercy of others—to design your website, handle your IT needs, coordinate your social networking feeds.

We've reached a point where you're either on the bus or you're off the bus, and I suggest you pay the fare and get on board. Take a couple classes and get yourself up to speed, because these jobs are not about to come looking for you.

KEEP THE POWER

Know this: no matter how old you are, the *power of broke* never leaves you. It's not something you outgrow, outpace, or out-earn. It's not something you can shake once you get a couple bucks in the bank. No, it gets in your DNA—and that's a good thing, because you'll almost certainly need to call on it throughout your career.

Anyway, it's sure in *my* DNA, and I can't imagine a time when I'll look out at the world in a different way—although, got to admit, I've slipped from time to time. I'll give you an example: My first year on *Shark Tank*, I lost a bunch of money because I found myself making decisions in ways I'd never made them before. I was spread thin, with all these new demands on my time, so a lot of times I would just throw money at a problem and hope that would take care of it. But of course, that's not how it works, right?

Another thing—the deal flow that first season wasn't what it would become. A lot of the pitches we were hearing were pretty thin. And a lot of the start-ups we were seeing on the show hadn't really started up just yet. Either the concepts were way out there or the proof of concept wasn't where it needed to be or the people behind these young businesses needed just a little more time to get things going. The show's producers have gotten better over the years at vetting the entrepreneurs who come on the air, but back then we were kind of scrambling. Still, each of us on the panel made a number of deals, and we had to do our due diligence on them and follow through. That first year, I think I closed about 50 percent of the deals I'd reached on the show—meaning, after the entrepreneur had been in the Tank with us, everything checked out in only about half the cases, and so we only ended up going into business with that 50 percent after the cameras stopped rolling. Some of those deals unraveled owing to a simple case of buyer's remorse—I was learning that the excitement of the show could sometimes lead to a bidding war among us Sharks—but most of them fell apart because the numbers didn't check out.

In all, I put in about $750,000 of my own money that first year that I've yet to get back. Why? Because I let the *power of broke* get away from me. How? Well, for one thing, I was getting killed on the legal end. For those first deals, I was using the law firm I always used, but they weren't really set up to help me vet these small companies. The firm was happy to take my money, but I was paying way more for their services than the deals themselves could justify—and the services they were offering didn't really cover everything I needed. Nothing against this one firm (hey, I continue to use them for the rest of my business), but this wasn't their strength. No, I needed to work with a venture capital firm, where they had software and systems in place to do this kind of thing, only I didn't realize the value they would bring, because they do it all at a fraction of the cost. So, by the second season, I was able to cut my legal bills down from $200,000 to about $30,000—a major savings just in terms of raw dollars, but an *enormous* difference on a percentage basis.

Also, I realized I needed to hire a support staff to assist me in running these small companies. I needed someone to help me on the licensing front, on the marketing front, on the social media front. All these different experts, when I was hiring them on an as-needed basis that first year, their fees were killing me. It's not that these good people were overcharging me, because these were the market rates, but I was definitely overpaying. Can you see the difference? Plus, it was tough to keep track of it all. I needed to bring all those businesses, all those opportunities, under one roof. All along, I should have put together a full-time team, given my people some sweat equity in these companies, and kept my costs down.

Me of all people, I should have known this going in, because I'd lost a bunch of money in previous years on similar deals and partnerships when I didn't have this kind of support in place. It started out, I was just throwing money at this new situation, but it wasn't until I was watching all that money slip through my fingers that I realized I had to change things up. In other words, it took being *broke* to get me to look for another way to grow my business. And the bonus here was that, once I had my team in place—a licensing expert, a business affairs person, a lawyer, a digital marketing person, someone to ride herd on contracts, someone to run point and interference for me—I was able to pursue similar deals away from the show, growing my business in ways I hadn't even anticipated and helping to spread those overhead costs across a number of different properties.

It took me a while, but I figured it out eventually—so that's why I say the *power of broke* never leaves you. It might run and hide every once in a while, and you might get a little too full of yourself to call on it, but it's *there*. Better believe it, it's there.

Before I let you go and reflect on the lessons of the powerful people you've met in this book—people who are *just like you,* one way or another—I want to introduce you to one last person: Mark Burnett, who's been my boss these past few years as the producer of *Shark Tank*. (Yeah, you heard me . . . my *boss*! Everybody answers to somebody, right? But I'll let you in on a little secret. Mark's not my toughest boss—not even close. That honor? It goes to my number-one boss—the customer.)

Anyway, I'm closing with Mark's story because there are a ton of similarities to my own, as you're about to see. He comes from a neighborhood of hardworking families. His folks had to sometimes work two or three jobs just to keep food on the table. He learned, early on, the power of positive thinking, goal-setting, perseverance . . . all that good stuff. From his mother, he learned that regret can be a powerful motivator too—he was always hearing about the opportunities his parents had let slip away. And like me, he didn't want to grow up telling those same stories on himself. He was inspired by people like Tony Robbins and Donald Trump, just like me. He got his start selling T-shirts, just like me. And out of all that, he found a way to build on his spirit of adventure to become the most successful producer in the history of reality television—in fact, a lot of folks credit him with actually *creating* the genre, and I'm not about to argue with them.

So take a look at how Mark got to where he is today, which in a sidelong way has a lot to do with how *I* got here.

SURVIVE AND THRIVE

MARK BURNETT

TELEVISION PRODUCER, BESTSELLING AUTHOR

If you're smarter than a fifth grader, you can become an apprentice.

Then, a contender.

Out of that, hopefully, you'll be put through your paces and become a survivor.

By the time you become a Shark, you will have certainly found your voice. . . .

Okay, so here is where I get to suck up to the boss—only, not really, because Mark Burnett has more *broke* in his backstory than just about anybody in this book. These days, you might know Mark as one of the most successful television producers in the business—*Time* magazine calls him one of the world's most influential people, with almost 3,000 hours of prime-time content to his credit, including shows like *Shark Tank, Survivor, The Apprentice,* and *The Voice*—but what most fans of these shows don't know is that he started out in a working-class suburb of London with just enough to get by. His father worked the night shift at the local Ford plant; his mother worked the late shift in the car battery factory next door. Basically, he grew up in a factory town, where almost every house was identical—folks had the same jobs, the same dreams, the same circumstances.

"I never noticed that we didn't have any money," he says, "because everyone was in the same boat."

That's how it is in a lot of hardworking families. Mom and Dad work like crazy to put food on the table and keep a roof overhead, and the kids don't even notice the sacrifice—at least, not right away. When money's tight, they take on extra work, and the kids don't always notice that either. But Mark noticed. Even as a kid, he paid attention to the details, to the "story behind the story." That's one of the skills that make him such a success in television; he's such a great storyteller, and here he's got a great story to tell . . . his own.

One of the stories behind the story he picked up on was a theme of regret that seemed to run through his house. "My mom was always talking about how they should have started a business," he remembers. "Or they should have saved their money and opened up a pub. She was always dreaming about something bigger, something better."

The takeaway for Mark was that he didn't want to have those same feelings of regret when it came to making his own way in the world. That fear of missing out, of leaving an opportunity on the table . . . it's what drove him, he says.

"A lot of people, they're afraid to try something new because they're afraid to fail," he reflects. "For them, the fear of failure is so great, they wind up taking ordinary jobs, living ordinary lives. But my fear was something else. Everybody has a fear, right? Most people, they're either rushing towards a pleasure experience, or they're running away from a fear experience. And you have to decide, what's your motivator? My motivator was the fear of looking back and regretting that I didn't take one of these risks my mom was always talking about. My pain was the fear of future regret, so I didn't care so much whether things worked out. I only cared that I took the action and tried."

DON'T LOOK BACK

Mark's first course of action was a stint in the military—in a parachute regiment, where the work ethic he'd learned from his parents was kicked into an even higher gear. He was surrounded by hard-charger, no-excuses types—he even saw some action in Northern Ireland and in the Falklands—and this environment, too, set him up for his future role as a television producer, where an entire production team would be looking to him for leadership.

At the end of his service, Mark started thinking about his next move, and what he kept coming back to was what he *didn't* want to do. Like lot of folks just starting out, he could rule things out, but he couldn't focus in on any one goal. Basically, he knew he didn't want to work in a factory like his parents. He didn't want to miss out on any opportunities.

"My dad worked all his life," Mark says, "and he was getting paid forty pounds a week, the same pay I was making in the army. I thought there had to be something more."

Now, here's where Mark's path took a surprising turn—at least, that's how it seemed to me when I first heard the story. You see, following his military service, he took a job as a live-in housekeeper-slash-nanny for a family in Malibu. How's that for a pivot? A guy with his background, a badass who'd served in two wars, moving into some rich family's house to work as a domestic? But to hear Mark tell it, the move made perfect sense, once he'd decided to re-locate to Los Angeles. He had no money, no car, no place to live. By his calculations, it was exactly the sort of job he should be taking, so he grabbed at it. Really, he didn't care if he was flipping burgers, cleaning toilets, or taking care of kids and a big old house . . . long as he was moving toward something. And here it worked out that the guy he was working for owned an insurance company, so Mark started working for him at the office too.

This wasn't the best fit, Mark soon realized. "I'd never sold anything in my life," he says, "and I didn't like the idea of asking people for money, so I was starting to think it might not work out." But what Mark saw early on was that he had an ability to connect with people, and soon he found himself putting that ability to work along a stretch of Venice Beach.

Doing what? Selling T-shirts, baby! Just like his future "Shark" used to do outside the New York Coliseum—way, way, way before FUBU. You see, Mark wasn't prepared to give up on this insurance company gig just yet, but he was determined to make some extra money, build up his nut, so he figured out a way to make money slinging clothes. The way it worked was, he'd go to downtown Los Angeles and seek out these damaged shirts from well-known brands that were selling in Macy's and Nordstrom. For two bucks, he could get a shirt that would typically sell for $30 or $40. Slightly damaged, he could usually get half-price—meaning $15 or $20. Not a bad markup.

It started out, he was just selling on the weekends, but the money got too good to limit himself to Saturdays and Sundays. Trouble was, expanding his business meant taking on some additional costs—and cutting off the "sure thing" with his insurance gig. First, the additional costs: he needed to "rent" fifteen feet of linear space in front of someone's garden fence on one of the main drags by the beach. It was the cost of doing business, basically. There was a ton of foot traffic, and he could hang his display shirts on the fence to catch people's attention. Also, the longer he was outside with his inventory, the more he had to deal with weather damage, and dirt, and wear-and-tear.

"I'd make a great profit on about half those shirts," he says, "but then I'd have to get rid of the rest, whatever I could get, because those shirts would get so grubby, people trying them on, I was happy to get just a dollar or two on those and regenerate the money."

DO THE MATH

The only way Mark could justify the $1,500 monthly rent was to work every day. He figured $50 a day was a reasonable overhead, working seven days a week. Compare that to just two days a week and it came out to a day rate of about $150—a tough number to justify.

Finally, it got to where Mark had to go to his boss and tell him how much he appreciated the opportunity, selling insurance, but that he had to move on. "I was so nervous telling him I wanted to leave," Mark remembers, "after all the kindness he'd shown to me, but I was making more money on this T-shirt thing just on the weekends when I was just starting out than I was making the whole week working in this guy's office."

Turned out the guy couldn't have been happier for Mark, couldn't have been more proud. Mark, still relatively new to the United States, thought this mind-set was typical of his adopted country. He says, "Here's the perfect example of an American so happy for someone else's success. It's a nation of encouragers, really. It's a nation, I think, built on two things. Faith and free enterprise. Funnily enough, in my job, I went on to produce *The Bible* and *Shark Tank*, so I'm in both worlds, but this philosophy I had of wanting to take chances and not worrying about it if it didn't work out, it might have come from the example of my parents, but it was reinforced here in America."

During this time, on slow days at the beach, Mark used to read business and self-help books between customers. He was reading Donald Trump's *The Art of the Deal*, never imagining he would work with The Donald one day on *The Apprentice* franchise. He also scraped together enough money to attend a couple Tony Robbins seminars, never imagining he would one day count Tony among his closest friends.

"Tony's thing was to write down a list," Mark tells me, "an outrageous list of your hopes and dreams and what excites you." At the top of the list, Mark wrote down "adventure"—only, he didn't quite know what to do with that word. For now, he just filed it away, but because he'd taken the time to write it down, it stayed with him, in a meaningful way.

At some point, Mark realized he wasn't going to get rich selling T-shirts. He could make good money, but there was a ceiling to it, and he wasn't interested in a ceiling. "Look where I came from," he says. "I started out making one hundred and twenty-five dollars a week as a nanny, living in someone's house, taking care of their kids, and now I was making a couple thousand dollars a week, with a place of my own. I was living the American Dream, but I wasn't done dreaming."

One of the great motivators for Mark? Women—hey, let's tell it like it is. He was out and about one night with a guy who had a development deal at Sony. The guy had never made a movie, but he had a development deal, so he could go to parties and clubs and say he was in the movie business. Mark could say he sold T-shirts. Guess who got the most play?

"That guy made less money than I made," Mark remembers, "but he certainly had an office on a movie lot, so naturally I thought that'd be a really cool business to be in. The girls I was meeting, they weren't interested in a guy who sold T-shirts."

Meanwhile, in the back of his mind, Mark kept thinking of that word *adventure*—and now he tried to attach it in some way to the entertainment business. This thirst for adventure took him to the famous Raid adventure race in Costa Rica, after he'd read an article about the event's founder in the *Los Angeles Times*. He put together a team and entered the competition—again, driven by that "no regrets" motto that runs through his whole life.

He ended up competing in two Raid events, and somewhere in there he got an idea to license the format and stage a similar event in North America. Out of that, he started the Eco-Challenge, a premier adventure competition that required five-person teams to kayak, trek, horseback-ride, and mountain-bike over a rugged 300-mile course. The first event was held in a Utah desert in 1995, and it proved so popular that Mark found a way to sell the rights to cable television.

Here Mark's *power of broke* attitude kicked into high gear, because he had a clear idea how he wanted to capture the event on camera. He wanted the show to look unlike anything else on television, to show the thrill of the chase . . . the adventure. To do this, he decided, he needed to hire a helicopter to shoot from the sky. But the folks at the Discovery Channel who controlled the budget wouldn't authorize the shoot. So what did Mark do? He charged the helicopter to his credit card. He didn't have the money to pay for it, but he really, really wanted that helicopter shot, and so he figured he would sort it out later.

"These days, you can use a drone for a lot less money," he says, "but I felt we needed that shot. We needed to have a different look. In the end, you have to go with your instincts. No regrets, right? You just step to it and go."

GO OUT OF YOUR WAY

Jump ahead a bunch of years to *Survivor,* which, as you may have guessed by now, basically came out of those Eco-Challenge broadcasts, and Mark was still trying to stretch his budget in a way that would make his show stand out. Remember, one of the great conceits of *Survivor* was that each season was filmed in a different exotic location—a premise he borrowed from his Eco-Challenge format, by the way—but for the first season he was scrambling.

Once again, he called on the *power of broke.*

"Basically, I needed to find an island," he says, "and I needed to get someone else to pay for it. And as I was researching and re-searching, I saw that Malaysia had just started a tourism campaign, so I made a call to the Malaysian government."

He didn't just make a call. He made an ask—a big ask. "I told them I needed five business-class tickets, five hotel rooms, and the use of a helicopter to scout locations," he says. The response? He got everything he asked for—and a little bit more besides. The tourism board also kicked in a location manager to help Mark and his team tour the country.

The reason Mark got what he needed on this? It was the art of the pitch—he found a way to match his needs to the needs of the Malaysian government. He knew that a prime-time CBS television show highlighting exotic Malaysian locations would be a boon to the country's tourism industry, so he could pitch a win-win situation.

End of the day, Mark believes his success in television flows directly from the fear of regret that has driven him his entire life. Also, his thirst for adventure—and his determination to surround himself with people who share in that thirst. "That's the one fac-tor I look for in deciding to work with someone," he says. "I want to see energy. I learned that in the army. I learned that doing the Eco-Challenge. I learned that with *Survivor*. I learned that from my friend Donald Trump, who once told me it's the one quality he looks for in a new hire. He said you could have a great education, a degree from Harvard, but what he wants to know most of all is if that person has limitless energy. Will he keep going, no matter what?"

POWER FACT: 97 percent of the entrepreneurs who give up become employed by the 3 percent who never quit.... *Not sure this one even needs a comment from me—agreed?*

That kind of relentless energy—it's really about perseverance, right? And here Mark reaches for one of his favorite biblical passages, from the book of Romans, to illustrate:

Suffering produces perseverance;
perseverance, character; and character, hope.

"Really," he says, "if you have hope, in anything you do, you can make it."

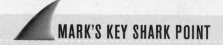

MARK'S KEY SHARK POINT

ADORE WHAT YOU DO. With Mark, it's all about the adventure. He knew he wasn't cut out for a desk job. He knew he wanted to make money, see the world, soak in new experiences. He took the example of his parents—hard work and discipline—and went another way with it. Oh, he works harder than anyone I know, he's got more discipline than anyone I know, but he comes at the work from a place of joy. He's one of those guys who is up for anything—and this, too, comes from his parents, only here it comes from making sure he doesn't have any of their regrets. That's a powerful motivator, don't you think?

Look back at all these SHARK Points throughout the book, and you'll see that each and every one of them can be applied to each and every one of the innovators and entrepreneurs we've met in these pages. And, since this is the last profile in the book, I'm hoping you get it by now—that each and every one of these SHARK Points can also apply to you.

Set a goal.

Do your homework.

Adore what you do.

Remember, you are the brand.

Keep swimming.

And know that the *power of broke* can take you to the same levels of success that found these good people.

So what are you waiting for?

For more information and resources, check out
www.DaymondJohn.com/PowerofBroke/Mark

BRINGING IT ALL HOME

BEFORE I SIGN off, I want to help you take some of the stories and principles we've covered in this book and find a way to attach them to your own lives. After all, the great lessons of the game-changing individuals you've met in these pages are intended to inspire you to do some game-changing of your own.

Okay, so what's the big takeaway here? Well, the bottom-line message beneath each mega-success story is that broke only breaks you if you let it. But broke can make you too . . . if you let it. And, even better, if you find a way to leverage the *power of broke*, it can become a mammoth springboard and a driver of unimaginable business, financial, and personal achievement.

Hopefully, in reading between the lines and looking behind the curtain at the lives of these pioneering individuals, you've gone from a place of uncertainty, wondering just how you'll get from zero to sixty when zero seems to have a hold on you, to a place of infinite possibility. Through these real profiles of real people accomplishing really, really cool things, you've seen how these remarkably resilient, resourceful, and relentlessly driven individuals have used the *power of broke* to fuel their resolve and to help them build an iconic billion-dollar brand, an outrageously successful chain of cupcake shops, and a compelling social media platform. . . . And you've seen how in each case, they've harnessed the *power of broke* to change their attitude and altitude of vision, possibility, and focus.

And so as we prepare to close the book on these lessons, let's take this final opportunity to highlight our main points so you can carry these lessons forward, and build your own high-performance/high-achievement growth strategies to serve you mightily in your business, in your relationships, in your performance potential, and in any part of your life. If you're like me, you'll want to take these lessons and post them on your bathroom mirror, on your refrigerator, on your dashboard, on your desktop . . . wherever it is that they will catch your full attention on a daily basis because, hey, there's nothing like constant reinforcement to get you going.

So here we go. Here are the Broke Power Principles pulled from the lives of the trailblazing individuals I've just introduced to you.

BROKE POWER PRINCIPLE #1: Use all of the resources available to you, but don't expect to just flip a switch and get them all cranking on autopilot. No. You've got to learn how to best use these resources to your smartest advantage, especially if you're tapping into those OPM—type resources my good friend Jay Abraham talked about earlier—other people's money, other people's mind-set, and other people's magic.

BROKE POWER PRINCIPLE #2: Keep it real. Strive for authenticity in everything you do. At the end of the day, the more humility and integrity you put out into the world, the more you'll connect with others who'll want to help you succeed.

BROKE POWER PRINCIPLE #3: Learn (and embrace!) the power of optimization. By that I mean make the very best use of your time, energy, actions, opportunity costs, and capital. One of the most precious resources available to you, at absolutely no cost, is time—don't waste it.

BROKE POWER PRINCIPLE #4: Understand that you will be rewarded for solving other people's problems or filling holes in the marketplace, just as you will be rewarded for helping others reach their desired objectives. In other words, if you can figure out how to do something better, faster, easier, and more efficiently than anybody else, and if you can make somebody else's life a little smoother in the bargain, you're way ahead of the game.

BROKE POWER PRINCIPLE #5: Put all your passion and purpose behind whatever it is you're doing. If you don't believe in yourself, in your product, your service, or your business, you can't expect anyone else to either. That said, you don't want to come across as a nut, so don't be fanatical or unreasonably optimistic. Remember that you're selling people on the idea of trusting in you, because people invest in people, not just in a product or service.

BROKE POWER PRINCIPLE #6: Take the time to understand and appreciate everyone you meet on your path to success. Investor, distributor, vendor, prospective buyer, or customer...whoever it is, show him or her that you get how things are from their perspective. Tell them that you're rooting for them. Show them that you have their best interests in mind. They will respect you for respecting their reality. And who knows, maybe they'll go out of their way to do the same for you.

BROKE POWER PRINCIPLE #7: Think beyond the moment. This can be tough to do, especially when you're up against it. Find a way to support your vision with logic, data, and realistic projections. Wishful thinking and conjecture have a way of working against you, and breaking you in a bad way.

BROKE POWER PRINCIPLE #8: Make the probability of your success a natural part of your thinking. Expect it...will it so. Why? Because good things come to those who expect them. Now, that doesn't mean that we only make room in our thinking for pie-in-the-sky outcomes. (See Broke Power Principle #7.) No, this means you need to train yourself to keep your goals in sight and in reach. It means that you must believe wholeheartedly that your success is within you. Keep this thought at the front of your mind. Let it drive every action you take. Learn from the stories I've shared with you, and model your approach after these successful individuals. Each and every one of them had a low point, and yet each and every one of them found a way to pick themselves up and move on. Know that you can too. Know that you must.

Tell me, what are your Broke Power Principles? I encourage you to share them with me at DaymondJohn.com/PowerofBroke, and I promise to pass them along and share them with all of you—together with a whole bunch of new ones I'm sure I'll come up with . . . now that I'm thinking along these lines.

Are you ready to put these principles to work? That's great! Before I let you go, I want to ask you to look one more time at the SHARK Points we've hit on in each of these profiles. They're basic—so basic, in fact, that you should probably find a way to hard-wire your thinking to make room for them. In some way or other, they should be at the heart of everything you do:

- Set a goal . . .
- Do your homework . . .
- Adore what you do . . .

- Remember, you are the brand . . .
- Keep swimming . . .

Now, I don't expect you to master each of these points and principles right away, so why not start by picking one that you believe
is within reach. Imprint it on your brain. Commit to it fully. Then
go out and put it to work for you, and once you've got that one
done, get to work on another one. And as you do so, expect it to
be a little bit hard; it's not always easy to try something new. Anything beyond your comfort level or outside your experience will
take some getting used to, but I'm betting on you to figure it all out
and go at your own pace and get up to speed before too, too long.
We were all babies once, right? We've all taken baby steps. That's
how we learned to walk, to talk, to eat, to ride a bicycle, and to
program our smart phones. There's no shame in taking baby steps
here either; build up to your first goal and work at it until you get
it right—until it becomes natural, perpetual, and authentic. And
then, once you've got it down, once you're feeling comfortable and
competent, you can move on to the next one, and the next.

Do this and you'll do yourself and your business a massive
solid—trust me on this.

Do this and you'll push yourself closer to where you want to be.

Do this and you'll have tapped into the true *power of broke*
and turned your iron will and boundless creative energy into the
engines of your success.

I'm super excited to be on this journey with you, and proud to
share these stories to help you discover the power, possibility, and
profit potential you actually have in being broke. Just look at me:
a dyslexic kid from Queens who was raised by a hardworking, no-
nonsense single mother who found a way to instill in me an ability
to think in big, bold strokes. To think without limits, even though
there are all kinds of limits on my resources. To think beyond my

circumstances, which, I got to say, was pretty bleak at times. Out of that thinking, I somehow found a way to build a $6 billion clothing brand, and an unexpected second career as a brand-building entrepreneur and star of a hit television show. And get this, I've even been tapped by President Barack Obama to serve as an ambassador of his groundbreaking Presidential Ambassador for Global Entrepreneurship program (PAGE). Pretty cool, right? But underneath the tremendous kick and great honor comes an enormous responsibility to help spread the power of entrepreneurship all over the world. And, here again, the *power of broke* is a big part of that for me.

Now, I don't set this out to boast or strut—just to show that if I can accomplish these things, then you can too. It doesn't matter how broke you are. Broke is broke, and believe me, I don't meet too many people in my travels today who were more broke than I was when I was growing up. But we were rich in possibility, rich in hopes and dreams, rich in determination . . . and that's the whole point of this book. That's what drove all these fine success stories—from a place of desperation to a place of inspiration.

So now is the time in our relationship as writer and reader for you to start believing in yourself. Now is the time for you to take action, and the best way to start is to take a final look at the subtitle of this book: HOW EMPTY POCKETS, A TIGHT BUDGET, AND A HUNGER FOR SUCCESS CAN BECOME YOUR GREATEST COMPETITIVE ADVANTAGE.

Are your pockets empty?

Are you working on a tight budget?

Are you hungry for success?

Well, then . . . you're good to go. And even if you aren't literally up with your back against the wall, act like it.

So, what do you say? Are you ready to put the *power of broke* to work for you?

ACKNOWLEDGMENTS

THERE ARE A great many people I want to thank for their extra efforts in helping me to get to this place in my life and career—and the good news is that I'm not waiting around for the publication of my book to give them the props they deserve. I thank them at every opportunity and let them know how much I appreciate them whenever I can, but I do want to give a few of them a special shout-out in these pages.

First and foremost, I want to thank my mother, who taught me the spirit of entrepreneurship. I want to thank my amazing family: my beautiful daughters and my ex-wife, who have always supported me as I've chased my many ventures and adventures. Of course, the "chase" would have meant nothing without my friends and partners Carl, Keith, and J—my brothers for life. Also, my partners Norman and Bruce were instrumental on the FUBU front, and in almost every other aspect of my professional life. So I owe them a great debt as well.

I want to thank my amazing staff. There are too many individuals to mention, so I don't want to run through a list because I don't want to leave anyone out. Let's just say that over the past twenty years I've been blessed to have good, dedicated, thoughtful people working with me in support of my dreams. And lately, they help me to push my new and improved dreams, and the dreams of so many others. That said, I do want to highlight one member of my team, my head of business development at Shark Branding, Ted Kingsbery, who's played a key role in the launch and development of this book.

A special thank you to LL Cool J, for believing in me early, and to all the amazing artists and individuals who believed in me along the way.

I want to acknowledge everyone in my television family, from the executives at ABC, Sony, and Mark Burnett Productions to Holly, Jamie, Yun, and Clay. Mostly, I want to thank Mark Burnett himself, who saw something in me when he plucked a relatively unknown fashion designer and decided to put me on the air. And as much as I joke about them (and as much as they joke about me), I'm grateful for the friendship and collaborative energy of the distinctive panel of Sharks on the show. No matter how many deals my fellow panelists have taken from me, no matter how many I've taken from them, we have each other's backs. It's one of the great blessings in my life, the way we're able to draw from one another and learn from one another on our incredible shared journey.

Of course, our show would be nothing without the bold entrepreneurs who appear before us and risk their reputations and their bottom lines. I'm not certain that I'd have the guts to put myself out there like that (in fact, I'm pretty sure I don't), but they're the heart and soul of the show. Right up there with them, I'd have to put the fans and supporters of the show, who really rallied when it was announced that ABC was considering cancelling us, and watched the show religiously every single night in bigger and bigger numbers.

Thanks, too, to CNBC, for airing *Shark Tank* in heavy rotation, as if we were the Kardashians of the network.

And just to close out this television circle, let me shine a light on my *Shark Tank* partners who've listened to me when they probably shouldn't have and ignored me when they probably shouldn't have—that's what partners do, right?

I'm also grateful to my management team: Eric Ortner of Vector Management, and my entire team at William Morris Endeavor who've helped to grow my business and my brand these past several years. And, a special tip of the hat to President Barack Obama and the members of his administration who tapped me to participate in their powerful and empowering My Brother's Keeper initiative, and for giving me the honor of naming me a Presidential Ambassador for Global Entrepreneurship.

Thanks to all of my strategic partners in licensing, manufacturing, and financing across the board. Really, I have so many amazing partners working with me on my various *Shark Tank* investments. Together they keep all the balls I'm juggling from falling to the ground.

On the book front, I want to thank Dan Paisner for standing by me and helping me express myself in ways nobody else can. This is our third book together, and I'm grateful for this strategic partnership. This time around, we were helped along the way by Kirsten Neuhaus at Foundry Media and Talia Krohn and the entire team at the Crown Publishing Group, who saw something in this *power of broke* idea before Dan and I really had a chance to develop the concept that would drive this book. Thank you, thank you.

Heather, the love of my life, thank you for believing in me, for supporting me, for nourishing me.

Also, I want to salute our veterans—past, present, and future—who put everything on the line and fight to give us the freedom to be entrepreneurs, to make things happen here at home.

There are also a great many "intrapreneurs" who make things

happen across corporate America in an inside way. Those of us on the outside need supporting players on the inside who share our vision, so thank you.

Thank you as well to the countless teachers, mentors, and community leaders who help to inspire us, ground us, and inform us. They might not be entrepreneurs themselves, but very often we find our first sparks in folks like them, such as my amazing mentor, Jay Abraham, and my father, Steve Sirota.

I'm grateful to the many organizations I work with and consult with, including, but not limited to, Understood.org, Starkey Hearing Technologies, and the Yale Center for Dyslexia and Creativity.

To all my friends who have passed through my life, going all the way back to grade school and high school, who realize I haven't changed. I'm still the same dude who used to run around with them in the neighborhood, and every once in a while we'll get together and pick up right where we left off. We might let a bunch of time pass between visits, but when we're together, it's like nothing has changed. So they get a nod here too. I love them all.

In the end, I want to give it up to the man above . . . without Him, none of this would be possible.

AS A SHARK on ABC's *Shark Tank,* Daymond John is no stranger to entrepreneurship. During the past twenty years, Daymond has gone from sewing logos on hats in his basement to establishing an international clothing empire, earning himself the iconic title God-father of Urban Fashion. In addition to his success in style, Daymond has become one of the world's most sought-after branding experts and motivational speakers.

As president, CEO, and founder of FUBU, Daymond revolutionized the sportswear industry in the 1990s with a distinctive line of fashionable attire that transcended the underserved urban market and became wildly popular in the mainstream teen market. Daymond has since gone on to own and operate several other lines, including Crown Holder, Kappa USA, Coogi, and Heatherette.

Daymond's first foray into the apparel market came in the early 1990s. He was looking to purchase a tie-top hat but was put off by the high prices. Taking this discovery as an opportunity, Daymond began to spend his mornings producing his own tie-top hats and his nights selling them on the streets of his Queens neighborhood. Daymond recruited his friends to help him with the production, and after making an $800 profit in the first day of his new venture, it became clear that they had discovered an untapped market. Daymond and Co. soon created the distinctive FUBU logo and began sewing it on hockey jerseys, sweatshirts, and T-shirts. Soon, famed entertainer LL Cool J, a neighborhood friend of Daymond and music idol of the time, agreed to wear one of Daymond's shirts in a picture that would become the centerpiece of FUBU's first promotional campaign. In 1992, FUBU premiered at the MAGIC fashion trade show in Las Vegas. The line of distinctively cut and vibrantly colored sportswear was an instant hit, garnering $300,000 in orders and securing the company a contract with New York City–based department store powerhouse Macy's. A landmark distribution deal with Korean conglomerate Samsung soon followed, allowing FUBU to be manufactured and distributed on a massive scale. In 1998, FUBU made $350 million in revenue, and Daymond John's neighborhood tie–top hat business was suddenly in direct competition with well-known brands like Donna Karan New York and Tommy Hilfiger.

Daymond is often touted as a "branding genius" in the marketing world, and his services have been courted by Fortune 500 companies such as AT&T, Turner Networks, and Nike. In response to this demand, Daymond established the branding firm, Shark Branding, separate from his apparel businesses. Specializing in brand strategies, brand development, licensing, artist relations, and marketing, Daymond and Shark Branding have perfected the methods for ingraining companies, brands, and products into the social consciousness. The thriving marketing company recently added a celebrity brand management division anchored by Daymond's extensive experience working with superstars such as Muhammad Ali, Pitbull, Idris Elba, Lennox Lewis, and the Kardashians.

In 2007, Daymond entered the literary world with his first

book, *Display of Power: How FUBU Changed a World of Fashion, Branding and Lifestyle*. A road map for success in business and in life, Daymond's first pass as an author was selected by *Library Journal* as one of the best books of 2007. Daymond went on to release a second nonfiction offering from his bestselling Display of Power series, *The Brand Within: How We Brand Ourselves, from Birth to the Boardroom*, an examination of celebrity-fueled brand loyalty, consumer impulses, and purchasing habits.

In addition to his ventures in the fashion, branding, and literary worlds, Daymond is an active angel investor in a range of businesses from fashion to health clubs to his new priority, technology. He has also lent his business acumen to famed institutions, including Brandeis University, the University of Southern California, and Harvard Business School. He has also served as Entrepreneur in Residence at the prestigious Babson College.

Daymond's revolutionary contributions to fashion and American business have been recognized by many esteemed organizations that have honored him over the years. His achievements include Brandweek Marketer of the Year (1999), the Advertising Age Marketing 1000 Award for Outstanding Ad Campaign (1999), the NAACP Entrepreneur of the Year Award (1999), Crain's Business of Forty Under Forty Award (2002), and Ernst & Young's New York Entrepreneur of the Year Award (2003). In 1999, FUBU the Collection became the first company to receive the ESSENCE Achievement Award.

For additional content and resources mentioned throughout this book, check out DaymondJohn.com/PowerofBroke.

INDEX

MAKE POWER PART
OF YOUR PORTFOLIO WITH THE
DISPLAY OF POWER SERIES

"Daymond John brings his signature style to the world of books, and *Display of Power* is a must-read for anyone wondering how a kid from Hollis, Queens, could climb to the very top rungs of the fashion industry."

—Montel Williams, television talk show host on *Display of Power*

"A must-read for anyone who wants their brand to walk into the room long before they do."

—Kevin O'Leary, renowned entrepreneur and venture capitalist on *The Brand Within*

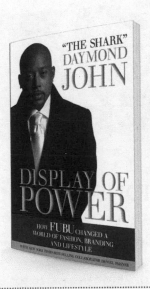 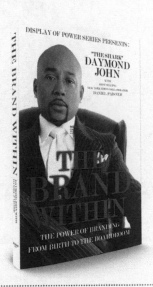

From branding to back-alley hustling, from street corners to corner offices, Daymond John explores how power transformed his life, and how it can revolutionize your business today.

DAYMONDJOHN.COM

RISE & GRIND
COMING IN JANUARY 2018

IN MY TRAVELS as an entrepreneur, investor, "Shark" and Presidential Ambassador, I've noticed a common trait in the supersuccessful people I meet: every single one of them—whether a woman, whether a man—has got a killer work ethic. They're up and at it each and every day, and they're at it *hard*.

As I write this, it's 1:00 A.M. I've been on the road for the past three weeks at various speaking engagements, consulting gigs, or promotional appearances. I just wrapped my third consecutive twelve-hour day of shooting *Shark Tank,* and after I set these thoughts to paper I plan to send out voice-notes to my key team members—because, hey, after all, even in the middle of all this, I've still got my businesses to run. Tomorrow morning (*this* morning!), I have a call time of 6:45 A.M. back on set.

In chapter two of *The Power of Broke* you read about why my motto in life boils down to three little words: rise and grind. Because those three words remind me that the choice of whether to succeed—*or not*—is all mine. All this makes for a fast-paced life, that's for sure. But I wouldn't have it any other way—and neither would any of the creative, thriving, striving, crazy-talented people I hope to introduce to readers in my next book. My thing is, it helps to hear from these people directly, so we can lift ourselves up by their example. So-called experts can share their lists of top secrets, tell you all about their winning strategies, sell you into expensive seminars . . . but at the end of the day you need to put in the work. You need to out-think, out-hustle, out-perform every one of your competitors. You need to work so hard you'll wonder how far you can push yourself.

You need to *Rise & Grind* each and every day.

The best way to inspire people is to show them how it's done. Let somebody else give you the textbook, the playbook. Me. I want you to learn from the very best. So in my new book I will be talking to some of the world's top business executives, athletes, musicians, thought leaders, and influencers; talking about how they built great careers, amazing brands, and an incredible body of work, all of it in a painstaking, grind-it-out sort of way. I will take an up-close-and-personal look at the hard-charging routines of some of our greatest game-changers who have *risen* to the challenges in their lives and careers and *grinded* their way to the very tops of their fields. And I'll share my own insights and experiences on what it takes to get and keep ahead.

If there's one thing I've learned on my journey as poor kid from the streets of Hollis, Queens, to now—growing FUBU from a kitchen-table operation into a $6 billion brand to mentoring rising and grinding entrepreneurs of all ages and backgrounds both in my role as "The People's Shark" on *Shark Tank* and as one of President Obama's Ambassadors for Entrepreneurship—it's that there's no such thing as overnight success. Your goals don't just up and find *you*. No, you've got to "rise and grind" to meet them. And you've got to be relentless about it. Because when you do, you find the power to do anything, to get past anything, and to become anything.

Let's be clear. We don't get where we're going by standing still. We've got to move the needle every day. We've got to keep reaching, pushing, because whatever it is we're doing, whatever dreams we're chasing, there's somebody out there reaching and pushing and chasing the same damn dream. I'm excited to inspire readers across the country to find their own way to RISE AND GRIND.